S0-ADJ-360

Data Preparation for Data Mining Using SAS

The Morgan Kaufmann Series in Data Management Systems

Series Editor: Jim Gray, Microsoft Research

DATA PREPARATION FOR DATA MINING USING SAS

MAMDOUH REFAAT

QA
76.9
. D343
R43
2007

AMSTERDAM • BOSTON • HEIDELBERG • LONDON
NEW YORK • OXFORD • PARIS • SAN DIEGO
SAN FRANCISCO • SINGAPORE • SYDNEY • TOKYO
Morgan Kaufmann Publishers is an imprint of Elsevier

ELSEVIER

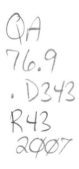

MORGAN KAUFMANN PUBLISHERS

Publisher: Diane D. Cerra
Assistant Editor: Asma Palmeiro
Publishing Services Manager: George Morrison
Project Manager: Marilyn E. Rash
Cover Design: Eric DeCicco
Cover Image: Qettyimages
Composition: diacriTech
Copyeditor: Joan Flaherty
Proofreader: Dianne Wood
Indexer: Ted Laux
Interior printer: The Maple Press Company
Cover printer: Phoenix Color Corp.

I P F W
WITHDRAWN APR 8 2008
HELMKE LIBRARY

Morgan Kaufmann Publishers is an imprint of Elsevier.
500 Sansome Street, Suite 400, San Francisco, CA 94111

This book is printed on acid-free paper.

ⓒ 2007 by Elsevier Inc. All rights reserved.

Designations used by companies to distinguish their products are often claimed as trademarks or registered trademarks. In all instances in which Morgan Kaufmann Publishers is aware of a claim, the product names appear in initial capital or all capital letters. Readers, however, should contact the appropriate companies for more complete information regarding trademarks and registration.

No part of this publication may be reproduced, stored in a retrieval system, or transmitted in any form or by any means—electronic, mechanical, photocopying, scanning, or otherwise—without prior written permission of the publisher.

Permissions may be sought directly from Elsevier's Science & Technology Rights Department in Oxford, UK: phone: (+44) 1865 843830, fax: (+44) 1865 853333, E-mail: permissions@elsevier.com. You may also complete your request on-line via the Elsevier homepage (http://elsevier.com), by selecting "Support & Contact" then "Copyright and Permission" and then "Obtaining Permissions."

Library of Congress Cataloging-in-Publication Data
Refaat, Mamdouh.
  Data preparation for data mining using SAS / Mamdouh Rafaat.
    p. cm.
  Includes bibliographical references and index.
  ISBN-13: 978-0-12-373577-5 (alk. paper)
  ISBN-10: 0-12-373577-7 (alk. paper)
1. Data mining. 2. SAS (Computer file) 1. Title.
  QA76.9.D343R43 2007
  006.3'12—dc22   2006023681

ISBN 13: 978-0-12-373577-5
ISBN 10: 0-12-373577-7

For information on all Morgan Kaufmann publications, visit our
Web site at *www.mkp.com* or *www.books.elsevier.com*

Printed in the United States of America
06 07 08 09 10   5 4 3 2 1

Working together to grow
libraries in developing countries

www.elsevier.com | www.bookaid.org | www.sabre.org

ELSEVIER   BOOK AID International   Sabre Foundation

CONTENTS

CHAPTER
1

INTRODUCTION   1

CHAPTER
2

TASKS AND DATA FLOW   7

CHAPTER
3

REVIEW OF DATA MINING MODELING TECHNIQUES   15

CHAPTER

6

INTEGRITY CHECKS   63

CHAPTER

7

EXPLORATORY DATA ANALYSIS   83

CHAPTER
11

TREATMENT OF MISSING VALUES   171

CHAPTER
12

PREDICTIVE POWER AND VARIABLE
REDUCTION I   207

CHAPTER
13

ANALYSIS OF NOMINAL AND ORDINAL VARIABLES   211

CHAPTER
14

ANALYSIS OF CONTINUOUS VARIABLES   233

CHAPTER
15

PRINCIPAL COMPONENT ANALYSIS   247

CHAPTER
16

FACTOR ANALYSIS 257

CHAPTER
17

PREDICTIVE POWER AND VARIABLE REDUCTION II 267

LIST OF FIGURES

LIST OF TABLES

PREFACE

The use of data mining modeling in different areas of business has moved over the last two decades from the domain of a few academic researchers to that of a large number of business and quantitative analysts in commercial organizations. This move has been accelerated by the rapid development of reliable commercial data mining software suites that allow easy implementation of many data mining algorithms such as regression, decision trees, neural networks, and cluster analysis.

However, data mining analysts spend up to 80% of their time, not doing actual modeling, but *preparing data*. This is due to three main reasons. First, all current modeling methods assume the data is in the form of a matrix containing the analysis variables, which somehow have been cleaned and prepared for modeling from their original source. The second reason is the nature of data sources. Almost all business data today is stored in relational form, either in a database, in a data warehouse, or in the back end of operational systems. Therefore, collecting the data from several tables from the relational form and converting data into the final matrix form is an essential task. Finally, the quality of the resulting models always depends on the quality of the data. This is not a surprise or a deviation from the familiar warning: *Garbage in, garbage out!* So, it turns out that data mining is mostly about data preparation.

Therefore, increasing the efficiency as well as the quality of data preparation procedures is at least as, if not more, important as making sure that the modeling algorithms are used to their fullest potential. This is the focus of this book.

This book is intended as a book of recipes. It provides the explanation of each data preparation procedure, as well as the SAS implementations, in the form of a macro that is suitable for task automation. Much of the code presented in this book can also be implemented in other data manipulation tools such as SQL. However, I have chosen SAS because of its dominance in today's data mining environment.

Although the focus of the book is on developing good mining views for data mining modeling, the presented techniques could also be used for the purpose of the other complementary task of reporting. Indeed, one of the essential data mining tasks is the generation of reports, both before and after the development and deployment of models.

One final note: this is not a book to teach readers how to use SAS or to do macro programming. It is a book about data preparation for data mining; therefore, a basic knowledge of the SAS system is assumed.

DATA PREPARATION FOR DATA MINING USING SAS

CHAPTER 1
INTRODUCTION

1.1 THE DATA MINING PROCESS

The procedure used to perform data mining modeling and analysis has undergone a long transformation from the domain of academic research to a systematic industrial process performed by business and quantitative analysts. Several methodologies have been proposed to cast the steps of developing and deploying data mining models into a standardized process.

This chapter summarizes the main features of these methodologies and highlights the role of the data preparation steps. Furthermore, it presents in detail the definition and contents of the the mining view and the scoring view.

1.2 METHODOLOGIES OF DATA MINING

Different methodologies of data mining attempt to mold the activities the analyst performs in a typical data mining engagement into a set of logical steps or tasks. To date, two major methodologies dominate the practice of data mining: CRISP and SEMMA.

CRISP, which stands for Cross Industry Standard Process for data mining, is an initiative by a consortium of software vendors and industry users of data mining technology to standardize the data mining process. The original CRISP documents can be found on *http://www.crisp-dm.org/*. On the other hand, SEMMA, which stands for Sample, Explore, Modify, Model, Assess, has been championed by SAS Institute. SAS has launched a data mining software platform (SAS Enterprise Miner) that implements SEMMA. For a complete description of SEMMA and SAS Enterprise Miner, visit the SAS web site: *http://www.sas.com/*.

In addition to SEMMA and CRISP, numerous other methodologies attempt to do the same thing, that is, to break the data mining process into a sequence of steps to be followed by analysts for the purpose of promoting best practices and standardizing the steps and results.

This book does not delve into the philosophical arguments about the advantages of each methodology. It extracts from them the basic steps to be performed in any data mining engagement to lay out a roadmap for the remaining chapters of this book.

All methodologies contain the following set of main tasks in one form or another.

1. Relevant data elements are extracted from a database or a data warehouse into one table containing *all* the variables needed for modeling. This table is commonly known as the *mining view*, or *rollup file*. In the case when the size of the data cannot be handled efficiently by available data modeling tools, which is frequently the case, sampling is used.

2. A set of data exploration steps are performed to gain some insight about the relationships among the data and to create a summary of the properties. This is known as EDA (Exploratory Data Analysis).

3. Based on the results of EDA, some transformation procedures are invoked to highlight and take advantage of the relationships among the variables in the planned models.

4. A set of data mining models are then developed using different techniques, depending on the objective of the exercise and the types of variables involved. Not all the available variables are used in the modeling phase. Therefore, a data reduction procedure is often invoked to select the most useful set of variables.

5. The data mining models are evaluated and the best performing model is selected according to some performance criteria.

6. The population of data intended for the application of the model is prepared in an identical process to that used in the preparation of the mining view to create what is known as the *scoring view*. The selected optimal (best) model is used to score the scoring view and produce the *scores*. These scores are used by the different business units to achieve the required business objective, such as selecting the targeted customers for marketing campaigns or to receive a loan or a credit card.

Typically, these steps are performed iteratively, and not necessarily in the presented linear order. For example, one might extract the mining view, perform EDA, build a set of models, and then, based on the evaluation results of these models, decide to introduce a set of transformations and data reduction steps in an attempt to improve the model performance.

Of the six steps in the data mining process, the data extraction and preparation steps could occupy up to 80% of the project time. In addition, to avoid a "garbage in, garbage out" situation, we have to make sure that we have extracted the right and most useful data. Therefore, data extraction and preparation should have the priority in planning and executing data mining projects. Therefore, this book!

1.3 THE MINING VIEW

Most, if not all, data mining algorithms deal with the data in the form of a single matrix (a two-dimensional array). However, the raw data, which contains the information needed for modeling, is rarely stored in such form. Most data is stored in relational databases, where the data is scattered over several tables. Therefore, the first step in collecting the data is to roll up the different tables and aggregate the data to the required rectangular form in anticipation of using mining algorithms. This last table, with all the elements needed, or suspected to be needed, for the modeling work is known as the *mining view*, *rollup file*, or *modeling table*. The tools used to aggregate the data elements into the mining view are usually data management tools such as SQL queries, SAS procedures, or, in the case of legacy systems, custom programs (e.g., in C, C++, and Java).

The mining view is defined as the aggregated modeling data on the specified *entity* level. The data is assembled in the form of columns, with the entity being unique on the row level. The meaning of the *entity* in the preceding definition is related to the business objective of modeling. In most business applications, the entity level is the *customer level*. In this case, we assemble all the relevant data for each customer in the form of columns and ensure that each row represents a unique customer with all the data related to this customer included. Examples of customer-level mining views are customer acquisition, cross selling, customer retention, and customer lifetime value.

In other situations, the entity is defined as the *transaction*. For example, we try to create a fraud detection system, say for online credit card shopping. In this case, the entity level is the purchase transaction and not the customer. This is because we attempt to stop fraudulent *transactions*. Similarly, the entity level may be defined as the *product level*. This could be necessary, for example, in the case of segmentation modeling of products for a supermarket chain where hundreds, or even thousands, of products exist.

The mining view usually undergoes a series of data cleaning and transformation steps before it is ready for use by the modeling algorithm. These operations achieve two purposes:

1. Clean the data of errors, missing values, and outliers.

2. Attempt to create new variables through a set of transformations, which could lead to better models.

Data errors and missing values always occur as a result of data collection and transformation from one data system to another. There are many techniques for cleaning the data from such errors and substituting or imputing the missing values.

Typically, the required data transformations are discovered over several iterations of data preparation, exploration, and pilot modeling. In other words, not all the needed data preparation steps are, or could be, known in advance. This is the nature of knowledge discovery in data mining modeling. However, once specific transformations have been established and tested for a particular dataset for a certain model, they must be recorded in order to be used again on the data to be scored by the model. This leads us to the next view: the *scoring view*.

1.4 THE SCORING VIEW

The scoring view is very similar to the mining view except that the dependent variable (variable to be predicted) is not included. The following are other differences between the mining view and the scoring view.

1. The scoring view is usually much larger than the mining view. The mining view is only a sample from the data population; the scoring view is the population itself. This has implications on the requirements of the hardware and software needed to manipulate the scoring view and perform the necessary transformations on it before using it in scoring.

2. The scoring view may contain only one record. This is the case of online scoring, in which one record is read at a time and its score is calculated. The mining view, for obvious reasons, must have many records to be useful in developing a model.

3. The variables needed to make the mining view are determined by attempting to collect all conceivable variables that may have association with the quantity being predicted or have a relationship to the problem being modeled. The scoring view, on the other hand, contains only the variables that were used to create the model. The model may contain derived and transformed variables. These variables must also be in the scoring view. It is expected, therefore, that the scoring view would have significantly fewer variables than the mining view.

The only special case in which the mining view becomes the scoring view as well is the development of time series models for forecasting. In this case, the mining view is used to fit the predictive model and simultaneously to predict future values, thus removing the distinction between the mining view and the scoring view. We do not deal with data preparation for time series modeling in this book.

The next chapter provides a more detailed description of both the mining view and the scoring view.

1.5 NOTES ON DATA MINING SOFTWARE

Many software packages are used to develop data mining models. The procedures developed in this text for data preparation are independent of the tool used for the actual model building. Some of these tools include data preparation capabilities, thus allowing analysts to perform functions similar to some of the procedures described in this book. Most analysts prefer to separate the procedures of data preparation and modeling. We have adopted this attitude by developing the procedures described in this book as SAS macros to be implemented independently of the modeling software.

However, the techniques and procedures described in the book could also be applied using many of the data manipulation capabilities of these modeling tools.

TASKS AND 2
DATA FLOW

2.1 DATA MINING TASKS

Data mining is often defined as a set of mathematical models and data manipulation techniques that perform functions aiming at the discovery of new knowledge in databases. The functions, or *tasks*, performed by these techniques can be classified in terms of either the analytical function they entail or their implementation focus. The first classification scheme takes the point of view of the data mining analyst. In this case, the analyst would classify the tasks on the basis of the problem type as one of the following.

1. *Classification*

   In these problems, the operative is to assign each record in the database a particular class or a category label from a finite set of predefined class labels. For example, a bank would be interested in classifying each of its customers as potentially interested in a new credit card or not. All decisions involving Yes/No selection, such as classifying insurance claims according to the possibility of fraud, also belong to classification problems. Classification problems may involve three or more levels, such as "high," "medium," and "low." The main point is that the number of classes is finite. Note that there could be an implicit order relationship in the definition of the classes, such as "high," "medium," and "low."

2. *Estimation*

   These problems are focused on estimating the unknown value of a continuous variable. For example, taxation authorities might be interested in estimating the *real income* of households. The number of possible outcomes of an estimation problem is infinite by definition.

3. *Prediction*

   Prediction is the task of estimating a value in the future. Typical examples include attempting to predict stock prices, prices of commodities, and future values of air pollution indices.

4. *Clustering*

   Clustering, which is also known as *segmentation*, is the task of dividing a heterogeneous population into a number of more or less homogeneous subgroups or clusters. It is also sometimes defined as *finding islands of simplicity in the data*. Typical examples include customer and market segmentation. In dealing with very large datasets, clustering is also used as an initial analysis tool to simplify the data into smaller groups or to generate hypotheses about the data.

5. *Affinity Analysis*

   Other names for affinity analysis include *market basket analysis* and *association analysis*. It is concerned with finding *things* that usually go together. These *things* could be products, transactions, sequences of operations, or any objects stored in a database. A typical example is the analysis of the supermarket basket, where we attempt to find the likelihood of specific products being purchased together in the same basket. For example, we might be interested to know whether chicken and barbecue sauce are more likely to be purchased together than, say, chicken and canned soup.

The preceding classification scheme of data mining tasks focuses on their analytical nature. Businesses, on the other hand, define data mining in terms of the application. For example, in banking and finance one speaks about *credit scoring* and *risk analysis*, and in marketing applications, data mining is described as the tool for modeling *customer behavior*, *churn analysis*, *customer acquisition*, and *cross-selling*. We can set a simple framework for the classification of data mining tasks in terms of the *business view* by dividing the applications into the following three areas of interest.

- *Sales and marketing:* This domain includes CRM (customer relationship management) applications such as customer acquisition, cross-selling, customer service, churn and retention, product affinity, and lifetime value estimation.

- *Operations management:* This classification applies to areas such as process control, inventory management, supply chain management, financial risk analysis, and maintenance.

- *Finance:* This category includes areas such as prediction and management of cash flow, loans and mortgages, credit card issuing, and assignment of credit limits.

A second business-based view of data mining tasks could be structured by grouping applications that relate to the management of "Products," "Operations," or "Customers." These three domains cover almost all aspects of any business. For example, customer retention is related to management of customers, and risk management belongs to operations.

The range of problems for which data mining modeling has been used outside business applications is too wide to classify into specific categories. For example, clustering methods have been used to identify star formations in astronomy, and classification models are used to select jury members. Other applications include weather prediction, clinical trials, drug discovery, genetic engineering, and social studies, to mention a few.

2.2   Data Mining Competencies

A successful implementation of data mining modeling requires competencies in three areas.

1. *Understanding the Problem Domain*

   This first requirement necessitates the full understanding of the objectives of the project, the value added by the engagement and the expected return on investment (ROI), and how the business processes is being impacted by the implementation of the data mining technology. For example, in credit card risk scoring applications, the analyst must understand the basics of credit card risk management strategies and the basics of the legal as well as the business procedures involved.

2. *Understanding the Data*

   Understanding the data is not limited to the names and descriptions of fields in the database or data warehouse, but also concerns the content of the fields, the meaning of each category, the meaning of outliers, missing values, any preprocessing that has been done on the data, and the sources of the data.

3. *Data Mining Modeling Methods and Software*

   This area of competency covers the methodology of data mining, the strengths and limitations of each data mining technique, and the modeling software. The analyst should know which technique to use, with which dataset, and when.

Although nobody is an expert in everything, to achieve good results using data mining modeling, these three areas of competency are necessary. Therefore, in large organizations, where no single individual could possess high competency in all these areas, data mining is performed by a team consisting of business domain experts, data analysts and programmers, and modelers.

Many good textbooks provide the details of the business aspect of data mining and how modeling fits in the general scheme of things. Similarly, numerous good texts are dedicated to the explanation of the different data mining algorithms and software. We will not dwell much on these two areas.

2.3 THE DATA FLOW

Figure 2.1 depicts the typical stages of data flow. In this process, many of the steps may be repeated several times in order to fit the flow of operations within a certain data mining methodology. The process can be described as follows.

1. The data is extracted from the database or the data warehouse to the mining view. The mining view is the dataset that will be used to create the predictive models.

2. The data in the mining view is divided into three partitions for training, validation, and testing of the different models. Often, only two partitions are used: training and validation.

3. A scoring view is extracted from the database or data warehouse. The scoring view is similar to the mining view, except that it contains only the fields necessary to calculate the score by the trained and validated predictive model(s). The scoring view does not contain the value of the dependent variable.

4. One or more of the trained and tested predictive models is used to produce scores using the data of the scoring view. The scores may take the form of discrete

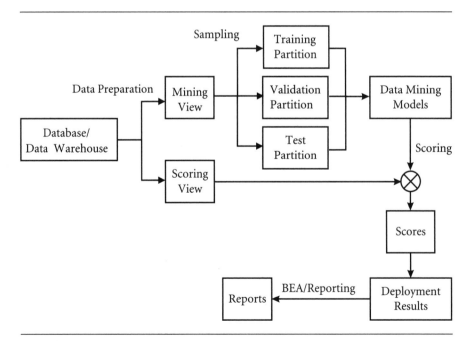

Figure 2.1   Steps of data flow.

values (1/0, Yes/No), probabilities (in the range 0–1), real values (predicted sales), or segment indexes (e.g., 1 to 9).

5. The scores, along with additional information that would be collected from the results of implementing the model (e.g., in a campaign), are then used to compile business reports.

6. After the deployment of the model and collection of the actual response or the predicted value, a Back End Analysis (BEA) is conducted to assess the model and the business process performance.

A closer examination of the preceding steps reveals that all the procedures that reshape the data can be categorized into three groups.

1. Procedures for extracting, integrating, and reshaping the mining and scoring views

2. Procedures for sampling

3. Procedures for reporting

We next discuss in more detail the types of variables and the contents of the mining and scoring views.

2.4 Types of Variables

In general, we can categorize the variables that would be included in the mining and scoring views into the following groups.

1. *Dependent Variables*

   The dependent variables (DVs) contain the quantities being estimated or predicted. In the cases of clustering and association rule models, there is no dependent variable. In all other models (classification, estimation, and prediction models), there is at least one dependent variable. Sometimes, the mining view can be used to model different objectives simultaneously (e.g., calculating the risk of loan default as well as estimating the amount to be lost in such loans).

2. *Independent Variables*

   The independent variables (IVs) are used to build the model. In the case of classification, estimation, or prediction models, these variables are the "predictors" of the dependent variable.

3. *Record Identification Variables*

   The identification (ID) variables allow the analyst to revert to the data to identify the records that show certain interesting features. For example, the ID variable in a loan default model would allow the analyst to identify the details of data on the customers who have been flagged by the model as high-risk customers.

4. *Explanation Variables*

The explanation variables (labels) provide extra information on each record. They are not to be used, however, in the modeling process. For example, one may find a product variable having the categories (AK1, ASU3). A descriptive variable indicating that AK1 is "long-distance package A with calling feature package K" would not add value to analysis and is too long to be used in the model, but it is useful to keep in the mining view to make understanding the data easier.

5. *Sample Weights*

Sample weights should be included in all samples in order to allow the proper calculation of the population statistical properties, and for use in the modeling algorithms.

2.5 THE MINING VIEW AND THE SCORING VIEW

The mining view is a table or, in the case of SAS, a dataset that contains the following fields.

- Identification fields: Typical examples of ID fields include customer number and transaction number.

- Independent variables: These are only *possible* predictors because one of the tasks of building a good predictive model is to identify the best predictors and use them in the model. Therefore, the mining view will contain many candidate IVs that may not be used in the development of the model.

- Dependent variables: As mentioned, with the exception of the clustering and association models, we always have one or more dependent variable in the model. In cases of classification models, it is always better to have the DV in a binary form (1/0). In spite of the fact that most classification techniques (decision trees, neural networks, logistic regression) allow the multicategory DVs, when the DV has more than two categories, the quality of the models using each output separately is better than that achieved by using all the categories simultaneously.

- Explanation variables.

- Sample weights.

- *Other reporting fields:* The mining view can include other fields that would be used for producing reports.

The scoring view is a table that contains the following fields.

- ID fields

- All the predictors that were used in the predictive model(s) to calculate the score or the predicted value, or the actual model IVs

- Description variables

- Reporting variables

Therefore, the scoring view is very similar to the mining view with the following exceptions.

- It contains only the IVs that were used in the development of the final predictive model used for scoring. Not all the other possible IVs, which were eliminated from the model, need be included.

- It does not contain the DV field. This will be the result of the scoring process.

- It usually contains many fewer fields but far more records.

2.6 STEPS OF DATA PREPARATION

The typical steps involved in the preparation of the mining view include the following.

1. Extracting and sampling data from the operational database or the data warehouse; at this stage, the data may be spread among several datasets.

2. Checking the integrity of the extracted and sampled data: These checks may be performed on the individual datasets or after the integration of all data elements into one dataset, which is the next step.

3. Integrating data: In this step, the different elements of the mining view are integrated into one table or view.

4. Transforming the data and creating new variables (analytical variables): This operation can also be performed on each table extracted from the data warehouse before the integration of the data. This can sometimes result in improved model performance.

5. Removing independent variables that have low or no predictive power.

This order of steps may be altered to improve performance and to accommodate the specific needs of the data warehouse or the data sources.

The preparation of the scoring view is always much easier than that for the mining view. However, because the number of records in the scoring view is usually much larger than that in the mining view, the execution of the data preparation programs could be slower.

In today's practical business applications of data mining, the most common models are classification models, followed by estimation models. Clustering models are also popular as a first step of analysis to reduce the data or describe large populations in terms of smaller segments.

CHAPTER 3

REVIEW OF DATA MINING MODELING TECHNIQUES

3.1 INTRODUCTION

A large number of modeling techniques are labeled "data mining" techniques. This chapter provides a short review of a selected number of these techniques. Our choice was guided by two factors:

1. Frequency of use: We focus on the most currently used models in industry.
2. Relevance to the book's scope: We review the modeling methods most likely to benefit from the data preparation procedures in this book.

The review in this chapter only highlights some of the features of different techniques and how they influence, and benefit from, the data preparation procedures presented in the remaining chapters of the book. We do not present a complete exposition of the mathematical details of the algorithms, or their SAS implementations, to keep the focus of the book on data preparation.

3.2 REGRESSION MODELS

Regression models are the oldest and most used models in data mining. Most data mining software packages include regression capabilities. They are also the most understood models in terms of performance, mathematics, and diagnostic measures for model quality and goodness of fit. Regression models have been applied to a very wide range of problems in finance, engineering, environment, medicine, agriculture, economics, military, and marketing, to mention a few.

Two forms of regression are of particular interest to data mining applications: linear regression and logistic regression.

3.2.1 LINEAR REGRESSION

Linear regression models are used primarily in *estimation* tasks, that is, to predict a continuous value. It assumes that the dependent variable y can be calculated from a *linear* form of the independent variables $x_1, \ldots, x_p$, as follows (Johnson and Wichern 2001):

$$y = a_0 + a_1 x_1 + \cdots + a_p x_p. \tag{3.1}$$

In the language of data mining, the model training process involves finding the values of $p + 1$ constants, also known as the *model parameters*, $a_0, a_1, \ldots, a_p$, by fitting Equation 3.1 to the training portion of the mining view. There are several methods to fit the data to the form of 3.1. The most common is known as *ordinary least squares* (OLS). PROC REG of SAS/STAT implements OLS to fit linear regression models. It also provides a comprehensive set of diagnostic measures to assess the model and data quality.

There are several requirements that linear regression models impose on the data and that, therefore, our data preparation procedures should consider:

- Linear regression requires that *all* the predictors (i.e., variables $x_1, \ldots, x_p$) be numeric, and preferably continuous. Therefore, nominal variables have to be converted to something else. The transformations described in Section 9.4 are typically used to do just that.

- Linear regression models are not designed to deal with missing values. Therefore, missing values need to be replaced with something or the models would simply ignore these records. Replacing missing values always runs the risk of introducing some bias in the model. On the other hand, ignoring records with missing values can lead to a model based on a significantly smaller number of observations that do not represent the problem. The best available compromise is to *impute* the missing values. The complete coverage of the issue of missing values and multiple imputation is presented in Chapter 11. We strongly recommend considering imputing missing values before attempting to build a regression model, especially when the records containing missing values represent a significant portion of the modeling data, that is, more than 20%.

- When one or more of the independent variables can be expressed as a linear combination of other independent variables, the basic regression formulation fails to find a unique solution. This problem is known as *multi-collinearity*, and the variables are said to be collinear. PROC REG, as well as most other regression procedures in SAS/STAT, performs a collinearity test by default and eliminates from the model some of the variables suspected to be the cause of the problem. This is particularly the case when some of the independent variables were generated using linear forms as part of the data preparation transformations. Data transformations are dealt with in detail in Chapter 9, including the generation of new variables. The issue here is to remember not to use linear forms to generate new variables and then use them, along with all their components, as predictors in a linear regression model.

■ Most real-life data contains outliers. Techniques of detecting outliers are presented in Section 7.5. The main problem with outliers is that they result in large *residuals*. OLS models fit the model parameters by minimizing the sum of the squares of the residuals. Therefore, outliers could lead to a large bias in the model parameters. In this case, *robust regression*, which is a modified regression formulation, is specifically designed to fit linear models while minimizing the effect of outliers. In fact, one of the methods used to identify outliers depends on building a robust regression model and labeling the observations that were rejected by the model as outliers. This technique for detecting outliers is presented in Section 7.5.2.

■ Although linear regression is designed to fit a *linear* model form, it can be easily extended to fit model forms that are *nonlinear* in the independent variables. For example, we may consider a model form that is nonlinear in the predictors x_1, x_2, x_3, as follows:

$$y = a_0 + a_1 x_1 + a_2 x_2 + a_3 x_3 + a_4 x_1 x_2 + a_5 x_2 x_3 + a_6 x_3 x_1$$
$$+ a_7 x_1^2 + a_8 x_2^2 + a_9 x_3^2. \tag{3.2}$$

Equation 3.2 represents a regression model that is nonlinear in the independent variables x_1, x_2, x_3, but still linear in the parameters $a_1, \ldots, a_9$. PROC REG does not allow the specification of an equation of this form directly. Therefore, we need to create new variables to represent the terms that involve higher interaction among variables, *interaction terms*, or higher orders of the same variable. The techniques described in Section 9.3.2 can be used to automate the process of generating these variables as part of the data preparation process.

■ Sometimes we need to develop more than one model on the basis of some classification variable. For example, we may need to develop models to estimate the profitability of banking customers using their transaction and investment history, but for separate geographical regions or separate business units of the bank. The last case is more common because many retail banks offer the same services under several brand names as a result of mergers and acquisitions. In this case, we need to develop several models, all having the same structure and fitted with similar data, but for disjoint subsets of the data using a classification variable. In this case, the classification variable would include the name of the business unit or the geographical region. This is one of the features of all regression implementations in SAS, which is specified using the CLASS statement.

The importance of this feature is that it facilitates the data preparation procedures because we could prepare a single mining view for *all* the data, and identify the different groups aimed for different models later, through the definition of the CLASS variable(s).

- One last feature of linear regression, which is important from the point of view of data preparation, is the model building process. Linear regression models, as well as logistic regression model, offer the capability of iterative *selection* of the best combination of independent variables. There are several strategies and criteria for such variable selection. PROC REG documentation provides the details of these methods. The method known as *stepwise* selection of variables is one of the most popular and reliable methods. It depends on adding and removing variables iteratively until no significant improvement in the model quality is observed. Another recommended method is based on maximizing the R^2, known as the coefficient of multiple determination, which measures the extent to which the independent variables *explain* the variability in the dependent variable.

  The result of variable selection schemes is that the initial set of independent variables, provided by the mining view, is reduced to a smaller set. The reduced set is all that will be needed in the scoring view. Therefore, building good regression models that use the minimum set of independent variables has a positive impact on the time and effort needed to prepare the scoring view. Models that attempt to use the smallest set of independent variables are called *parsimonious* models.

Most of these issues apply also to other models, and in particular logistic regression, which is the next topic.

3.2.2 LOGISTIC REGRESSION

At the time of writing this book, logistic regression is by far the most popular classification algorithm. The majority of classification models in finance, marketing, and customer relationship management employ logistic regression.

Logistic regression is used when the response variable is binary, multicategory nominal, or ordinal (Hosmer and Lemeshow 1989). The model equation takes many forms depending on the type of response variable. In the case of the binary dependent variable, as in the most common case of classification tasks, the model is given as

$$g(\pi) = a_0 + a_1 x_1 + \cdots + a_p x_p, \tag{3.3}$$

where $x_1, \ldots, x_p$ are the independent variables, $a_0, a_1, \ldots, a_p$ are their associated model parameters, π is the probability of one of the two events of the binary dependent variable y, and $g(\cdot)$ is a transformation function, called the *link function*. The most commonly used link function is the *logit* function, defined as

$$g(\pi) = \log\left(\frac{\pi}{1 - \pi}\right). \tag{3.4}$$

π is usually taken as the probability of success, that is, $y = 1$.

In the case of the dependent variable y being ordinal, taking values of $1, \ldots, k+1$, the model is defined as

$$g(Pr\{y \le i\}) = a_{0i} + a_1 x_1 + \cdots + a_p x_p, \qquad i = 1, \ldots, k. \tag{3.5}$$

Equation 3.5 is similar to the model of Equation 3.3, except it defines k constant terms, and not only a single constant a_0.

Finally, in order to model multicategory nominal dependent variable, with $k + 1$ categories, the model in Equation 3.5 is modified to have a total of k model equations, given as

$$\log \left(\frac{Pr\{y = i\}}{Pr\{y = k + 1\}} \right) = a_{0i} + a_{1i}x_1 + \cdots + a_{pi}x_p, \quad i = 1, \ldots, k. \tag{3.6}$$

In this case, the link function is restricted to the *log* function and the model is called the *generalized logit model*. Note that on the left side of Equation 3.6, the denominator is the probability of the last category of the dependent variable. Since there is no order relationship among the categories, we can select any DV category to replace the denominator. The last category was chosen only for convenience.

Several link functions can be used in Equations 3.3 and 3.5 for modeling binary and ordinal dependent variables. PROC LOGISTIC offers the following options:

- The *logit* function, which is the inverse of the cumulative logistic distribution function

- The *probit*, or *normit*, function, which is the inverse of the cumulative standard normal distribution function

- The *complementary log–log* function, which is the inverse of the cumulative extreme-value function (also called the Gompertz distribution)

The difference among these link functions is the range and scale of the probabilities they produce. In most practical cases discussed in this book, the dependent variable is binary and the *logit* link function is appropriate.

Logistic regression attempts to estimate the *probability* of the events of the dependent variable, therefore, the method of *maximum likelihood* (ML) is used to solve for the model parameters. Furthermore, because the model equations involve nonlinear link functions, the estimation procedure involves the iterative solution of a set of nonlinear equations. Therefore, for tasks involving large training datasets with a large number of variables, logistic regression takes longer to execute than the equivalent linear regression.

Similar to the case of linear regression, implementing logistic regression raises several issues that may impact the procedures of data preparation. The following is a summary of these issues.

- Unlike linear regression, logistic regression implementation in PROC LOGISTIC, and many other modeling packages, allows the use of nominal predictors. This advantage may remove the need to map nominal predictors to indicator variables (see Section 9.4). However, most implementations, indeed in PROC LOGISTIC when utilizing different methods of variable selection, such as stepwise selection, can use either all the categories of the variable in the model or none. In most cases, this is not an issue. However, explicit mapping of nominal variables to indicator variables overcomes this limitation easily.

- As in the case of linear regression, collinearity of independent variables will lead to models that ignore some of the variables.

- Logistic regression cannot deal with missing values. Therefore, we need to either impute or replace missing values before training the model. Observations with missing values are ignored.

- Logistic regression is more robust to outliers than linear regression. However, it is still recommended that we check for outliers, especially in the predictors (i.e., what are known as *leverage points*) before training the model. See Section 7.5 for the methods of detecting outliers.

- Similar to the case of linear regression, interaction and higher order terms can be used in logistic regression models by defining new variables to hold the values of these terms. The techniques in Section 9.3.2 can be used to generate these variables. Alternatively, PROC LOGISTIC allows the direct definition of interaction terms in the model equation (MODEL statement). We recommend defining new variables to hold the values of interaction terms explicitly in order to facilitate the scoring process.

- PROC LOGISTIC also offers the ability to build different models using a CLASS variable as well as selecting the best set of predictors using several selection criteria. The most common selection method is STEPWISE selection. The result of the variable selection is the reduced set of predictors to be used in the scoring view.

- Logistic regression cannot model datasets that are *linearly separable*. A dataset is said to be linearly separable when we can find a set of constants, $b_1, \ldots, b_q$, not all zeros, such that a linear expression of the form $b_1 x_1 + \cdots + b_q x_1 \geq 0$ for all the observations where $y = 1$ and $b_1 x_1 + \cdots + b_q x_1 < 0$ for all the observations where $y = 0$. In this case, we say the data of the variables $x_1, \ldots, x_1$ classifies the response variable y perfectly. It can be demonstrated that there exists no maximum likelihood solution for the logistic regression equations. PROC LOGISTIC, and most other implementations in data mining packages, would still give some solution in these cases, with a warning message.

  Unfortunately, there is no easy way to check on the presence of linear separability in datasets before attempting to use them in logistic regression. However, experience has shown that linear separability is more likely to exist in datasets (1) that have a medium to small number of observations, or observations free of missing values, relative to the number of variables; and (2) in which a large proportion of the independent variables is nominal or binary.

  The good news is that when logistic regression fails because of linear separability, neural networks attain their best performance, and therefore, provide a good alternative.

3.3 DECISION TREES

Decision tree models are used for both classification and estimation tasks. Therefore, dependent variables could be binary, nominal, ordinal, or continuous. The independent variables could be also of all these types (Breiman et al. 1998).

The main decision tree algorithm works by attempting to *split* the data using one of the independent variables to separate the data into subgroups that are more homogeneous, in terms of some measure related to the dependent variable, than the original dataset. The splitting process continues recursively until no significant splits can be made. The final form of the tree can be translated to a set of If-Then-Else rules.

Decision trees are popular because of the graphical user interface offered by many vendors of data mining packages. These packages allow easy manipulation of the tree during the tree growth, including the manual intervention of the analyst to override the algorithm choice of splits. Figure 3.1 shows one such tree.

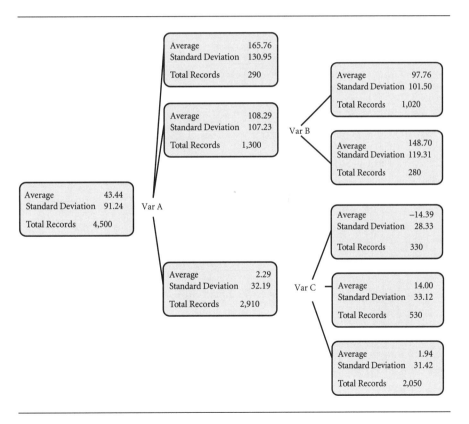

Figure 3.1   Decision tree diagram.

Decision trees offer the following advantages over regression models.

- The interactive features offered by almost all software packages make it easier to use than writing code for regression models.

- The representation of the data in tree form gives the *illusion* of understanding the *causes* of the observed behavior of the dependent variable. Of course, like all data mining models, the tree model cannot determine or prove causality, but the tree diagram helps to explains *how* the model determined the estimated probability (in the case of classification) or the mean value (in the case of estimation problems) of the dependent variable.

- The final tree can be translated to a simple code, in either SAS or other programming language, to execute the scoring code.

- The tree model can naturally handle all types of variables, even with missing values.

- Collinearity and linear separability problems do not affect tree performance.

- Most implementations of tree algorithms are faster, in terms of execution time, than logistic regression for the same problem size.

However, decision tree algorithms do not enjoy the large number of diagnostic tests and measures available for linear and logistic regression. Furthermore, decision tree algorithms bin continuous variables to use them as categories, with or without accounting for the order. This binning leads to some loss of information. This becomes apparent in some estimation problems when the underlying relationship between the dependent variable and the predictors is genuinely linear; then decision trees cannot match the performance of that of linear regression. Therefore, it is always recommended that we use as many model types as possible and use the model showing the best validation results.

Decision trees do not impose special restrictions or requirements on the data preparation procedures. On the other hand, the following data preparation techniques are based on the same formulations of decision tree splits.

- Reduction of cardinality of nominal variables, Section 10.2.5.

- Optimal binning of continuous variables, Section 10.3.3.

- Methods of variable reduction using X^2, Gini, and Entropy variance methods, Chapter 17.

3.4 NEURAL NETWORKS

Neural networks are powerful mathematical models suitable for almost all data mining tasks, with special emphasis on classification and estimation problems. They have their origins in attempts to simulate the behavior of brain cells, but that is where the relationship ends. There are numerous formulations of neural networks, some of which are specialized to solve specific problems, such as self-organizing maps (SOM), which is a special formulation suitable for clustering. The most common neural network formulation is that of the *multilayered perceptron* (MLP).

The MLP formulation is based on the definition of a mathematical object, called a neuron, that transforms the *sum* of its input data to an output according to some *activation function*. Figure 3.2 shows the representation of a single neuron with two inputs and one output.

Mathematically, we express the output of the neuron of Figure 3.2 as

$$y = f\left(\sum_i x_i\right). \tag{3.7}$$

The activation function $f(\cdot)$ could be any function that saturates for both the low and high levels of its input. Common activation functions are

- The logistic function (the inverse of the logit function)

- The inverse cumulative normal function

- The complementary log–log function

- The log–log function

The multilayered perceptron neural network uses neurons arranged in layers, as shown in Figure 3.3. Figure 3.3 shows a network with a single *hidden layer* and a

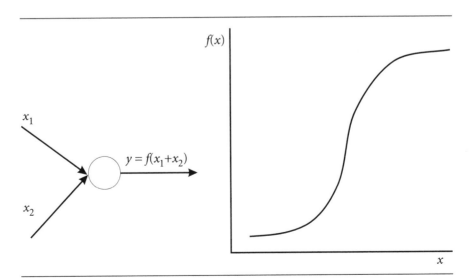

Figure 3.2   A single neuron.

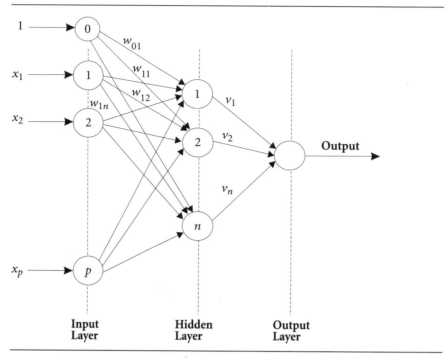

Figure 3.3   Multilayered perceptron network with a single output.

single output. The neurons in the input layer are always defined with identity activation functions; all the other neurons are defined with a function in the preceding list. For most practical applications, one hidden layer is sufficient. The connections between the different layers carry multiplicative weights, the w's and the v's. For example, neuron 1 in the hidden layer of Figure 3.3 has a total input of $1 \cdot w_{01} + x_1 w_{11} + x_2 w_{12} + \cdots + x_p w_{1p}$. This input is transformed by the activation function of this neuron in the hidden layer. The output of this neuron is then multiplied by the weight v_1 to be fed to the output neuron. Therefore, the output of the network shown in Figure 3.3 is given by

$$y = f\left(\sum_{j=1}^{n} \left(v_j \cdot f\left(\sum_{i=0}^{p} w_{ij} \cdot x_i \right) \right) \right). \tag{3.8}$$

Note that the input to neuron 0 represents a constant in the model and is known as the *bias*. The process of model training, or fitting, is simply to find the values of the weights w_{ij}, v_j, where $i = 0, \ldots, p$, and $j = 1, \ldots, n$. The process of model fitting, or training, is obtained by minimizing the sum of the squared error between the predicted and the actual output for the training dataset. There are many algorithms for solving this optimization problem. Refer to Bishop (1996) for the details of solution algorithms and other network configurations. Furthermore, the MLP just described can be extended to allow for more than a single output.

Examination of the neural network formulation reveals that it is only a complex form of nonlinear regression. In fact, inspection of Equation 3.8 shows that linear and logistic regressions are special cases of MLP. Specifically, when all the activation functions, in all the layers, are defined as the identity function, Equation 3.8 becomes the linear regression equation. Similarly, when the activation function of the neurons of the hidden layer is the identity function, and that of the output neuron is the logistic function, Equation 3.8 reduces to the logistic regression equation.

The advantages of neural networks is that they usually outperform all other models because of their complex structure. They are not sensitive to outliers and provide even better performance when the data is separable.

However, because of the mathematical complexity and the lack of clear graphical representation of the results (compared to, say, decision trees), neural networks are not as popular as regression and tree models. They also lack the extensive diagnostic measures offered by regression models. Therefore, many analysts consider them *black box* models, which are to be used only as a last resort.

Similar to linear regression models, MLP requires all the variables to be numeric with no missing values. Therefore, nominal variables have to be mapped and missing values have to be either replaced with other values or imputed; see Section 9.4 and Chapter 11. Some implementations of MLP use iterative variable selection algorithms similar to those used in linear and logistic regression. In this case, only the selected set of variables is used for scoring.

3.5 CLUSTER ANALYSIS

Cluster analysis is concerned with finding subgroups of the population that "belong" together. In other words, we are looking for *islands of simplicity* in the data. Clustering techniques work by calculating a multivariate distance measure between observations. Observations that are *close* to each other are then grouped in one cluster. Clustering algorithms belong to three broad categories: agglomeration methods, divisive methods, and *k*-clustering.

In divisive methods, we start by considering the entire dataset as one cluster and then divide it recursively into several smaller clusters. Ultimately, each observation becomes a cluster on its own. The final relationships among the records are represented in a *tree*, or a *dendrogram*.

In the case of agglomerative methods, each observation is initially considered a cluster by itself. Then using the distance measure, the clusters are merged into larger ones until the entire dataset is one cluster. It is the opposite of the divisive strategy.

Finally, the *k*-clustering approach is based on attempting to cluster the dataset into a fixed integer number of clusters *k*. The algorithm in this case starts with *k* observations, at random, as the centers of the clusters, and then attempts to group all the other observations into these clusters. The process iteratively adds and removes observations to and from the different clusters until no significant improvement is achieved.

Because all cluster analysis methods rely on the calculation of some *distance measure*, all variables must be numeric. Ordinal variables are converted to continuous variables on a scale, and nominal variables are converted to dummy or indicator variables, at least internally during the calculation of the distance measure. Clearly, missing values need to be either replaced or imputed before using cluster analysis, or they can be treated as a category of their own that would be mapped to an indicator variable. See Section 9.4 and Chapter 11 for more details on mapping of nominal variables and treatment of missing values.

From the data preparation point of view, *k*-clustering methods can be used for initial segmentation to reduce very large datasets to smaller more homogeneous sets. *K*-means, which is a *k*-clustering method, is sensitive to outliers. Therefore, we use it in Section 7.5.3 as a method for detecting candidate outliers.

3.6 ASSOCIATION RULES

Association rules are a set of techniques, as the name implies, that aim to find association relationships in the data (Adamo 2001). A typical application of association rules is the analysis of retail transaction data. For example, the analysis would aim to find the likelihood that when a customer buys Product X, she would also buy Product Y. This is why association rules are frequently called *Market Basket Analysis*.

Association rule algorithms can also be formulated to look for sequential patterns. They would provide results such as: a customer buys Product X, then Product Y, then Product Z (in this sequence).

The data usually needed for association analysis algorithms is the *transaction* data, for example, data that represent the purchasing baskets of the customers over a certain time frame. Typically, the data volumes are very large. Some of the techniques presented in the book are relevant to association analysis. The methods of data acquisition and integration, Chapter 5, and integrity checks, Chapter 6, are the most relevant.

3.7 TIME SERIES ANALYSIS

Time series analysis is concerned with making predictions (Box, Jenkins, and Reinsel 1994). Typical applications include analysis of stock prices, market trends, and sales forecasting. Because of the time dependence of the data, the data preparation procedures for time series data are different from the main theme of this book. However, some basic procedures might be of interest to the analyst in this field. See the chapters on data acquisition (5), integrity checks (6), and some parts of data transformations (9).

3.8 SUPPORT VECTOR MACHINES

Support vector machines (SVM) are machine learning algorithms based on statistical learning theory (Cristianini and Shawe-Taylor 2000). SVMs are similar to neural networks in the sense that they are used for estimation as well as classification problems. Also, when the dataset is linearly separable, they perform even better. Furthermore, SVMs are not susceptible to collinear data, as regression methods are. Although SVMs are relatively young compared to other data mining methods, there are a number of good commercial software implementations. SVMs usually do not require the generation of interaction or higher order terms, as regression methods do. This should save some data preparation steps. However, like neural network models, they work only with numeric non-missing data. Therefore, the techniques of Chapter 11 are typically useful.

CHAPTER 4

SAS MACROS: A QUICK START

4.1 INTRODUCTION: WHY MACROS?

This chapter provides readers unfamiliar with the SAS macro language a quick review of the basic elements of SAS macro programming. This is not a comprehensive guide, but rather it contains the minimum requirements to write reasonably efficient macros.

In providing this brief introduction, we adopted a learning strategy based on *What do I need to learn to be able to ... ?* The "..." represents different scenarios we intend to cover in our data preparation journey in this book. In these scenarios, we will need to write effective macros to facilitate performing the following tasks:

1. Write a SAS code with variable names and dataset names that are themselves parameters to allow reuse of the code with other datasets and variables. This requires familiarity with replacing text in regular SAS code. Furthermore, the text may need additional manipulation before using it in the final code. For example, the name of the SAS library will need to be concatenated to the name of the dataset before being referenced in a DATA step.

2. Perform some calculations before replacing the text. These calculations could be performed on either a string or numerical values. We may also need to call some of the mathematical functions provided by SAS. For example, we may wish to count the number of variables in the dataset and iterate on each of them to determine some univariate statistics as part of the EDA process.

3. Allow the code to be controlled by some programming logic, such as conditional execution of some parts of it depending on the nature of the data. For example, we may decide to determine the type of a variable as either categorical or continuous and treat each type differently.

4.2 THE BASICS: THE MACRO AND ITS VARIABLES

Writing SAS macros can be simplified by thinking of it as a way to replace the text of the SAS code with dynamic content. So let us start with a simple example. The following DATA step code reads the dataset DS1 into DS2:

```
DATA DS2;
 SET DS1;
RUN;
```

We can turn this simple code to create a macro that copies the contents of the dataset (call it DS_Original) to a new dataset, (DS_Copy). The way to do that is to use macro variables to express the names of the datasets in the DATA step instead of the static names DS1 and DS2. We can accomplish this as follows:

```
DATA &DS_Copy;
 SET &DS_Original;
  RUN;
```

Notice that we used the operator & to let SAS substitute the "contents" of the variables DS_Copy and DS_Original in those exact locations in the code. Then all we need to do each time we want to use this code is to *set* the value of these variables to the actual names of the datasets. This is accomplished using the keyword %LET . Note the percent sign that precedes the keyword LET. This percent sign always precedes *all* SAS macro keywords. The syntax used to define a macro variable and set its value is

```
%LET DS_Original = DS1;
%LET DS_Copy = DS2;
```

Now, we can define the two variables DS_Original and DS_Copy and give them their respective values as the names of the datasets DS1 and DS2, respectively, and we are ready to use the code that copies DS_Original into DS_Copy.

Finally, we add one more twist to this example. In order to *package* the copying code into a *SAS macro*, we enclose the code between two statements: one uses the keyword %MACRO ; the second ends the macro definition using the keyword %MEND. The syntax for the %MACRO statement includes the name of the macro and the list of parameters being passed to this macro enclosed in parentheses, as in the following example:

```
%MACRO CP_DS(DS_Original, DS_Copy);
... (the code goes here)
%MEND CP_DS;
```

The final code of the macro, then, is as follows:

```
%MACRO CP_DS(DS_Original, DS_Copy);
DATA &DS_Copy;
  SET &DS_Original;
  RUN;
%MEND CP_DS;
```

Note that the name of the macro in the %MEND statement is optional and will be ignored in most of our code.

And just as in all programming languages, we first define the function and then use it. In the case of SAS macros, we first define the macro and then use it. To use a macro, we need only to invoke its name preceded by the % and pass the appropriate values to its parameters. So, in our example, we invoke the dataset copying macro as follows:

```
%CP_DS(DS1, DS2);
```

The limitations on the names that can be used to define macro variables and macros are the same limitations that apply to general SAS programming language. Although recent versions of SAS allow longer variable names, we advise avoiding excessively long variable names. We also recommend that the user consult the most recent documentation on SAS macro language to review the limitations on naming macros and macro variables.

Within the body of the SAS macro, we can include almost any regular SAS code. However, this code will be executed only when the macro is invoked.

Variables declared within a macro are *local*, in the sense that their scope of definition is limited within the macro and cannot be reached from the open code area. Once the program execution leaves the macro, these variables will no longer be defined. Variables that are used as arguments in the macro name are local by definition. Macro variables declared outside any macro are *global*, and all macros can *see* these variables and use them. It is a good practice to limit the number of such variables and try to define all the variables within the macros to limit the chances of errors that can result from unintentionally overwriting values to the same variables. And as might be expected, a list of macro variables can be declared local or global by preceding them with the keywords %LOCAL and %GLOBAL, as follows:

```
%LOCAL Local_Var1 Local_Var2;     /* Local variables  */
%GLOBAL Global_Var1 Global_Var2;  /* Global variables */
```

We will get back to the issue of local and global macro variables later in this chapter. Please make sure that you read the section on common macro patterns before you start writing macros that call other macros.

To summarize the basic features of macros:

- Macro variables are defined using the %LET statement, which assigns a text to the contents of the variable. The value of the variable can be restored in the code using the & operator.

- Macros can be defined by enclosing the macro code within the statements %MACRO and %MEND. The name of the macro is mandatory for the %MACRO statement but optional for the %MEND statement.

- Variables within a macro can be declared global or local. By default all variables created within a macro as well as the macro arguments are local. Variables created in the open code area are global.

4.3 DOING CALCULATIONS

The SAS macro language provides a wide variety of commands to facilitate calculations. The simplest one is the function %EVAL(), which evaluates an *integer* expression. For example, to increase the value of a counter by 1, we can write:

```
%LET Counter = 1;
%LET Counter = %EVAL(&Counter+1);
```

Again, notice that we did not forget to use the & before the variable Counter inside the expression to let the macro compiler substitute its previous value. The result of the above calculation would be to set the value of the variable Counter to 2.

A useful command to print the value of any macro variable to the SAS Log is the command %PUT. To display the final value of the variable Counter of the preceding calculation, we would use the %PUT at the end of the code. The final code would be as follows:

```
%LET Counter = 1;
%LET Counter = %EVAL(&Counter+1);
%PUT &Counter;
```

To do floating point calculations, the function %SYSEVALF() is used. The following example shows how to use this function to calculate the area of a circle using its radius.

```
%LET Radius = 10;
%LET PI = 3.14159;

%LET Area = %SYSEVALF(&PI * &Radius * &Radius );
%PUT &Area;
```

Finally, SAS provides a very useful macro function: %SYSFUNC(,). This function can take two arguments. The first is any regular SAS function, and the second is the SAS format to use to present the result. The following example sets the value of the variable Date_Today to the current date in words.

```
%let Date_Today = %Sysfunc(Date(), worddate.);
%put &Date_Today;
```

The second formatting argument is optional and can be omitted if no formatting is required. There are some restrictions on the SAS functions that can be called using this function. Please refer to the SAS Macro manual or SAS online help to learn about SAS functions that cannot be called using %SYSFUNC(). The good news is that all regular mathematical functions and data conversion functions can be used with %SYSFUNC(). The importance of this function is that it extends the scope of the numerous SAS functions to the macro language.

4.4 PROGRAMMING LOGIC

Almost all programming languages provide a set of statements for creating programs that express complex logic through three basic categories of statement.

1. Iterations through a set of statements a predefined number of times. This is similar to the DATA step DO loop in regular SAS language.

2. Statements that create loops that keep iterating until or while a certain condition is valid. This is similar to the DO–WHILE and DO–UNTIL loops in the SAS DATA step.

3. Statements that make decisions based on checking the validity of conditions. This is similar to IF–THEN–ELSE conditions used in the SAS DATA step.

All these categories of statement are supported in the SAS macro language. The syntax is almost the same as that used in the DATA step, with the exception that in the case of macros we use the % before *all* the key words.

For example, the syntax for a DO loop in the macro language is

```
%do i=1 %to 10;
... (some statements go here)
%end;
```

The DO–WHILE, DO–UNTIL, and IF–THEN–ELSE statements share the fact that they require the testing of some logical condition. For example, define two macro variables and write a simple IF–THEN statement.

```
%LET A=10;
%LET B=20;
```

```
%IF &A>&B %THEN %LET C = A;
        %ELSE %LET C = B;
```

The code defines two variables, A and B. It then compares them and sets a variable C to the name of the larger one. Notice that we used the & operator to restore the values of the variables A and B before comparing their values. If we did not do so, the condition A > B would compare the two "texts" "A" and "B" and would result in an error.

A logical condition in SAS macros must compare two numerical values. In fact, it compares two integer values. If one of the values is real (i.e., contains numbers to the right of the decimal point), we must use the function %SYSEVALF() to enclose the condition. For example, let us assign noninteger values to A and B and rewrite the code.

```
%LET A=5.3;
%LET B=12.5;

%IF %SYSEVALF(&A>&B) %THEN %LET C=A;
                    %ELSE %LET C=B;
```

The syntax for the %DO–%WHILE and %DO–%UNTIL loops is straightforward. The following examples show how to use these two statements.

```
%macro TenIterations;
/* This macro iterates 10 times and writes
   the iteration number to the SAS Log. */
%let Iter=0;                  /* intialize i to zero */
%do %while (&Iter<10);        /* loop while i<10     */
 %let Iter=%Eval(&iter+1);    /* increment i         */
 %put &iter;                  /* write it to the log */
%end;
%mend;
```

This example performs the same function but uses the %DO–%UNTIL structure.

```
%macro TenIterations;
  %let Iter=0;
  %do %Until (&Iter =10 );
    %let Iter = %eval(&Iter +1);
    %put &Iter;
%end;
%mend;
```

Note the use of a different logical condition to stop the iterations in the two macros.

Before we move on to the next topic, we emphasize a very important fact about the preceding programming logic structures in SAS macros:

All the programming logic statements, such as %IF–%THEN–%ELSE, %DO–%UNTIL, and %DO–%WHILE, are valid *only within* the body of a macro. We cannot write these statements in open program code.

4.5 WORKING WITH STRINGS

The SAS macro language provides a long list of functions to manipulate string values. These functions allow for removing quotation marks, trimming strings, searching for sequences of characters in them, and so on. Of this long list, the most used functions are %LENGTH() and %SCAN(). The following is a brief description of these two functions.

The %LENGTH() function, as expected, evaluates the length of a string. For example, consider the following code:

```
%let X=this is a string.;
%let L = %length(&X);
%put Length of X is: &L characters;
```

The code would result in the variable L storing the value 17. (Remember that the period at the end of the string stored in the variable X and the spaces count as characters).

The function %SCAN() is used to extract the next word from a string starting from a certain position. The delimiters used to separate words can be specified as one of the arguments. The syntax of %SCAN is as follows:

```
%SCAN (String to search, word number, list of delimiters)
```

The first argument is the string to examine and it is mandatory. The word number is optional (1 by default) and determines the word number to extract. For example, using three extracts the third word in the expression. The list of delimiters is also optional; the default delimiters are the space, the comma, and the semicolon. The following code is a macro that decomposes a string into its words and prints them in the log.

```
%macro Decompose(List);
%let i=1;
%let condition = 0;

%do %until (&condition =1);
  %let Word=%scan(&List,&i);
  %if &Word =  %then %let condition =1;
             %else %do;

  /*** This part prints the word to the log */
      %put &Word;
  /***/

  %let i = %Eval(&i+1);
                %end;  /* end of the do */
  %end; /* end of the until loop */
%mend;

%let MyList = This is a list of several words;
%Decompose (&MyList);
```

Another common string macro function, which is usually useful when comparing two strings, is the %UPCASE() function. As the name implies, it converts all the characters of the input string to uppercase. This makes it easy to compare two strings while ignoring the case. The function %LOWCASE() converts all the characters to lowercase. Neither of these functions are real functions; they are called "macro calls"; they are built-in macros provided by SAS. However, we do not need to be concerned with this fine distinction.

4.6 MACROS THAT CALL OTHER MACROS

When macro programs become more complex, it is easier to divide the program into several macros and have a main macro that calls all the bits and pieces. For example, the following code shows the macro Main(), which calls two other macros.

```
%macro Main();

  ... /* some statements */
  %local x1 x2 x3;
  %let x1=7; %let x2=89; %let x3=92;
  %Func1(&x1, &x2);
  ... /* more statements */
  %Func2(&x3, &x2);
  ... /* more statements */
%mend;
```

The only precaution is that the macros Func1() and Func2() shown in the code have to be defined *before* using them in the macro Main(). This can be achieved by simply putting the definition of Func1() and Func2() *above* the code of Main() in the same file. This way, during execution, the SAS compiler will compile the macros Func1() and Func2() before attempting to compile and execute Main().

When the called modules, such as Func1() and Func2(), are themselves calling other modules, or when they are large macros with lengthy code, then it is more convenient to store the macros in different files. In this case, we can *include* a particular macro before it is used by another macro using the statement %INCLUDE, as follows:

```
%INCLUDE 'C:\Macros\Macro_Func1.sas';
```

This statement instructs SAS to include the contents of the file C:\Macros\ Macro_Func1.SAS. The filename could be enclosed in either single quotes (') or double quotes ("). When double quotes are used, we can substitute in them the values of some macro variables. For example, we could define the directory name as a variable and then add the filename to it, as follows:

```
%let Dir=C:\Macros\;
%include "&Dir.Macro_Func1.sas";
```

Note the dot at the end of the macro variable Dir. It tells the compiler to resolve the value of Dir before appending Macro_Func1.SAS to it.

In this way, we can write general programs that would work on, say, both UNIX and Windows file structures using simple logic, as follows:

```
%let OS=WIN; /* specify the Operating system */
/* if in UNIX use: %let OS=UNIX; */

%let dirWin=C:\MyMacros\;
%let dirUNIX=/myroot/sasfiles/mymacros/;

%if &OS=WIN  %then %let Dir=&dirWin;
%if &OS=UNIX %then %let Dir=&dirUNIX;

%include "&Dir.macro_A.sas";
```

We recommend that each macro be written in its own file so that when we need to call this file in a program or a macro, we can simply call it using the %INCLUDE statement. For example, the Main() macro mentioned would call its submodules Func1() and Func2(), as follows:

```
%include "C:\Macros\Func1.sas";
%include "C:\Macros\Func1.sas";

%macro Main();
 ...
 %Func1(&x1, &x2);
 ...
 %Func2(&x3,&x2);
 ...
%mend;
```

Finally, the %INCLUDE statement can be used to combine any usual SAS code that is spread over several physical files. Many of the macros presented in this book use other macros. The dependency between these macros is provided in Section A.2.

4.7   Common Macro Patterns and Caveats

In writing SAS macros, certain common tasks always arise. This section provides the details of some of these patterns.

4.7.1   Generating a List of Macro Variables

This task arises, for example, when we decompose a list of string tokens, such as the list of variables to be included in a model, and we want to keep these variables in a list of macro variables. The required variables should be easy to increment through. For example, we would like to generate a list of variables called X1, X2, ... up to XN, where N is their number, an integer, and is already stored in a macro variable.

This is usually achieved using the following pattern:

```
%do i=1 %to &N;
  %let X&i = { here goes the definition of variable x(i) }
    ... {other statements}
%end;
```

The loop shows that we iterated through the *N* values and generated a list of variables using the %LET x&i statement. The SAS macro compiler resolves the values of the variables generated by this statement first, such that the pattern is equivalent to writing *N* %LET statements as

```
%let X1 = ...
%let X2 = ...
  ... { up to XN}
```

In other parts of the macro, to access the values stored in these variables, we use a %DO loop to iterate through them. The values stored in each of these variables are accessed through the *double ampersand*, &&, convention, as follows:

```
%do j=1 %to &N;
  /* store the value of Var_j in a new variable y_j */
  %let y_&j = &&Var_&j;
    ... (other statements)
%end;
```

In the preceding code, the second part of the %LET statement (&&Var_&j) reads as follows: resolve the value of j first, then resolve the value of the resulting variable. For example, during the third iteration of the %DO loop (j=3), the part &&Var_&j will first resolve j to the value of 3 then resolves the value of Var_3. This logic is illustrated in Figure 4.1 when the value of the variable Var_3 is the string My Text.

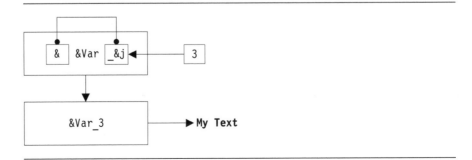

Figure 4.1   Resolution of macro variables with double coding.

4.7.2 Double Coding

Double coding means having a macro variable that holds the name of another macro variable. For example, we wish to have two macro variables that hold the names of the categories of a variable, such as the values `Female` and `Male` of the variable `Gender`. We can do that as follows:

```
%let V1=Female;
%let V2=Male;
```

Now, let's have another macro variable called X that could have either the values V1 or V2.

```
... (some statements)
%let X=V1;
... (some statements)
%let X=V2;
... (some statements)
```

At a later stage in the macro, we need to resolve the value of the macro variable included in X directly, that is the value of `Gender` (`Male` or `Female`). We do that as follows:

```
%let Xg= &&&X;
```

The three ampersands are interpreted over two steps, as follows:

- First resolve the value of &X to give either V1 or V2.

- Then resolve the resulting value (V1 or V2;) as a macro variable. This should give the required value (`Female` or `Male`).

The double coding pattern is useful in cases that involve automatically generated macro variables.

4.7.3 Using Local Variables

Some of the macros presented in this book involve calling other macros. In these cases, we have to be careful to declare *all* the variables in each macro as *local*. Failing to do this could lead to errors that are difficult to debug.

For example, consider the macro `Parent` that calls another macro, `Child`, as follows:

```
%macro Child;
 %do i=1 %to 2;
   %put --- Now in Child --Message &i;
 %end;
 %mend Child;

%macro Parent;
 %do i=1 %to 5;
```

```
    %Child;
  %end;
%mend Parent;
```

The macro `Child` appears to be an innocent macro that prints only two messages to the SAS Log.

If we invoke the macro `Parent`, we would expect a total of 10 messages to be printed to the SAS Log (5 times for the loop in `Parent` X, twice in each call of `Child`). However, we will discover that attempting to run the macro `Parent` will result in an endless loop of messages on the SAS Log. (Try it yourself and be prepared to press the Stop button!)

The reason for such a problem is that the macro `Child` *modifies* the value of the counter variable i, which is used in a loop in the macro `Parent`. Every time `Child` is called, i loops from 1 to 2. But the loop in `Parent` will not stop until i reaches a value of 5, which it will never do.

To remedy this situation, we declare i a local variable in *both* macros (at least in `Child`, but we opt for both to be on the safe side). Therefore, a good code that will behave as expected would be as follows:

```
%macro Child;
%local i;
 %do i=1 %to 2;
   %put --- Now in Child --Message &i;
 %end;
 %mend Child;
\midskip
%macro Parent;
%local i;
 %do i=1 %to 5;
   %Child;
 %end;
%mend Parent;
```

Note that if i were declared as local only in `Parent`, it would still run properly; but it is actually a sloppy programming practice because we allow a submodule to create global variables that could have an impact later on some other macro.

This behavior is especially critical for variables used as loop counters. Some symbols are popular for that function such as $i, j, k,$ ..., and so on. Therefore, we recommend that while you are writing a macro, declare *all* the variables as local the minute they are created. In this way, you minimize the chances that any of them gets forgotten. Therefore, I actually consider it good programming practice to use several %LOCAL statements in a macro, although some die-hard idealists insist on putting all the %LOCAL declarations at the begining of the macro.

4.7.4 FROM A DATA STEP TO MACRO VARIABLES

We should not think of macro variables and macros as clever tools to control the standard SAS programs, such as DATA steps and the different PROCs. We regularly need to feed back values read from datasets into macro variables. The way to do this is to use the system call CALL SYMPUT. (Note the CALL part of it.) In these cases, we are not really interested in processing the data in the DATA step by generating a new dataset; we are merely interested in reading the values in sequence from the dataset until we reach the required condition to set the value of the macro variable.

For example, assume that we want to find the observation number of the last observation that has a missing value in a variable called X in a dataset called DUMP. Furthermore, we need to store this value in a macro variable we will call LastMiss. We do this using the NULL dataset of SAS, which has the fixed name _NULL_, as follows:

```
DATA _NULL_;
 SET DUMP;
 IF X=. THEN CALL SYMPUT('LastMiss',_N_);
run;
```

In the DATA step, we used the system call SYMPUT, which stores the value of the SAS variable _N_, that counts the observations read so far to the dataset _NULL_. This call will be executed only if the value of variable X is missing. If variable X does not have missing values, then the macro variable LastMiss will not be created. In case the dataset DUMP has several observations with X missing, the variable LastMiss will store the observation number of the *last* one, which is what we want to do.

This pattern appears very often to read values from a dataset into macro variables. Often we use it in situations where we know that the IF condition will occur *only once* in the entire dataset or when the dataset has only one observation.

4.8 WHERE TO GO FROM HERE

With this introduction to SAS macro language, we believe that you can write relatively complex macros that can turn simple code into powerful analysis tools. To explore more features of SAS macro programming, consult the *SAS Macro Programming Language Manual* or one of the many books available on the subject. For suggestions on good books dedicated to writing SAS macros, please refer to the official SAS website for guidance (*www.sas.com*).

CHAPTER 5

DATA ACQUISITION AND INTEGRATION

5.1 INTRODUCTION

This chapter first provides a brief review of data sources and types of variables from the point of view of data mining. Then it presents the most common procedures of data rollup and aggregation, sampling, and partitioning.

5.2 SOURCES OF DATA

In most organizations today data is stored in relational databases. The quality and utility of the data as well as the amount of effort needed to transform the data to a form suitable for data mining depends on the types of the applications the databases serve. These relational databases serve as data repositories for the following applications.

5.2.1 OPERATIONAL SYSTEMS

Operational systems process the transactions that make an organization work. The data from these systems is, by nature, transient and keeps accumulating in the repository. A typical example of these systems is any banking transaction processing system that keeps records of opened and closed accounts, deposits, withdrawals, balances, and all other values related to the money moving among accounts, clients, and the outside world. Data extracted from such operational systems is the most *raw* form of data, in the sense that it has not been transformed, cleansed, or changed. It may contain errors due to data entry procedures or applications and usually has many missing values. It is also usually scattered over several tables and files. However, it is the most honest representation of the status of any business.

5.2.2 DATA WAREHOUSES AND DATA MARTS

Data warehouses and data marts were conceived as a means to facilitate the compilation of regular reports on the status of the business by continuously collecting, cleaning, and summarizing the core data of the organization. Data warehouses provide a clean and organized source of data for data mining. In most cases, however, data warehouses were not created to prepare data for data modelers; they were rather created with a certain set of reporting functions in mind. Therefore, data residing in them might have been augmented or processed in a special way to facilitate those functions. Ideally, a specialized data mart should be created to house the data needed for data mining modeling and scoring processes.

5.2.3 OLAP APPLICATIONS

OLAP, which stands for On Line Analytical Processing, and similar software are often given the name *Business Intelligence* tools. These applications reside in the data warehouse, or have their own data warehouse, and provide a graphical interface to navigate, explore, and "slice and dice" the data. The data structures that OLAP applications operate on are called *cubes.* They also provide comprehensive reporting capabilities. OLAP systems could be a source of data for data mining because of the interactive exploration capabilities that they offer the user. Therefore, the user would find the interesting data elements related to the problem through OLAP applications and then apply data mining modeling for prediction.

Alternatively, data mining can offer the identification of the significant variables that govern the behavior of some business measure (such as profit), and then OLAP can use these variables (as dimensions) to navigate and get qualitative insight into existing relationships. Data extracted from OLAP cubes may not be granular enough for data mining. This is because continuous variables are usually *binned* before they can be used as dimensions in OLAP cubes. This binning process results in the loss of some information, which may have a significant impact on the performance of data mining algorithms.

5.2.4 SURVEYS

Surveys are perhaps the most expensive source of data because they require direct interaction with customers. Surveys collect data through different communication channels with customers, such as mail, email, interviews, and forms on websites. There are many anecdotes about the accuracy and validity of the data collected from the different forms of surveys. However, they all share the following two common features:

- The number of customers who participate in the survey is usually limited because of the cost and the number of customers willing to participate.

- The questions asked in the survey can be designed to directly address the objective of the planned model. For example, if the objective is to market new products, the survey would ask customers about their preferences in these products, whether they would buy them, and what price would they pay for them.

These two points highlight the fact that, if well designed and executed, surveys are indeed the most accurate representation of possible customer behavior. However, they usually generate a limited amount of data because of the cost involved.

5.2.5 Household and Demographic Databases

In most countries, there are commercially available databases that contain detailed information on consumers of different products and services. The most common type is demographic databases based on a national census, where the general demographic profile of each residential area is surveyed and summarized. Data obtained from such database providers is usually clean and information-rich. Their only limitation is that data is not provided on the individual customer or record level, but rather averaged over a group of customers, for example, on the level of a postal (zip) code. Such limitations are usually set by privacy laws aimed at protecting individuals from abuse of such data.

The use of averaged data in models could lead to *diluting* the model's ability to accurately define a target group. For example, extensive use of census-like variables in a customer segmentation model would eventually lead to a model that clusters the population on the basis of the used census demographics and not in relation to the originally envisaged rate of usage or buying habits of the planned products or services.

It is not uncommon that analysts collect data from more than one source to form the initial mining view and for the scoring of mining models.

5.3 Variable Types

Designers of applications that use databases and different file systems attempt to optimize their applications in terms of the space required to keep the data and the speed of processing and accessing the data. Because of these considerations, the data extracted from databases is very often not in optimal form from the point of view of data mining algorithms. In order to appreciate this issue, we provide the following discussion of the types of variables that most data mining algorithms deal with.

5.3.1 Nominal Variables

Nominal, or *categorical*, variables describe values that lack the properties of order, scale, or distance between them. For example, the variables representing the type of a housing unit can take the categories House, Apartment, Shared Accommodation.

One cannot enforce any meaning of order or scale on these values. Other examples include Gender (Male, Female), Account Type (Savings, Checking), and type of Credit Card (VISA, MasterCard, American Express, Diners Club, EuroCard, Discover, . . .).

From the point of view of data mining algorithms, it is important to retain the *lack* of order or scale in categorical variables. Therefore, it is not desirable that a category be represented in the data by a series of integers. For example, if the type of a house variable is represented by the integers 1–4 (1 = Detached, 2 = Semi-detached, 3 = Townhome, 4 = Bungalow), a numerical algorithm may inadvertently add the numbers 1 and 2, resulting implicitly in the erroneous and meaningless statement of "Detached + Semi-detached = Townhome"! Other erroneous, and equally meaningless, implications that "Bungalow > Detached" or "Bungalow − Semi-detached = Townhome − Detached." The most convenient method of storing categorical variables in software applications is to use strings. This should force the application to interpret them as nominal variables.

5.3.2 ORDINAL VARIABLES

Ordinal, or *rank* or *ordered scalar*, variables are categorical variables with the notion of order added to them. For example, we may define the risk levels of defaulting on a credit card payment into three levels (Low, Medium, High). We can assert the order relationships High $\geq$ Medium $\geq$ Low. However, we cannot establish the notion of scale. In other words, we cannot accurately say that the difference between *High* and *Medium* is the same as the difference between *Medium* and *Low* levels of risk.

Based on the definition of ordinal variables, we can realize the problem that would arise when such variables are represented by a series of integers. For example, in the case of the risk level variable, representing these levels with numbers from 1 to 3 such that (Low = 1, Medium = 2, High = 3) would result in the imposition of an invalid notion of distance between the different values. In addition, this definition would impose the definition of scale on the values by implying that Medium risk is double the risk of Low, and High risk is three times the risk of Low.

Some ordinal variables come with the scale and distance notions added to them. These are best represented by a series of positive integers. They usually measure the frequency of occurrence of an event. Examples of such ordinal measures are number of local telephone calls within a month, number of people using a credit card in a week, and number of cars purchased by a prospective customer in her or his lifetime.

A typical problem, especially in data warehouses, exists in the representation of ordinal measures. Some ordinal measures are often subjected to "binning" to reduce the values we need to store and deal with. For example, a data warehouse may bin the number of times a customer uses a credit card per month to the representation 0–5 $\rightarrow$ 1, 6–10 $\rightarrow$ 2, 11–20 $\rightarrow$ 3, more than 20 $\rightarrow$ 4. Although this leads to a more compact representation of the variables, it may be detrimental to data mining algorithms for two reasons: (1) It reduces the granularity level of the data, which may result in a reduction in the predictive model accuracy, and (2) it distorts the ordinal nature of the original quantity being measured.

5.3.3   REAL MEASURES

Real measures, or *continuous variables*, are the easiest to use and interpret. Continuous variables have all the desirable properties of variables: order, scale, and distance. They also have the meanings of zero and negative values defined. There could be some constraints imposed on the definition of continuous variables. For example, the age of a person cannot be negative and the monthly bill of a telephone line cannot be less than the subscription fees. Real measures are represented by real numbers, with any reasonably required precision.

The use of ratios in constrained continuous variables is sometimes troublesome. For example, if we allow the balance of a customer to be negative or positive, then the ratio between $ −10,000.00 and $ −5,000.00 is the same as that between $ +10,000.00 and $ +5,000.00. Therefore, some analysts like to distinguish between the so-called interval and ratio variables. We do not make that distinction here because in most cases the context of the implementation is clear. For example, if we wished to use the ratio of balances, we would restrict the balances to positive values only; if negative values occurred, we would devise another measure to signify that fact.

With the three types of variable from the mining point of view, the first task the analyst should consider, when acquiring the data, is to decide on the type of data to be used for each variable depending on its meaning. Of special interest are variables that represent *dates* and *times*. With the exception of time series analysis, dates and times are not useful in their raw form. One of the most effective methods of dealing with date and time values is to convert them to a *period* measure, that is, calculate the *difference* between the values and a fixed *reference* value. For example, instead of dealing with the date of opening an account, we deal with total tenure as the difference between today's date and the date of opening the account. In fact, we use this method every day by referring to the age of a person instead of her or his birth date. In this way, we convert dates and times to real measures, with some constraint if necessary, as in the case of a person's age. (Negative age is not well defined!)

5.4   DATA ROLLUP

The simplest definition of data rollup is that we convert categories to variables. Let us consider an illustrative example.

Table 5.1 shows some records from the transaction table of a bank where deposits are denoted by positive amounts and withdrawals are shown as negative amounts.

We further assume that we are building the mining view as a *customer view*. Since the first requirement is to have one, and only one, row per customer, we create a new view such that each unique Customer ID appears in one and only one row. To *roll up* the multiple records on the customer level, we create a set of new variables to represent the combination of the account type and the month of the transaction. This is illustrated in Figure 5.1. The result of the rollup is shown in Table 5.2.

Table 5.1   A sample of banking transactions.

Customer ID	Date	Amount	Account type
1100-55555	11Jun2003	114.56	Savings
1100-55555	21Jun2003	−56.78	Checking
1100-55555	07Jul2003	359.31	Savings
1100-55555	19Jul2003	89.56	Checking
1100-55555	03Aug2003	1000.00	Savings
1100-55555	17Aug2003	−1200.00	Checking
1100-88888	14June2003	122.51	Savings
1100-88888	27June2003	42.07	Checking
1100-88888	09July2003	−146.30	Savings
1100-88888	09July2003	−1254.48	Checking
1100-88888	10Aug2003	400.00	Savings
1100-88888	11Aug 2003	500.00	Checking
. . .			

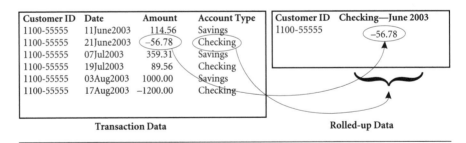

Figure 5.1   Data rollup.

Table 5.1 shows that we managed to aggregate the values of the transactions in the different accounts and months into new variables. The only issue is what to do when we have more than one transaction per account per month. In this case, which is the more realistic one, we have to summarize the data in some form. For example, we can calculate the sum of the transactions values, or their average, or even create a new set of variables giving the count of such transactions for each month–account type combination.

It is obvious that this process will lead to the generation of possibly hundreds, if not thousands, of variables in any data-rich business applications. Dealing with such

Table 5.2   Result of rolling up the data of Table 5.1.

Cust. ID	C-6	C-7	C-8	S-6	S-7	S-8
1100-55555	−56.78	89.56	−1200.00	114.56	359.30	1000.00
1100-88888	42.07	−1254.00	500.00	122.51	−146.30	400.00

a large number of fields could present a challenge for the data preparation and data mining software tools. It is therefore required that we keep the number of these new fields to a minimum while keeping as much information about the nature of the data as possible. Unfortunately, there is no magic recipe to achieve this balance. However, a closer look at the preceding data reveals that the key to controlling the number of new variables is to decide on the level of granularity required to perform the rollup. For example, is it necessary to roll up the transactions of each month, or is it enough to roll up the data per quarter? Similarly, in our simplified case, we had only two categories for the account type, but typically, there would be many more categories. Then comes the question of which categories we can group together, or even ignore, to reduce the number of new variables.

In the end, even with careful selection of the categories and resolution of combining the different categories to form new variables, we usually end up with a relatively large number of variables, which most implementations of data mining algorithms cannot handle adequately. However, we should not worry too much about this problem for the moment because data reduction is a basic step in our planned approach. In later chapters, we will investigate techniques to reduce the number of variables.

In the last example demonstrating the rollup process, we performed the rollup on the level of two variables: the account type and the transaction month. This is usually called *multilevel rollup*. On the other hand, if we had had only one type of account, say only savings, then we could have performed a simpler rollup using only the transaction month as the summation variable. This type of rollup is called *simple rollup*. In fact, multilevel rollup is only an aggregation of several simple rollups on the row level, which is the customer ID in our example. Therefore, data preparation procedures, in either SAS or SQL, can utilize this property to simplify the implementation by performing several simple rollups for each combination of the summarization variables and combining them. This is the approach we will adopt in developing our macro to demonstrate the rollup of our sample dataset.

Now let us describe how to perform the rollup operation using SAS. We will do this using our simple example first and then generalize the code using macros to facilitate its use with other datasets. We stress again that in writing the code we preferred to keep the code simple and readable at the occasional price of efficiency of execution and the use of memory resources. You are welcome to modify the code to make it more efficient or general as required.

We use Table 5.1 to create the dataset as follows.

```
Data Transaction;
Informat CustID $10.;
Informat TransDate date9.;
format TransDate Date9.;
input CustID $  TransDate Amount AccountType$;
Cards;
55555    11Jun2003     114.56     Savings
55555    12Jun2003     119.56     Savings
55555    21Jun2003     -56.78     Checking
55555    07Jul2003     359.31     Savings
55555    19Jul2003      89.56     Checking
55555    03Aug2003    1000.00     Savings
66666    22Feb2003     549.56     Checking
77777    03Dec2003     645.21     Savings
55555    17Aug2003   -1200.00     Checking
88888    14Jun2003     122.51     Savings
88888    27Jun2003      42.07     Checking
88888    09Jul2003    -146.30     Savings
88888    09Jul2003   -1254.48     Checking
88888    10Aug2003     400.00     Savings
88888    11Aug2003     500.00     Checking
;
run;
```

The next step is to create the month field using the SAS month function.

```
data Trans;
 set Transaction;
  Month = month(TransDate);
run;
```

Then we accumulate the transactions into a new field to represent the balance in each account.

```
proc sort data=Trans;
  by CustID month AccountType;
run;

/* Create cumulative balances for each of the accounts */
data Trans2;
 retain Balance 0;
 set Trans;
  by CustID month AccountType;
  if first.AccountType then Balance=0;
   Balance = Balance + Amount;
   if last.AccountType then output;
   drop amount;
run;
```

Finally, we use PROC TRANSPOSE to roll up the data in each account type and merge the two resulting datasets into the final file.

```
/* Prepare for the transpose */
proc sort data=trans2;
 by CustID accounttype;
 run;

proc transpose data =Trans2 out=rolled_C prefix=C_;
 by CustID accounttype;
ID month ;
var balance ;
where AccountType='Checking';
run;

proc transpose data =Trans2 out=rolled_S prefix=S_;
by CustID accounttype;
ID month ;
var balance ;
where AccountType='Savings';
run;

data Rollup;
 merge Rolled_S Rolled_C;
 by CustID;
 drop AccountType _Name_;
run;
```

To pack this procedure in a general macro using the combination of two variables, one for transaction categories and one for time, we simply replace the Month variable with a TimeVar, the customer ID with IDVar, and the AccountType with TypeVar. We also specify the number of characters to be used from the category variable to prefix the time values. Finally, we replace the two repeated TRANSPOSE code segments with a %do loop that iterates over the categories of the TypeVar (which requires extracting these categories and counting them). The following is the resulting macro.

Step 1
Sort the transaction file using the ID, Time, and Type variables.

```
proc sort data=&TDS;
by &IDVar &TimeVar &TypeVar;
run;
```

Step 2
Accumulate the values over time to a temporary _Tot variable in the temporary table Temp1 (see Table 5.3). Then sort Temp1 using the ID and the Type variables.

Table 5.3   Parameters of macro `TBRollup()`.

Header	`TBRollup(TDS, IDVar, TimeVar, TypeVar, Nchars, Value, RDS)`
Parameter	*Description*
`TDS`	Input transaction dataset
`IDVar`	ID variable
`TimeVar`	Time variable
`TypeVar`	Quantity being rolled up
`Nchars`	Number of characters to be used in rollup
`Value`	Values to be accumulated
`RDS`	The output rolled up dataset

```
data Temp1;
retain _TOT 0;
set &TDS;
by &IDVar &TimeVar &TypeVar;
if first.&TypeVar then _TOT=0;
_TOT = _TOT + &Value;
if last.&TypeVar  then output;
drop &Value;
    run;
proc sort data=Temp1;
by &IDVar &TypeVar;
run;
```

Step 3
Extract the categories of the Type variable, using PROC FREQ, and store them in macro variables.

```
proc freq data =Temp1 noprint;
tables &TypeVar /out=Types ;
run;

data _null_;
set Types nobs=Ncount;
if &typeVar ne " then
call symput('Cat_'||left(_n_), &TypeVar);
if _N_=Ncount  then call symput('N', Ncount);
run;
```

Step 4
Loop over these N categories and generate their rollup part.

```
%do i=1 %to &N;
proc transpose
data =Temp1
out=_R_&i
prefix=%substr(&&Cat_&i, 1, &Nchars)_;
by &IDVar &TypeVar;
ID &TimeVar ;
var _TOT ;
where &TypeVar="&&Cat_&i";
run;
%end;
```

Step 5
Finally, assemble the parts using the ID variable.

```
data &RDS;
merge %do i=1 %to &N; _R_&i %end ; ;
by &IDVar;
drop &TypeVar _Name_;
run;
```

Step 6
Clean the workspace and finish the macro.

```
proc datasets library=work nodetails;
delete Temp1 Types %do i=1 %to &N; _R_&i  %end; ;
run;
quit;

%mend;
```

We can now call this macro to roll up the previous example Transaction dataset using the following code:

```
data Trans;
set Transaction;
Month = month(TransDate);
drop transdate;
run;

  %let IDVar    = CustID;      /* The row ID variable */
  %let TimeVar  = Month;       /* The time variable */
  %let TypeVar  = AccountType; /* The Type variable */
  %let Value    = Amount;      /* The time measurement variable */
  %let NChars   = 1;           /* Number of letters in Prefix */
  %let TDS      = Trans;       /* The value variable */
  %let RDS      = Rollup;      /* the rollup file */
```

```
%TBRollup(&TDS, &IDVar, &TimeVar, &TypeVar, &Nchars,
          &Value, &RDS);
```

The result of this call is shown in Table 5.4.

Table 5.4   Result of rollup macro.

CustID	C_6	C_7	C_8	C_{12}	S_6	S_7	S_8	S_{12}
5555	−56.78	89.56	−1200	.	234.12	359.31	1000	.
6666	.	.	.	549.56	.	.	.	.
7777	.	.	.	.	.	.	.	645.21
8888	42.07	−1254.48	500	.	122.51	−146.3	400	.

5.5 ROLLUP WITH SUMS, AVERAGES, AND COUNTS

In addition to finding the sum of a value variable during the rollup, it may also be more meaningful sometimes to calculate average value and/or the number of records that represent certain events—for example, number of deposits, number of withdrawals, or number of mailings a customer received responding to an offer.

In our rollup macro, these requirements would alter only the middle part of our code, where we calculated the cumulative value of the Value variable. The following code segment would modify the macro to calculate the average value and the number of transactions for each account type instead of the total.

Step 2

```
data _Temp1;
retain _TOT 0;
retain _NT 0;
set &TDS;
by &IDVar &TimeVar &TypeVar;
if first.&TypeVar then _TOT=0;
_TOT = _TOT + &Value;
if &Value ne . then _NT=_NT+1;
if last.&TypeVar  then
do;
_AVG=_TOT/_NT;
output;
_NT=0;
end;
drop &Value;
run;
```

Furthermore, the code inside the %do loop should also reflect our interest in transposing the values of the average variable, _AVG. Therefore, the code will be as follows

Step 4

```
%do i=1 %to &N;
Oproc transpose
data = _Temp1
out=_R_&i
prefix=%substr(&&Cat_&i, 1, &Nchars)_;
by &IDVar &TypeVar;
ID &TimeVar;
var _AVG;
where &TypeVar="&&Cat_&i";
run;
%end;
```

The complete code for the modified code to roll up the average value is included in the macro ABRollup().

5.6 CALCULATION OF THE MODE

Another useful summary statistic is the mode, which is used in both the rollup stage and the EDA (see Chapter 7). The mode is the most common category of transaction. The mode for nominal variables is equivalent to the use of the average or the sum for the continuous case. For example, when customers use different payment methods, it may be beneficial to identify the payment method most frequently used by each customer.

The computation of the mode on the mining view entity level from a transaction dataset is a demanding task because we need to search for the frequencies of the different categories for *each* unique value of the entity variable. The macro shown in Table 5.5 is based on a *classic* SQL query for finding the mode on the entity level from a

Table 5.5   Parameters of macro VarMode().

Header	VarMode(TransDS, XVar, IDVar, OutDS)
Parameter	*Description*
TransDS	Input transaction dataset
XVar	Variable for which the mode is to be calculated
IDVar	ID variable
OutDS	The output dataset with the mode for unique IDs

transaction table. The variable being searched is XVar and the entity level is identified through the unique value of the variable IDVar.

```
%macro VarMode(TransDS, XVar, IDVar, OutDS);
/* A classic implementation of the mode of transactional
   data using SQL */
proc sql noprint;
create table &OutDS as
SELECT &IDVar , MIN(&XVar ) AS mode
FROM (
            SELECT &IDVar,  &XVar
            FROM &TransDS p1
            GROUP BY &IDVar, &XVar
            HAVING COUNT( * ) =
                  (SELECT MAX(CNT )
                   FROM (SELECT COUNT( * ) AS CNT
                         FROM &TransDS p2
                         WHERE p2.&IDVar= p1.&IDVar
                         GROUP BY p2.&XVar
                         ) AS p3
                  )
             ) AS p
      GROUP BY p.&IDVar;
quit;
%mend;
```

The query works by calculating a list holding the frequency of the XVar categories, identified as CNT, then using the maximum of these counts as the mode. The query then creates a new table containing IDVar and XVar where the XVar category frequency is equal to the maximum count, that is, the mode.

The preceding compound SELECT statement is computationally demanding because of the use of several layers of GROUP BY and HAVING clauses. Indexing should always be considered when dealing with large datasets. Sometimes it is even necessary to partition the transaction dataset into smaller datasets before applying such a query to overcome memory limitations.

5.7 DATA INTEGRATION

The data necessary to compile the mining view usually comes from many different tables. The rollup and summarization operations described in the last two sections can be performed on the data coming from each of these data sources independently. Finally, we would be required to assemble all these segments in one mining view. The most used assembly operations are *merging* and *concatenation*. Merging is used to collect data for the same key variable (e.g., customer ID) from different sources. Concatenation is used to assemble different portions of the same data fields for different segments of the key variable. It is most useful when preparing the scoring view with a very large number of observations (many millions). In this case, it is more efficient to partition the data into smaller segments, prepare each segment, and finally concatenate them together.

5.7.1 MERGING

SAS provides several options for merging and concatenating tables together using DATA step commands. However, we could also use SQL queries, through PROC SQL, to perform the same operations. In general, SAS DATA step options are more efficient in merging datasets than PROC SQL is. However, DATA step merging may require sorting of the datasets before merging them, which could be a slow process for large datasets. On the other hand, the performance of SQL queries can be enhanced significantly by creating indexes on the key variables used in merging.

Because of the requirement that the mining view have a unique record per category of key variable, most merging operations required to integrate different pieces of the mining view are of the type called *match-merge with non-matched observations*. We demonstrate this type of merging with a simple example.

EXAMPLE 5.1 We start with two datasets, Left and Right, as shown in Table 5.6.

Table 5.6   Two sample tables: Left and Right.

	Table: Left			*Table:* Right	
ID	Age	Status	ID	Balance	Status
1	30	Gold	2	3000	Gold
2	20	.	4	4000	Silver
4	40	Gold			
5	50	Silver			

The two tables can be joined using the MERGE–BY commands within a DATA step operation as follows:

```
DATA Left;
 INPUT ID Age Status $;
 datalines;
 1  30  Gold
 2  20  .
 4  40  Gold
 5  50  Silver
 ;
RUN;
```

```
DATA Right;
 INPUT ID Balance Status $;
 datalines;
 2  3000  Gold
 4  4000  Silver
 ;
RUN;

DATA Both;
 MERGE Left Right;
 BY ID;
RUN;

PROC PRINT DATA=Both;
RUN;
```

The result of the merging is the dataset Both given in Table 5.7, which shows that the MERGE-BY commands did merge the two datasets as needed using ID as the key variable. We also notice that the common file Status was overwritten by values from the Right dataset. Therefore, we have to be careful about this possible side effect. In most practical cases, common fields should have identical values. In our case, where the variable represented some customer designation status (Gold or Silver), the customer should have had the same status in different datasets. Therefore, checking these status values should be one of the data integrity tests to be performed before performing the merging.

Table 5.7   Result of merging: dataset Both.

Obs	ID	Age	Status	Balance
1	1	30	Gold	.
2	2	20	Gold	3000
3	4	40	Silver	4000
4	5	50	Silver	.

Merging datasets using this technique is very efficient. It can be used with more than two datasets as long as all the datasets in the MERGE statement have the common variable used in the BY statement. The only possible difficulty is that SAS requires that *all* the datasets be sorted by the BY variable. Sorting very large datasets can sometimes be slow.

◆

You have probably realized by now that writing a general macro to merge a *list* of datasets using an ID variable is a simple task. Assuming that all the datasets have been sorted using ID prior to attempting to merge them, the macro would simply be given as follows:

```
%macro MergeDS(List, IDVar, ALL);
DATA &ALL;
```

```
        MERGE &List;
        by &IDVar;
run;
%mend;
```

Finally, calling this macro to merge the two datasets in Table 5.6 would simply be as follows:

```
%let List=Left Right;
%let IDVar=ID;
%let ALL = Both;
%MergeDS(&List, &IDVar, &ALL);
```

5.7.2 CONCATENATION

Concatenation is used to attach the contents of one dataset to the end of another dataset without duplicating the common fields. Fields unique to one of the two files would be filled with missing values. Concatenating datasets in this fashion does not check on the uniqueness of the ID variable. However, if the data acquisition and rollup procedures were correctly performed, such a problem should not exist.

Performing concatenation in SAS is straightforward. We list the datasets to be concatenated in a SET statement within the destination dataset. This is illustrated in the following example.

EXAMPLE 5.2 Start with two datasets TOP and BOTTOM, as shown in Tables 5.8 and 5.9.

Table 5.8   Table: TOP.

Obs	ID	Age	Status
1	1	30	Gold
2	2	20	.
3	3	30	Silver
4	4	40	Gold
5	5	50	Silver

Table 5.9   Table: BOTTOM.

Obs	ID	Balance	Status
1	6	6000	Gold
2	7	7000	Silver

We then use the following code to implement the concatenation of the two datasets into a new dataset.

```
DATA TOP;
 input ID Age Status $;
 datalines;
1  30  Gold
2  20  .
3  30  Silver
4  40  Gold
5  50  Silver
 ;
run;
DATA BOTTOM;
input ID Balance Status $;
 datalines;
6  6000  Gold
7  7000  Silver
 ;
run;

DATA BOTH;
 SET TOP BOTTOM;
run;
```

The resulting dataset is shown in Table 5.10.

Table 5.10   Table: BOTH.

Obs	ID	Age	Status	Balance
1	1	30	Gold	.
2	2	20	.	.
3	3	30	Silver	.
4	4	40	Gold	.
5	5	50	Silver	.
6	6	.	Gold	6000
7	7	.	Silver	7000

As in the case of merging datasets, we may include a list of several datasets in the SET statement to concatenate. The resulting dataset will contain all the records of the contributing datasets in the same order in which they appear in the SET statement.

◆

The preceding process can be packed into the following macro.

```
%macro ConcatDS(List, ALL);
DATA &ALL;
 SET &List;
run;
%mend;
```

To use this macro to achieve the same result as in the previous example, we use the following calling code.

```
%let List=TOP BOTTOM;
%let ALL = BOTH;
%ConcatDS(&List, &ALL);
```

CHAPTER 6

INTEGRITY CHECKS

6.1 INTRODUCTION

Upon completion of data acquisition and integration, the first task the analyst should do is to make sure that the data passes through the first gate: integrity checks. Integrity checks should reveal errors or inconsistencies in the data because of either sampling or errors in the data acquisition procedures. When such errors are present, data cleansing procedures are necessary before proceeding.

Data warehouses and OLAP applications are currently commonplace. A fundamental step in building these systems is the process of data cleansing. This usually means removing errors and inconsistencies from the data. Although these procedures are beneficial to data mining modeling, they are not usually sufficient. The reason lies in the meaning of the terms *error* and *consistency*. The concepts of data errors and data consistency are heavily used in data warehousing, OLAP, and data mining. However, there is no unique or rigorous definition of these terms. Therefore, before we elaborate about data mining requirements of data cleansing, let us discuss these two concepts: *data errors* and *data consistency*.

One common definition of *errors* is an impossible or unacceptable value in a data field. For example, a gender field should accept values representing "Male," "Female," and "missing" (do not forget the "missing"!). However, due to possible errors in data entry, a value of "Tale" may be found. The data cleansing process in this case is defined as removing such values and replacing them with the most probable acceptable value, which is "Male" in this particular case.

Data *consistency*, on the other hand, is a more subtle concept and, therefore, more difficult to define. It may be defined in terms of consistent values among the different fields, as well as in the values of the same field over time. For example, consider the problem of checking the consistency of the values among the fields of "Transaction Value" and "Product Type" in typical retail data. Ideally, we would have a reasonable match between the two fields such that all records with high transaction values are generated from transactions involving expensive products. It is not reasonable to discover some transactions involving expensive product types with low transaction value.

The second common type of inconsistency within a field often occurs as a result of "redefining" the field representation over different periods. For example, over a certain period of time, the gender field is coded as Male=1, Female=2, and Missing=0, while in a later period the same field is coded as Male=M, Female=F, and Missing=[blank].

Typical data cleaning procedures targeted to data warehousing–oriented cleansing procedures that address data consistency issues are mostly based on replacing "inconsistent" values with the acceptable values based on a simple set of rules. The rules are extracted from extensive exploration of the data in search of such inconsistencies and errors.

From the point of view of data mining, these checks form a good necessary start. It is therefore usually a blessing when the data mining analyst has access to a cleaned and efficiently managed data warehouse or data repository.

However, additional effort is needed to perform more checks on the data. Simple replacement of errors and inconsistent values would allow the correct summarization and calculation of simple sums and averages, as used by OLAP and reporting applications. Additionally, most data mining algorithms pose their special requirements on the nature of the data to be used in building, validating, and deploying models. For example, many implementations of linear and logistic regression models cannot handle missing values, and they either ignore records with missing values or perform some missing value treatment operation (see Chapter 11 for more details). The point is that, although missing values are legitimate and consistent in terms of business meaning, they may not be acceptable to certain data mining algorithms.

We summarize here some of the most common data cleansing and integrity checks of the simple type:

- Detecting invalid characters and values in different fields. In most cases, these values are replaced by missing values. Invalid values are defined as those that are out of the permitted range. See Section 7.5 for a detailed discussion of outliers.

- Detecting outliers using a simple multiple of the standard deviation or by simply listing and excluding the lowest and highest N values, where N is a user-defined number based on the total number of observations and the understanding of the meaning of the variables. The outliers could also be identified using the *interquartile* ranges.

- Detecting missing and nonnumeric data in a numeric field.

- Detecting data with a missing or invalid row identifier (key).

- Identifying rows with fixed values, such as 999, which is sometimes used by databases and operational systems to code a missing or an invalid value.

- Identifying data with invalid dates. Because of the different standards for writing dates in different countries, dates usually pose their own special problems with data collected from different regions. Invalid dates may arise simply because the day or the year is not present in the field as a result of data entry problems or errors in loading the data from the database. Fields containing data before the year 2000 may not contain four digits in the year part and thus can cause the known Y2K problem.

- Identifying duplicate records and duplicate IDs.

- Identifying *unique* records. Unique records are those that appear exactly once in the database. For example, in credit card transaction data, if a certain credit card number (the ID) appears only once in the entire database, then most likely there is some error attached to this ID. The reason is that, even if the customer does not activate the card, the customer service center must have attempted to contact the customer to inquire about the reason for not activating it. This would generate at least two entries in the database, one for sending the card and one for each attempted contact.

- Identifying the integrity of date-triggered events. For example, the customer service center in the credit card example should have attempted to contact the customer *after* the date of sending the card.

- Checking sums and ratios when they come from different operational sources. For example, in direct marketing applications, the actual discount value should be equal to the properly calculated value as the purchase amount times the discount rate. This type of check should give allowance for simple numerical round-off errors, such as $0.01 in the case of money calculations.

- Checking on artificial data values entered by the users of operational systems to work around certain known system restrictions. For example, some department stores give special discounts to new subscribers to their charge cards. The sales-person may offer the customer immediate credit approval, thus allowing the customer to use the card with the benefit of a discount rate on the first purchase. To get around the requirement of a credit rating check, the salesperson may assign a temporary credit limit of $1.00 to the customer. However, this value stays in the database.

All these checks represent a limited set of examples where *rule-based procedures* should be employed to check and clean the data. Replacing or removing erroneous or inconsistent records should be a matter of a simple set of IF–THEN–ELSE statements in regular SAS code.

In addition to these checks, which are all based on checking particular fields, we should also check the integrity of (1) sampling and (2) the implicit assumption that the mining view and the scoring view have the same statistical properties. This leads us to consider not only comparing the values of a particular field against a set of rules, but also comparing the values from two or more datasets.

6.2 COMPARING DATASETS

We now focus our attention on the tests and checks used to ensure that the modeling data (mining view) represent the population (scoring view) and that the training and validation partitions (both parts of the mining view) have similar statistical properties.

There is a wealth of well-established statistical methods to compare two samples of data. Before we discuss some of the details of these methods, let us first create our wish list of the measures of similarity, which would increase our confidence that a sample or two datasets represent the same pool of data.

- *Dataset schema:* Both datasets should contain the same variables using the same data types.

- *Values and statistics:* For each of the continuous variables, both datasets should have similar maximums, minimums, averages, and modes. For each nominal and ordinal variable, both datasets should have the same categories.

- *Distributions:* Variables of both datasets should have similar distributions.

- *Cross-relationships:* All relationships among different variables should be the same in both datasets.

Although these measures are very general in scope, they provide the requirements that form the core of integrity check procedures. Let us discuss each of them in some detail.

One last remark on notation specific to datasets, samples, and population. Since the methods used to compare two datasets are the same whether we are comparing a sample to a population or a sample to a sample, we will not make that distinction anymore. We will simply talk about comparing two datasets.

6.3 DATASET SCHEMA CHECKS

6.3.1 DATASET VARIABLES

We have borrowed the expression *schema* from the field of relational databases to denote the structure of a dataset in terms of the type definition of its constituent fields. In most applications, modeling data is taken as a sample of the population. This can easily be achieved while preserving the field names and their type definitions. However, in some situations, it is possible that the data used for modeling comes from one source and the data used in scoring or model assessment comes from another. Therefore, one must make sure that the two datasets have the same schema.

Manual comparison of the names and variable types of two datasets is quite an easy task in the case of datasets with few variables. However, for datasets with many variables, it is time consuming and error prone. Also, in environments where a large number of models are being produced and made operational, many of the scoring procedures are automated.

The need to compare the schema of two datasets is rather the exception to the rule. Whenever such a situation arises, however, it becomes a major headache for the analyst. For that reason, we have implemented a simple macro that compares two datasets (A) and (B) to ascertain that *every* variable in B is present in A and is defined using the same data type. This implementation allows the possibility that A is a superset of B in terms of the constituting variables. If a perfect match between A and B were required, the user could invoke the macro twice to test if all the variables in B are in A and vice versa. A positive result of these two checks would then guarantee that both datasets contain the same variable names and are implementing the same type definitions.

Since our implementation is in SAS, we check for only two types of data definition—the two SAS data types, numeric and string. A slight modification of the comparison implementation can include other data types such as time and date. We leave that for you to do as a simple exercise, which can be easily achieved through the use of SAS FORMAT and INFORMAT specifications.

The presented implementation relies on *SAS Dictionary Tables,* which are a set of read-only tables that are accessible through PROC SQL and contain information about all the tables defined in the current SAS session. These tables contain all the required information about the fields and their definitions, which is exactly what we need. An alternative to this SQL-based implementation is to use the capabilities of PROC CONTENTS and manipulate the results using standard DATA step statements. However, I believe that the SQL-based implementation is easier to understand and modify.

Table 6.1   Parameters of macro SchCompare().

Header	SchCompare(A,B,Result, I_St);
Parameter	*Description*
A	Dataset A (the base)
B	Dataset B
Result	A dataset containing the status of the variables of B when they are compared to all the variables in A
I_St	A status indicator: 0: B is not part of A; 1: B is a part of A

Step 1
Create a table with the field names and types for datasets A and B.

```
proc sql noprint;
create table TA as
  select name,type from dictionary.columns
  where memname = "%upcase(&A)"
  order by name;
```

```
create table TB as
  select name,type from dictionary.columns
  where memname = "%upcase(&B)"
  order by name;
select count(*) into:N from TB;
run;
quit;
```

Step 2

Loop on each element in TB and attempt to find it in TA. We do that by converting the elements of TB into macro variables.

```
data _Null_;
 set TB;
   call symput('V_'||left(_n_),name);
   call symput('T_'||left(_n_),Type);
run;
```

Step 3

Loop on the N variables in TB and check if they exist in TA and create the entries in a Result dataset.

```
proc sql noprint;
 create table &Result (VarName char(32)
   , VarType char(8)
   , ExistInBase num
   , Comment char(80));
%do i=1 %to &N;
  select count(*) into: Ni from TA  where name="&&V_&i" ;
  %if &Ni eq 0 %then %do ; /* variable does not exist */
    %let Value=0;
    let Comment=Variable does not exist in Base Dataset.;
%goto NextVar;
   %end;
  select count(*) into: Ti from TA
where name="&&V_&i" and Type="&&T_&i";
%if &Ti gt 0 %then %do;  /* perfect match */
%let Value=1;
%let Comment=Variable exits in Base Dataset with the same
data type.;
        %end;
 %else %do; /*different type */
%let Value=0;
%let Comment=Variable exists in Base Dataset
but with the different data type.;
   %end;
```

Step 4
Record the entry in the `Result` dataset and get the next variable.

```
%NextVar:;
  insert into &Result values ("&&V_&i"
    , "&&T_&i"
    , &Value
    , "&Comment");
%end;
 select min(ExitsInBase) into: I from &Result;
run;
quit;
%let &I_ST=&I;
%mend;
```

Using this macro, we can confirm that dataset B is contained in dataset A with the same variable names and types. However, it does not check on the contents of the fields and their formats. For example, date fields are stored in SAS datasets as numeric fields. It is straightforward to modify the macro to check also on the formats used for fields. This can be accomplished using the field `format` in the `dictionary.columns` table.

6.3.2 VARIABLE TYPES

Since the key question in this set of checks is the variable type, our first task is to identify the type of each variable. In SAS, there are two variable types: string and numeric. It is reasonable to assume that if a field were defined as a string variable, then it would be treated as nominal. There are situations where a string variable does in fact contain only numeric data and should be treated as continuous, or at least as an ordinal variable.

The only reason that a continuous a variable was defined as a string field in the SAS dataset is that it originally came from a database where that field was stored in a text field, or during the transformation process it was decided that using a string field would be easier during data conversion. A simple method to convert a character is to use the function INPUT and store the returned values in a new variable, as in the following example:

```
data SS;
 x='1';output;
 x='a'; output;
run;
data NN;
  set SS;
  y=input(x,best10.);
  drop x;
run;
```

The variable y in the dataset NN will be of type numeric and will have the value of the variable x in dataset SS. It should be noted, however, that if the string variable contains characters other than numbers, these records will be filled by missing values and an error will be entered in the SAS Log.

We will assume from now on that string variables are in fact nominal variables. On the other hand, numeric fields can represent nominal, ordinal, or continuous variables. This is determined by the analyst based on the understanding of the contents of the data in the field and how to interpret it in terms of the business problem being modeled. For example, a numeric field taking only the values of 0 and 1 could be used as an ordinal variable or as a nominal variable. It could also be used as continuous when intermediate values would also be allowed.

We can summarize this information in a simple rule: The analyst has to specify the use of each numeric variable (nominal, ordinal, or continuous) during modeling.

6.4 NOMINAL VARIABLES

In the case of nominal variables, we conduct two checks.

1. Check that all the categories present in the first dataset are also present in the second.

2. Check that the proportions of all categories in the two datasets are close or, ideally, identical.

The first check is a simple, though essential, one because ignoring one or more categories of any of the variables may result in unpredictable results, at either the modeling or the deployment stage. For example, some decision tree implementations use the average value of the population for classification and estimation whenever the tree model does not contain a clear method for the treatment of this category. Other tree implementations simply generate a missing score.

To avoid the pitfalls of either case, it is better to make sure that *all* the categories of all the variables in the population can be accounted for and used in the modeling in some way or another. (One way of dealing with some categories is to eliminate them intentionally, but we have to find them and define the method of their elimination or replacement).

The second check is more involved and will determine the degree of similarity between the two datasets with respect to the distribution of one particular variable.

The following two subsections provide the details for the two checks.

6.4.1 TESTING THE PRESENCE OF ALL CATEGORIES

Obtaining the distinct categories of a nominal variable is a relatively simple task. SAS provides several routes to achieving just that. PROC FREQ obtains the categories of a variable as well as their frequencies. Alternatively, we can use PROC SQL to issue a SELECT statement and use the keyword DISTINCT to create a list of the distinct categories of a field in a dataset. In the latter case, if the frequencies of the categories are also required to be calculated, we can use the function COUNT and group the selection by the variable in question. The SELECT statement would then be in the following form:

```
SELECT DISTINCT Variable, COUNT(*)
 FROM MyDataSet
 GROUP BY Variable
```

The next task is to make sure that all the categories included in the population do in fact exist in the sample. Note that in the current case we start our checks with the population and not the sample. In the case of two partitions, we have to confirm that they both have the same categories for all nominal variables. The macro in Table 6.2 compares the categories of the variable Var in two datasets Base and Sample to check whether all the categories of this variable in the Base dataset exist in the Sample dataset.

Table 6.2   Parameters of macro CatCompare().

Header	CatCompare (Base, Sample, Var, V_Result, I_St);
Parameter	*Description*
Base	Base dataset
Sample	Sample dataset
Var	The variable for which the categories in the Base dataset are compared to the categories in the Sample dataset
V_result	A dataset containing the comparison summary
I_St	A status indicator set as follows:
	0: all categories of Var in Base exist in Sample
	1: Not all categories of Var in Base exist in Sample

Step 1
Obtain the categories and their count for both Base and Sample for Var.

```
Proc SQL noprint;
create table CatB as select distinct &Var from &Base;
select count(*) into:NB from CatB;
create table CatS as select distinct &Var from &Sample;
select count(*) into:NS from CatS;
create table &V_Result (Category Char(32)
```

```
           , ExistsInSample num
           , Comment char(80));
   run;
   quit;
```

Step 2
Convert all the categories of the dataset Base into macro variables for use in the comparison.

```
data _Null_;
 set CatB;
   call symput('C_'||left(_n_),&Var);
run;
```

Step 3
Loop over the Base categories and find whether all of them exist in Sample.

```
proc SQL ;
%do i=1 %to &NB;
   select count(*) into: Nx
     from CatS where &Var = "%trim(&&C_&i)";
%if &Nx =0 %then %do;
     Insert into &V_Result
      values("%trim(&&C_&i)",0
        ,'Category does not exist in sample.');
           %end;
%if &Nx>0 %then %do;
   Insert into &V_Result
     values("%trim(&&C_&i)",1
               ,'Category exists in sample.');
         %end;
%end;
```

Step 4
Calculate the I_St indicator.

```
select min(ExistsInSample) into: Status from &V_Result;
quit;
%let &I_St = &Status;
```

Step 5
Clean the workspace.

```
proc datasets nodetails  library = work;
delete CatB CatC;
quit;
%mend;
```

This macro can be called as many times as necessary to make sure that the values of all the nominal variables in the population exist in the sample (or in both the training and validation partitions).

6.4.2 TESTING THE SIMILARITY OF RATIOS

To test the similarity of the ratios in the sample and those in the population with respect to a particular nominal variable, we will implement the techniques used in the analysis of *contingency tables*. A contingency table is simply the result of cross-tabulating the frequencies of the categories of a variable with respect to different datasets. For example, consider the following two SAS code segments generating two samples: SampleA and SampleB.

```
data SampleA;
INPUT x $ y @@;
datalines;
A  3  A  2  A  2  B  3  B  2  B  1
B  2  B  3  B  3  C  1  C  1  C  2
C  2  C  2  C  1  A  3  A  2  A  1
A  3  A  2  A  2  B  1  B  2  B  1
B  1  B  3  B  2  C  3  C  1  C  1
C  2  C  1  C  3  A  2  A  2  A  1
A  2  A  2  A  3  B  3  B  2  B  1
B  2  B  3  B  2  C  3  C  1  C  2
C  3  C  2  C  3  A  3  A  3  A  2
A  1  A  1  A  3  B  1  B  3  B  1
;
run;
data SampleB;
INPUT x $ y @@;
datalines;
C  2  C  3  C  1  C  1  C  3  C  1
B  2  B  2  B  2  B  1  B  2  B  2
B  3  B  1  B  3  B  3  B  2  B  1
A  2  A  1  A  3  A  2  A  2  A  1
B  2  B  1  B  3  B  2  B  1  B  1
C  3  C  2  C  3  C  3  C  1  C  2
C  1  C  3  C  2  C  3  C  1  C  3
B  1  B  1  B  2  B  2  B  1  B  1
C  1  C  2  C  1  C  2  C  2  C  1
A  2  A  2  A  2  A  1  A  2  A  3
;
run;
```

We can analyze the frequencies of the categories of the variable X in each of these two datasets using PROC FREQ, as follows.

```
PROC FREQ DATA=Sample A;
 TABLES x;
run;

PROC FREQ DATA=Sample B;
 TABLES x;
run;
```

The results of this analysis are summarized in Table 6.3.

We can rearrange the results of the frequencies of the two datasets in the equivalent but important form as shown in Table 6.4.

Table 6.3   Results of PROC FREQ on SampleA and SampleB datasets.

	Sample A			Sample B	
X	Frequency	Percent	X	Frequency	Percent
A	21	35.00	A	12	20.00
B	21	35.00	B	24	40.00
C	18	30.00	C	24	40.00

Table 6.4   SampleA and SampleB frequencies as a contingency table.

X	Sample A	Sample B
A	21	12
B	21	24
C	18	24

The analysis of contingency Table 6.4 is focused on whether we can confirm that there is a *significant difference* between dataset SampleA and dataset SampleB with respect to the frequencies of the variable X. A detailed description of the mathematics behind this type of analysis is presented in Chapter 13. For now, we will contend with the idea that we are using the Chi-square test to confirm the similarity, or dissimilarity, of the two datasets.

The following macro extracts the comparison variable from the two datasets, adds labels to them, and calls a macro that tests the similarity of the distribution of the comparison variable (see Table 6.5). The heart of the comparison is another macro, ContnAna(), which is described in detail in Section 13.5.

Table 6.5   Parameters of macro `ChiSample()`.

Header	`ChiSample(DS1, DS2, VarC, p, M_Result);`
Parameter	*Description*
`DS1`	First dataset
`DS2`	Second dataset
`VarC`	Nominal variable used for comparison
`p`	*P*-value used to compare to the *p*-value of Chi-square test
`M_Result`	Result of comparison. If two datasets are the same with a probability of *p*, then `M_result` variable will be set to Yes; otherwise, will be set to No.

Step 1

Extract only the comparison variable in both datasets, create a dataset ID label variable, and concatenate the two sets in one temporary dataset.

```
DATA Temp_1;
 set &DS1;
 Keep &VarC DSId;
 DSId=1;
RUN;
DATA Temp_2;
 set &DS2;
 Keep &VarC DSId;
 DSId=2;
RUN;
DATA Temp_Both;
 set Temp_1 Temp_2;
RUN;
```

Step 2

Use macro `ContnAna()` to test the association between the dataset ID variable and the comparison variable.

```
%ContnAna(temp_Both, DSId, &VarC, Temp_Res);
```

Step 3

Get the *p*-value of the Chi-square test, compare it to the acceptance *p*-value, and set the results message accordingly.

```
data _null_;
 set temp_res;
```

```
   if SAS_Name="P_PCHI" then
     call symput ("P_actual", Value);
run;
%if %sysevalf(&P_Actual>=&P) %then %let &M_Result=Yes;
%else %let &M_Result=No;
```

Step 4
Clean the workspace.

```
/* clean workspace */
proc datasets library=work nolist;
 delete Temp_1 Temp_2 Temp_both Temp_res;
quit;
```

To demonstrate the use of this macro, test the similarity of the last two datasets (SampleA, SampleB).

```
%let DS1=SampleA;
%let DS2=SampleB;
%let VarC=x;
%let p=0.9;
%let Result=;
 %ChiSample(&DS1, &DS2, &VarC, &p, Result);
%put Result of Comparison= &Result;
```

In the preceding code, we used a probability level of 90% as the acceptance level of the similarity of the two datasets. The last %put statement will echo the result of comparison to the SAS Log. Run the code and test whether the two datasets are similar! (Answer: No, the two datasets are different).

6.5 CONTINUOUS VARIABLES

In the case of continuous variables, there are no distinct categories that can be checked, only a distribution of many values. Therefore, integrity checks attempt to ascertain that the basic distribution measures are similar in the two datasets.

The distribution of a continuous variable can be assessed using several measures, which can be classified into three categories: (1) measures of central tendency, (2) measures of dispersion, and (3) measures of the shape of the distribution. Table 6.6 shows the most common measures used in each category.

The calculation of these values for a continuous variable in a dataset using SAS is straightforward. Both PROC UNIVARIATE and MEANS calculate all these values and can store them in a new dataset using the statement OUTPUT. PROC MEANS is in general faster and requires less memory that PROC UNIVARIATE. PROC UNIVARIATE, on the other hand, provides more detailed tests on the variance, mean, and normality of the data. It also provides the ability to extract and present histograms using different methods.

Table 6.6   Common measures of quantifying the distribution of a continuous variable.

Category	Common measures
Central tendency	Mean, mode, median
Dispersion	Variance, range, relative dispersion
Shape of distribution	Maximum, minimum, P1, P5, P10, P50, P90, P95, P99, kurtosis, and skewness

The following code provides a wrapper for PROC UNIVARIATE to facilitate its use. The macro calls PROC UNIVARIATE and stores the values of the preceding measures in variables in an output dataset with the appropriate names.

```
%macro VarUnivar1(ds,varX, StatsDS);
 proc univariate data=&ds noprint;
 var &VarX;
 output out=&StatsDS
  N=Nx
  Mean=Vmean
  min=VMin
  max=VMax
  STD=VStd
  VAR=VVar
  mode=Vmode
  median=Vmedia
  P1=VP1
  P5=VP5
  P10=VP10
  P90=VP90
  P95=VP95
  P99=VP99
 ;
 run;
%mend;
```

Call the macro straightforwardly, as in the following code.

```
%let ds=test;      /* Name of data set */
%let varX=x;       /* Analysis variable */
%let StatsDS=unv;  /* Dataset used to store results */

%VarUnivar1(&ds,&varX, &StatsDS);
```

6.5.1 COMPARING MEASURES FROM TWO DATASETS

The macro VarUnivar1() calculates the most common univariate measures of a continuous variable. We can use it to determine these measures for a variable in two different datasets—for example, training and validation partitions. Because the variable in question is continuous, there might be sampling errors, and the two datasets might be very different, the results from these two datasets will almost always be different. But how different? That is the important question that we have to answer.

There are two approaches to assess the difference in the measures of continuous variables. The first one is to use statistical tests, such as Chi-square or *t*-tests, to make a statement about the significance of the differences among calculated values. The second, and simpler, approach is to calculate the percentage of differences between the values from the two datasets. Of course, the second method does not enjoy the sound statistical foundation of the first method, but, in view of the simplicity of implementation, it can be a valuable tool, especially when there are many variables to test. It is particularly useful to compare quantities other than the mean and variance. Although in those cases rigorous statistical measures exist, the interpretation of their results is not easy for nonstatisticians.

In this book, we implement both methods. Table 6.7 shows the plan for comparing the different measures.

Table 6.7   Comparision of measures of continuous variables.

Quantity	Method of comparison
Mean	*t*-test
Variance	χ^2 test
Others	Percentage difference

Note, however: there are well-established methods for computing the statistical distributions of other univariate outputs, such as the mode and the different quantiles (PROC UNIVARIATE provides many of these measures). But, to keep the required statistical theory to a minimum, we adopt the simpler approach of using percentage difference.

6.5.2   COMPARING THE MEANS, STANDARD DEVIATIONS, AND VARIANCES

To compare the previous measures in two datasets, we use the macro CVLimits(), which calculates the confidence intervals for the mean, standard deviation, and variance for a continuous variable in a dataset. The results are stored in an output dataset with one row. The macro uses PROC UNIVARIATE to calculate the base values and the additional confidence intervals from their original formulas. All the formulas are based on the assumption that the variable in question follows the normal distribution.

Step 1
We first use PROC UNIVARIATE to calculate the mean, standard deviation, and variance.

```
proc univariate data=&dsin all noprint;
var &VarX;
```

Table 6.8   Parameters of macro CVLimits().

Header	CVLimits(DSin, VarX, DSout, Alpha);
Parameter	Description
DSin	Input dataset
VarX	Calculation variable
DSout	Output dataset with the measures
Alpha	*p*-value for confidence interval calculations

```
    output out=temp_univ
    Var=&VarX._Var
    STD=&VarX._STD
    mean=&VarX._Mean
    N=n;
run;
```

Step 2
Calculate the confidence interval on the mean, variance, and standard deviation.

```
data &dsout;
set temp_Univ;
/* Alpha */
Alpha=&alpha;
MC=tinv(1-&alpha/2,n-1) * &VarX._Std / sqrt(n);

/* Lower and upper limits on the mean */
&VarX._Mean_U= &VarX._Mean + MC;
&VarX._Mean_L=&VarX._Mean - Mc;

/* Lower and upper limits on the variance */
&VarX._Var_U= &VarX._Var * (n-1)/cinv(1-&alpha/2,n-1);
&VarX._Var_L= &VarX._Var * (n-1)/cinv(  &alpha/2,n-1);

/* Lower and upper limits on Standard Deviation */
&VarX._STD_U = sqrt (&VarX._Var_U);
&VarX._STD_L = sqrt (&VarX._Var_L);

drop MC ;
run;
```

Step 3
Finish the macro.

```
%mend CVLimits;
```

Now that we can calculate the confidence limits on a variable in a dataset, the question is: How can we compare these quantities (mean, standard deviation, and variance) for two datasets? The answer to this question can be discovered by considering three possible scenarios.

- *Case 1:* We have drawn a sample dataset from a population, and we want to make sure that the mean, the standard deviation, and the variance of the sample represent the population. This will be a straightforward application of the results of the macro. We calculate the population mean, standard deviation, and variance and test if they all fall within the limits calculated from the sample.

- *Case 2:* We have two samples—training and validation partitions—drawn from a population. In this case, we repeat the procedures used in Case 1 for each sample.

- *Case 3:* We have two samples—training and validation but we cannot calculate the actual measures for the population, either because of the size of population or because we do not have the data. This is the most difficult case and will require us to resort to a somewhat more complex approach. One simple and efficient approach, although not based on rigorous mathematical foundation, is to calculate the confidence intervals for each measure and then find the *intersection* of these intervals. We then require that the datasets that we denote later as *the population* have their respective values within the intersection of the confidence intervals. This is particularly useful in the case of scoring. We can limit the resulting models as valid only for scoring views with means, standard deviations, and variances that satisfy these conditions.

6.5.3 THE CONFIDENCE-LEVEL CALCULATION ASSUMPTIONS

The macro presented in the previous section calculated the confidence intervals of the variable in question assuming that this variable follows the *normal distribution*.

How realistic is this assumption? In real datasets, very few raw variables have normal distributions. However, this does not mean that we do not use the preceding methods, for two reasons. First, these are the only simple methods we have to compare these variables. Second, there is a statistical theory, called the *central limit theory,* that shows that with a large number of observations, the distribution of continuous variables approaches that of a normal distribution. Therefore, in large datasets we can assume that the variable follows that of a normal distribution without a significant error.

Finally, in Chapter 9 we will present the *Box–Cox* transformations, which can transform variables so that they become almost normally distributed (Johnson and Wichern 2001).

In the preceding discussions, we assumed that we had settled on a reasonable value for the confidence limit. However, the choice of the confidence level parameter (α) is not based on rigorous scientific reasoning. α is commonly set at 0.10, 0.05, or 0.01. These values are only what statisticians and modelers usually use so that they have

90, 95, or 99% confidence, respectively, in the results. The point is, the choice among these three values is somewhat arbitrary.

6.5.4 Comparison of Other Measures

As discussed earlier, there are some rigorous techniques to test other measures using statistical tests, similar to those used for testing the values of the means and the variances. In most cases, we focus most of our attention on the mean and the variance of continuous variables.

Comparing the values obtained for the different measures, such as kurtosis or P95, is a simple task, almost trivial. For example, the following macro describes a simple implementation to compare two such values and provide the difference between then as percentage of the first, second, or average value.

Table 6.9   Parameters of macro CompareTwo().

Header	CompareTwo(Val1, Val2, Method, Diff);
Parameter	*Description*
Val1	First value
Val2	Second value
Method	Method of comparison: 1: use Val1 as the base value 2: use Val2 as the base value 0: use average of Val1 and Val2 as the base value
Diff	Percentage difference

We can apply this macro to test the percentage difference between any of these values (Table 6.9). Then we adopt a simple strategy of accepting the hypothesis that the two samples are similar if their respective measures differ no more than, say, 10%.

```
%if &Method=1 %then %do;
%let &diff = %sysevalf(100*(&val2-&val1)/&val1);
%end;
%else %if &Method=2 %then %do;
%let &diff = %sysevalf(100*(&val2-&val1)/&val2);
%end;
%else %if &Method=0 %then %do;
%let &diff = %sysevalf(200*(&val2-&val1)/(&val1+&val2));
%end;

%mend;
```

We should note that in the preceding implementation we allowed use of the average value of the two values as the base for comparison. This is useful when we compare two values from two samples or when the intended base value is zero. The following examples use this macro.

```
/* Examples */
%let x=0.05;
%let y=0.06;
%let d=;
%CompareTwo(&x,&y,1,d);
%put Method 1: difference =&d %;

%CompareTwo(&x,&y,2,d);
%put Method 2: difference =&d %;

%CompareTwo(&x,&y,0,d);
%put Method 0: difference =&d %;
```

EXPLORATORY DATA ANALYSIS

7.1 INTRODUCTION

In Section 1.2 data exploration, or Exploratory Data Analysis (EDA) was listed as one of the fundamental steps of the data mining process. EDA is a set of procedures aimed at understanding the data and the relationships among variables. It is usually performed interactively through the calculation of many measures and summary tables, as well as by using graphical representation of the data. Most data mining modeling packages have extensive EDA capabilities. In addition, there are many software packages dedicated to performing some EDA functions, such as SAS/Insight.

This chapter examines how EDA and procedures of data preparation influence each other. Specifically, in order to perform EDA effectively, the data need to be prepared for that purpose. Conversely, EDA results will suggest that certain transformations should be performed on the data to obtain better models and to reveal hidden structures. The methods presented in this chapter follow these two lines of thought.

It should be emphasized that the procedures presented here are supplementary to the graphical and interactive methods of EDA. Interactive graphical analysis of the data is probably the most important aspect of EDA. We only cover the procedures involving calculations that could be automated using SAS macros. Be warned, then, that even implementing *all* the macros presented or discussed in this chapter will not be enough to render a *complete* EDA.

7.2 COMMON EDA PROCEDURES

EDA was proposed, and so named, by Tukey (1977). Current practices in EDA involve the following procedures.

- Descriptive statistics—This involves the examination of the univariate statistics of each variable.

- Examination of the distribution of each variable (for all variable types) and testing normality assumptions (for continuous variables only).

- Calculation of the coefficients of correlation between the variables (for ordinal and continuous variables only).

- Detection of outliers.

- Exploration of nonlinear relationships among different variables using scatter plots.

- Counting missing values for each variable and examining the effect of the bias introduced by simple substitution schemes, such as substituting the mean or the median, or by deleting these observations.

- Testing the assumptions that different samples were made from the same population.

- Extracting and examining cross-tabulated frequencies of variables.

- Calculation of different statistics on cross-tabulation tables.

- Using multivariate methods, such as factor analysis and principal component analysis, to detect linear structures within the data.

Many of these steps can be performed by dedicated EDA or data mining modeling packages. However, performing them as part of the data preparation process could save some time and automate the process to reduce the interactive effort performed by the analyst.

The interaction of data preparation procedures and the results of EDA is evident from the preceding list. For example, the option of using a simple substitution scheme to treat missing values, and the consequent bias in the data, will have a direct impact on preparing the mining view and the scoring view. Similarly, examining the distribution of each variable (e.g., through histograms) will reveal the necessity of altering the distribution of some of the variables using data transformations.

We will start with macros that implement some of these operations to automate some of the EDA steps.

7.3 UNIVARIATE STATISTICS

The calculations of the univariate statistics were introduced in Section 6.5 through the macro VarUnivar(). The purpose there was to check these measures and compare them to those of the population using the macro CVLimits(). In the case of EDA, the univariate measures are calculated for their own sake. We are interested in calculating these measures to assess the different variables. The macro VarUnivar() implemented a wrapper on PROC UNIVARIATE. PROC UNIVARIATE offers another important feature that is useful in EDA, that is, the identification of extreme observations.

However, PROC UNIVARIATE does not provide an easy way to store these values in a dataset to facilitate further processing on them. The following code generates a dataset with 32 numbers between 0 and 4.0, in addition to four high values between 22 and 34. The number of extreme values, at either the lower limit or the upper limit, printed by PROC UNIVARIATE is determined by the parameter NEXTROBS, which takes a default value of 5.

```
data Extremes;
 input x @@;
 datalines;
 1.45  0.73  2.43  3.89
 3.86  3.96  2.41  2.29
 2.23  2.19  0.37  2.71
 0.77  0.83  3.61  1.71
 1.06  3.23  0.68  3.15
 1.83  3.37  1.60  1.17
 3.87  2.36  1.84  1.64
 3.97  2.23  2.21  1.93
22.00 33.00 23.00 34.00
 ;
run;
proc univariate data=extremes nextrobs=6;
 var x;
run;
```

The following is the part of the output where the extreme values are printed.

```
        The UNIVARIATE Procedure
             Variable:  x

        Extreme Observations

----Lowest----        ----Highest----

Value      Obs        Value      Obs

 0.37       11         3.96        6
 0.68       19         3.97       29
 0.73        2        22.00       33
 0.77       13        23.00       35
 0.83       14        33.00       34
 1.06       17        34.00       36
```

Note that because we have chosen to print six extreme values on either side of the variable distribution, some the values identified by PROC MEANS are not really of interest because they do not represent the inserted high values.

This shows that using PROC UNIVARIATE in this simplified manner would not properly identify *interesting* extreme values, that is, *outliers*, with respect to this particular variable. The reason is that PROC UNIVARIATE simply sorts the values and finds the NEXTROBS lowest and highest values. However, it does not test these observations to confirm that they are outliers. We discuss outliers in more details in Section 7.5.

7.4 Variable Distribution

In addition to examination of the univariate statistics, the distribution of each variable usually reveals any interesting characteristics or potential problems. Continuous variables are usually represented using histograms, and nominal and ordinal variables are represented using pie or bar charts.

Plotting histograms is often done by special software or by preparing the data such that the histogram data is based on the binned values. The binning of continuous variables is discussed in full detail in Section 10.3. Examination of the histogram of continuous variables could reveal that it is skewed to either end of the scale. In this case, the techniques described in Section 9.6 could be used to change the shape of the variable distribution.

In the case of nominal and ordinal variables, pie charts often show two potential issues. The first is that when one of the categories is dominating the variable distribution, with all the other categories having small frequencies. In this case, it may be worthwhile to group the *other* categories into a new group. The second situation is that there are a large number of categories in a nominal variable, high cardinality. The techniques described in Section 10.2 could be employed to remedy this problem.

7.5 Detection of Outliers

A basic assumption in data mining is that the data used for modeling, and later for scoring, is obtained from (or generated by) a process that has a specific (but unknown) mechanism (a functional form). Therefore, observations that seem not to follow this mechanism are defined to be outliers. Outliers can be a result of having errors in the data or having observations that do not comply with the hidden (or assumed) mechanism that generated the data. Since the mechanism that generated the data is unknown, the definition of outliers is subjective and speculative at best. Therefore, excluding observations that have been labeled as outliers from the mining view or scoring view should be done after careful examination.

There are three main approaches to identifying outliers.

- The first and simplest one is the specification of an *acceptable* range of values for each variable. The upper and lower limits of this range are determined using some simple statistical justification. Common implementations include specifying ±3 standard deviations from the mean value for continuous variables. In the case of nominal and ordinal variables, a minimum percentage of the frequency count of the category of 1% is commonly used. The SAS implementation of these methods is straighforward and will be presented shortly. These methods have the advantage of being simple to implement and interpret. However, they do not take into account the multivariate nature of the data; that is, they rely on the examination of each variable independently. Thus the interaction between the variables is ignored. Furthermore, applying some transformations on continuous variables could reshape the distribution, and observations that were deemed outliers could become normal again. Therefore, this technique should be used only after attempts to reshape the variable distribution and after considering the interaction among variables.

■ The second category of methods relies on using a dependent variable and a set of assumed independent variables to fit a candidate model such as a least-squares or regression. Observations that show large deviation from the fitted model are then deemed outliers. These methods remedy some of the disadvantages of the previous range-based methods—namely, taking into account the multivariate nature of the data. However, they are based on assuming a certain form of the model that generated the data. In typical data mining applications, the analyst experiments with different modeling techniques and model forms. Therefore, using one of these models to reject some observations because they do not fit well into that model could be misleading. For example, when one uses linear regression to find the outliers, and then uses a decision tree to develop the mining model, the removed outliers may have been useful in identifying a small node of importance in the decision tree.

■ The third category of methods uses clustering algorithms to group the data into smaller subsets (clusters). Clusters containing a very small number of observations, ideally one observation, are identified as outliers. This is perhaps the best method that combines the best of the two methods. This is justified as follows. Clustering algorithms group *similar* observations in the same cluster based on the *distance* between them. This is similar to the idea of specifying an acceptable range, but in this case the range is limited to within the cluster or to a smaller subset of the data.

The second feature is that clusters with very few observations are deemed outliers. This idea is conceptually equivalent to rejecting the observations that do not fit the model. The model here is defined as the set of clusters with a relatively large number of observations, that is, normal values. Finally, because the clusters are defined on the basis of *all* the variables, the issue of the multivariate nature of the data has been taken care of, without assuming a specific form or a structure of the model to be used.

Most of the methods used to test outliers assume that we are dealing with continuous variables. However, most data in data mining applications contains a large number of nominal and ordinal variables. Unfortunately, there are no equivalent methods for the identification of outliers for nominal or ordinal variables, other than simply specifying a minimum acceptable percentage of the frequency of each category. This is easily implemented using PROC FREQ and labeling the categories with low frequency as outliers.

On the other hand, accounting for the effect of the multivariate nature of the interaction between continuous and nominal variables, while using the methods used for continuous variables, is achieved by mapping nominal variables into indicator, or dummy, variables. The details of mapping methods are provided in Section 9.4.

The following subsections provide the SAS implementation of the three approaches just described.

7.5.1 IDENTIFICATION OF OUTLIERS USING RANGES

When a continuous variable follows a normal distribution, 99.7% of the observations fall within ±3 standard deviations from the mean. Based on this observation, we may attempt to identify the outliers by looking for the observations that fall outside this range. This is implemented in the following macro. The macro uses PROC UNIVARIATE to calculate the mean and the standard deviation and simply find the observation numbers that are outside this range.

Table 7.1   Parameters of macro Extremes1().

Header	Extremes1(DSin, VarX, NSigmas, DSout);
Parameter	*Description*
DSin	Input dataset
VarX	Continuous variable with outliers
NSigmas	Number of standard deviations used on each side of the mean to identify the outliers
DSout	Output dataset with observation numbers of the outliers and their values

Step 1

We begin by extracting the variable to a temporary dataset to speed up the manipulation. We also generate a variable to hold the observation number. Obviously, the variable itself is allowed to be anything other than ObsNo.

```
data temp;
 set &DSin;
 ObsNo=_N_;
 keep &VarX ObsNo;
run;
```

Step 2

We use PROC UNIVARIATE to calculate the mean and standard deviation of the variable. Then we extract these values to macro variables and calculate the upper and lower limits of the "normal" range. Values of the variable XVAR outside this range will be labeled as outliers.

```
/* calculate the mean and STD using proc univariate */
 proc univariate data=temp noprint;
 var &VarX;
 output out=temp_u   STD=VSTD   Mean=VMean;
run;

/* Extract the upper and lower limits
    into macro variables */
data _null_;
 set temp_u;
 call symput('STD', VSTD);
 call symput('Mean', VMean);
run;

%let ULimit=%sysevalf(&Mean + &NSigmas * &STD);
%let LLimit=%sysevalf(&Mean - &NSigmas * &STD);
```

Step 3

We generate the output dataset DSOUT by reading only the observations outside the normal range.

```
/* extract exteme observations outside these limits */
data &DSout;
 set temp;
 if &VarX < &Llimit or &VarX > &ULimit;
run;
```

Step 4

Finally, we clean the workspace and finish the macro.

```
/* clean workspace and finish the macro */
proc datasets library=work nodetails;
 delete temp temp_u;
quit;
%mend;
```

To illustrate the use of this macro, we use it with the dataset Extremes of Section 7.3, as follows:

```
%let DSin=extremes;
%let varX=x;
%let NSigmas=3;
%let DSout=ExtObs;

%Extremes1(&DSin, &VarX, &NSigmas, &DSout);
```

Executing the macro, using three standard deviations on each side of the mean, will result in an output dataset ExtObs with two observations for the values of 33 and 34. This is disappointing because we expected this approach to lead to the discovery of the outliers, which we inserted in this simple dataset.

The reason for the failure is that the mean and standard deviations calculated by PROC UNIVARIATE were calculated using *all* the nonmissing observations; that is, it included the outliers. Therefore, the mean as well as the standard deviation are biased because of these outliers. A simple remedy for this situation is to use *unbiased* measures for central tendency and dispersion for the variable in question.

It can be shown that the *median* is more robust to outliers than the mean. We can also use the *interquartile range* in place of the standard deviation as a measure for dispersion. The interquartile range is the difference between the values Q3 and Q1 of the variable, that is, the variable range that contains 50% of the values.

It is easy to modify macro Extremes1() to use the median and the interquartile range, as shown in the following macro, Extremes2(). The macro is identical to Extremes1() with the exception of the method of calculating the outliers range.

```
%macro Extremes2(DSin, VarX, NQRange, DSout);
/* Calculation of extreme values for a continuous variable
      outside the range of NQrange * QRange
      from the median. We use the median in place of the mean
      as a more robust estimate of the central tendency */

/* First, extract XVar to a temp dataset, and the
   observation number of the original dataset */
data temp;
 set &DSin;
 ObsNo=_N_;
 keep &VarX ObsNo;
run;

/* Calculate the median and QRange using proc univariate */
 proc univariate data=temp noprint;
 var &VarX;
 output out=temp_u    QRANGE=VQr    mode=Vmode;
run;
```

```
/* Extract the upper and lower limits into macro variables */
data _null_;
 set temp_u;
 call symput('QR', VQr);
 call symput('Mode', Vmode);
run;
%let ULimit=%sysevalf(&Mode + &NQrange * &QR);
%let LLimit=%sysevalf(&Mode - &NQRange * &QR);

/* Extract extreme observations outside these limits */
data &DSout;
 set temp;
 if &VarX < &Llimit or &VarX > &ULimit;
run;

/* Clean workspace and finish the macro */
proc datasets library=work nodetails;
delete temp temp_u;
quit;
%mend;
```

Macro Extremes2() can be invoked on the same dataset and print the resulting dataset, as follows:

```
%let DSin=extremes;
%let varX=x;
%let NQRange=3;
%let DSout=ExtObs;

%Extremes2(&DSin, &VarX, &NQRange, &DSout);

proc print data=extObs;
run;
```

Macro Extremes2() correctly identifies the outliers in this case as the four inserted values: 22, 33, 23, and 34.

The number of standard deviations to use in Extremes1(), or the interquartile ranges in Extremes2(), is subjective and is determined by experience with the particular data of the problem. Commonly, the value of 3 is taken in both cases as a starting point. We reiterate that graphical examination of the variable distribution (e.g., using a histogram) after and before the identification of the outliers will reveal the success or failure of using this method.

7.5.2 IDENTIFICATION OF OUTLIERS USING MODEL FITTING

PROC ROBUSTREG of SAS/STAT performs what is known as *robust regression*. Robust regression is a modified form of the usual least-squares linear regression. It relies on alternative forms of the model fitting criterion such that the effect of outliers is minimized. There are three possible situations in which outliers could be present in the data pertaining to a linear model:

- The outliers could be present in the dependent (response) variable only.

- The outliers could be present in the independent variables only. In this case, observations containing the outliers are called *leverage points*.

- The outliers could be in both the response and independent variables. In this case, they are called simply outliers.

Outliers in linear models lead to large residuals. The residuals are defined as the difference between the predicted and actual values. Therefore, the modification of the objective function to be minimized during the model fitting is the key to robust regression. Different schemes of modifying the objective function and the associated solution algorithm lead to the development of several robust regression formulations. PROC ROBUSTREG implements four of these models. They are known as (1) M estimation, (2) LTS estimation, (3) S estimation, and (4) MM estimation. The default method is M estimation. In addition to fitting the model, while minimizing the effect of the outliers, these methods also offer the identification of outliers after building the model by the calculation of some distance measure between the model and each point.

Without getting into the mathematical details of these methods, the MM estimation method offers a good compromise between statistical efficiency and the ability to identify outliers. When the percentage of the outliers in the dataset is small (i.e., less than 5%), all methods, more or less, give close results using the default parameters.

Since our attention is focused on the identification of outliers, and not on building the best linear regression model, we will use the minimum capabilities of PROC ROBUSTREG to *point* to candidate outliers. We should not forget that linear regression is only one of the techniques usually used by data mining models. Finally, the identification of a set of points as *candidate* outliers should always be confirmed by more than one method before taking a drastic action such as removing them from the mining or scoring view.

The general syntax of PROC ROBUSTREG is very similar to PROC REG, which is used for the usual linear regression. The following macro wraps the procedure to generate an output dataset with two variables indicating the location of outliers and leverage points.

```
%macro RobRegOL(DSin, DV, IVList, DSout);
 /* Extraction of "Candidate" outliers using robust regression */
 proc robustreg data=&DSin method=mm (inith=502 k0=1.8); ;
   model &DV = &IVList /leverage;
   output out=&DSout outlier=_Outlier_ Leverage=_Leverage_;
 run;
 %mend;
```

Table 7.2   Parameters of macro RobRegOL().

Header	RobRegOL(DSin, DV, IVList, DSout);
Parameter	*Description*
DSin	Input dataset
DV	Dependent variable
IVList	List of independent variables
DSout	Output dataset with outliers identified

To demonstrate the use of the macro RobRegOL(), we generate an artificial dataset with 5% outliers, together with a linear model.

```
data TestOL ;
 do ObsNo=1 to 1000;
   /* generate three random IVs and an error term */
   x1=rannor(0); x2=rannor(0);
   x3=rannor(0); e=rannor(0);
/* In the first 50 observations, bias the x1, x3 variables */
   if ObsNo <= 50 then do;
    x1=100 * rannor(0);
    x3=100 * rannor(0);
                       end;
/* and in the last 5% of the dataset, bias the DV */
  if ObsNo > 950 then y=100 + e;
/* otherwise, the use the model equation */
  else y= 5 + 6*x1 + 7*x2 + + 8*x3 +  .4 * e;
 output;
 end;
run;
```

This code will generate 50 leverage points at the beginning of the dataset and another 50 outliers at the end. We invoke macro RobRegOL() as follows:

```
%let DSin=TestOL;
%let DV=y;
%let IVList=x1 x2 x3;
%let DSout=Test_Out;
%RobRegOL(&DSin, &DV, &IVList, &DSout);
```

The dataset Test_Out contains the two new variables: _Outliers_ and _Leverage_, which indicate the location of *candidate* outliers and leverage points, respectively.

You have probably noticed by now that I insist on using the adjective *candidate* each time I refer to the results. This is to help you remember that there is no bullet-proof guarantee that these methods will discover the genuine outliers.

7.5.3 IDENTIFICATION OF OUTLIERS USING CLUSTERING

Section 3.5 introduced briefly the main methods of cluster analysis. One of these methods is *k*-clustering, with one of its most common algorithms: *K*-means. *K*-means clustering is sensitive to outliers. In the presence of outliers that are very far from other observations, it often results in a cluster with one observation in it. From the point of view of clustering, this is considered a weakness. However, it is considered a blessing for finding outliers. The *K*-means algorithm is implemented in PROC FASTCLUS using a variety of distance measures. It is suitable for clustering large datasets and identifying outliers. This is usually achieved by specifying a large number of clusters. Clusters that have very few or, ideally, one observation are considered outliers.

In our implementation macro, we use PROC FASTCLUS to create 50 clusters, find the clusters with low frequency, and flag them as outliers. The number of clusters is controlled using the parameter MAXC in the PROC FASTCLUS statement. The value 50 is usually suitable for most datasets with more than few thousand records. PROC FASTCLUS is very fast, even with large datasets. Perhaps the only performance issue with this macro implementation is that we sort the observations of the dataset once to match the cluster indexes.

Table 7.3   Parameters of macro ClustOL().

Header	ClustOL(DSin, VarList, Pmin, DSout);
Parameter	*Description*
DSin	Input dataset
VarList	List of variables used in clustering
Pmin	Size of cluster, as percentage of dataset, to label its observations as outliers
DSout	Output dataset with outliers identified

Step 1
Invoke PROC FASTCLUS to group the observations into 50 clusters. We then use PROC FREQ to identify the frequency of each cluster and store the results in the dataset Temp_freqs.

```
/* Build a cluster model with a default of
   50 clusters to identify outliers */

proc fastclus data=&DSin MaxC=50 maxiter=100
    cluster=_ClusterIndex_   out=Temp_clust noprint;
  var &VarList;
run;
```

```
/* Analyze temp_clust  */
proc freq data=temp_clust noprint;
  tables _ClusterIndex_ / out=temp_freqs;
run;
```

Step 2
Isolate the clusters with a size less than Pmin percent of the dataset size.

```
data temp_low;
 set temp_freqs;
 if PERCENT <= &Pmin;
 _Outlier_=1;
 keep _ClusterIndex_ _Outlier_;
run;
```

Step 3
Match-merge clusters with low numbers of observations with the clustering results using the cluster index variable _ClusterIndex_, which requires some sorting. Also change the outliers indicator from missing to zero where applicable.

```
proc sort data=temp_clust;
 by _ClusterIndex_;
run;
proc sort data=temp_low;
 by _ClusterIndex_;
run;

data &DSout;
 merge temp_clust temp_Low;
 by _ClusterIndex_;
 drop _ClusterIndex_ DISTANCE;
 if _outlier_ = . then _Outlier_=0;
run;
```

Step 4
Finally, clean up the workspace and finish the macro.

```
proc datasets library=work;
 delete temp_clust temp_freqs temp_low;
quit;
%mend;
```

Note that PROC FASTCLUS can output a dataset with the summary of the number of observations in each cluster directly through the option MEAN. However, we have elected to find the frequency in each cluster explicitly using PROC FREQ to make the implmentation more clear.

7.5.4 Notes on Outliers

As mentioned, the definition of outliers is subjective. Therefore, when we label some observations in the mining or scoring view as outliers, it does not mean that they should be deleted. In many cases, it might mean only that they follow a different distribution that might have a valid interpretation. Very often these outliers surface in a decision tree model as a persistent node with a small number of records. A persistent node in a decision tree is a node that keeps appearing even when the order of the splits is overridden manually.

On the other hand, when the number of observations labeled as outliers represents a large percentage of the data (i.e., more than 5%), this is a definite sign that there is more than one mechanism governing the data at hand. In this case, it is worth investigating developing a separate model for the outliers.

Finally, sometimes outliers are *the* interesting observation. This is particularly the case when the *interesting* event is rare in the population. Typical applications are fraud detection, searches for criminal activities, and investigating money laundering.

7.6 Testing Normality

Many statistical tests are based on assuming that the variable in question is normally distributed. PROC UNIVARIATE provides the capability to test the distribution of continuous variables against a variety of statistical distributions, including the normal distribution. The normality test is invoked by adding the option NORMAL in the PROC UNIVARIATE statement. For example, using the dataset TestOL (Section 7.5.2), we calculate the normality test statistics as follows.

```
proc univariate data=TestOL normal ;
 var x1;
run;
```

The following is the test of normality results portion of the output.

```
                 Tests for Normality

Test                --Statistic---  -----p Value------

Shapiro-Wilk        W    0.238644  Pr < W     <0.0001
Kolmogorov-Smirnov  D    0.425662  Pr > D     <0.0100
Cramer-von Mises    W-Sq 62.67828  Pr > W-Sq  <0.0050
Anderson-Darling    A-Sq 293.5579  Pr > A-Sq  <0.0050
```

The output provides four measures of normality. The most useful are the Shapiro-Wilk W and the Kolmogorov-Smirnov D. The Shapiro-Wilk W is calculated only when the number of observations is less than 2000. It takes values between 0 and 1, with large values indicating a close fit to the normal distribution. The Kolmogorov-Smirnov D also varies between 0 and 1, but with smaller values indicating a close fit to normality. The extraction of the values of the normality statistics is straightforward using an OUTPUT statement in PROC UNIVARIATE.

In addition to the normality tests, PROC UNIVARIATE provides many graphical options to plot the variable distribution and the normality plots. We refer you to the online SAS help to learn more about these features.

7.7 CROSS-TABULATION

Cross-tabulation is concerned with the construction of the tables of frequency counts of two or more variables. PROC TABULATE offers many options and methods of calculating and presenting these tables. It is one of the most versatile procedures of the BASE/SAS product. PROC FREQ also offers the calculation of frequency counts for one or more variables. A detailed exploration of the implementation of these two procedures in data exploration is beyond the scope and focus of this book. Refer to the SAS documentation and many of the good books available for basic data reporting using SAS. Please check the SAS website for a comprehensive list of these references.

7.8 INVESTIGATING DATA STRUCTURES

One of the objectives of data exploration that has a significant effect on the procedures of data preparation is the discovery of some structure within the data. Of particular interest are linear structures. Linear structures, when they exist, are typically investigated using Principal Component Analysis (PCA), and Factor Analysis (FA). Using these two techniques, we can achieve two objectives: (1) find possible interesting relationships between the variables and (2) reduce the number of variables.

In terms of data preparation procedures, the subject of this book, we focus more on the second objective. This is the subject of Chapters 15 and 16, respectively. PCA and FA as models that describe the structure of the data can be considered data mining models on their own. Refer to Johnson and Wichern (2001) for a detailed exposition of these two interesting subjects.

CHAPTER 8

SAMPLING AND PARTITIONING

8.1 INTRODUCTION

Sampling is used to facilitate the analysis and modeling of large datasets. There are several types of sampling schemes. Three of these schemes are commonly used in data mining: random sampling, balanced sampling, and stratified sampling (Levy and Lemeshow 1999).

In random sampling, a simple random sample, that is sampling without replacement, is drawn from the population to form the mining view. In balanced sampling, the user designs the sample such that the target variable, or some other predefined nominal or ordinal variable, is forced to have a certain composition (e.g., 90% non-responders and 10% responders). Forcing samples to have such composition must be accompanied by defining and populating a weight variable to revert the proportions to their original values in the population. For example, when investigating fraud, the population may contain only 1% records with fraudulent behavior in them. Using a balanced sample with 10% records containing fraudulent behavior requires the definition of a weight variable with a value of 0.10 for sample records with (fraud = yes) and 1.10 for records having (fraud = No). These simple weights allow the models to revert the proportions to their original value in the population.

A third, but less common, type of sampling is stratified sampling. In this method, the data is divided into strata using the categories of one or more variables. Then simple random sampling is applied to each stratum to draw the samples. A typical example of this method is used in obtaining stratified samples based on geography using the state or province as the basis for defining the different strata. Other examples include using age or income groups.

Partitioning, on the other hand, is used to set aside a set of records to test on the developed models. Therefore, in most cases the data is partitioned into two partitions: a training partition, which is used fit the model, and a validation partition to validate the model. A third partition may also be set aside for final testing of the model, as was shown in Figure 2.1.

In most cases, training and validation partitions are formed by random sampling from the mining view with specified percentages or numbers of records for each of them. Best practices suggest that in the case of using two partitions the training partition would contain 60 to 70% of the records of the mining view, with the remaining records used for the validation partition. These values are only guidelines out of experience without known theoretical foundation.

Fortunately, most data mining packages have dedicated algorithms for extracting samples and partitions from datasets. In the following, we present a simple macro built around the PROC SURVEYSELECT of SAS/STAT. This macro can be used to obtain random samples from large datasets. The macro simply wraps the SURVEYSELECT procedure.

```
%MACRO RandomSample(PopDS, SampleDS, SampleSize);
/* This macro performes simple random sampling */
    PROC SURVEYSELECT
        DATA=&PopDs
        METHOD=srs
        N=&SampleSize
        NOPRINT
        OUT=&SampleDS;
    RUN;
%MEND;
```

This macro can be easily used to extract random samples from the dataset that represent the population. In the following subsections, we will discuss the SAS implementation of the random and balanced sampling as well as other issues related to the use of sampling methods.

8.2 CONTENTS OF SAMPLES

Implementing sampling in SAS requires the processing of several DATA steps and the use of several procedures including SORT and SURVEYSELECT. In order to maximize the performance of these procedures, we attempt to reduce the data included in these datasets to a minimum. This is particularly important in all procedures where we attempt to sort the dataset. The reduction of the data can be achieved by removing all the variables from the datasets except the row ID variable (e.g., customer ID), and the value of the dependent variable (e.g., response variable), if the dataset contains one. After obtaining the samples, which contain only the ID field, it is an easy exercise to merge the rest of the variables from the original dataset. We will adopt this approach in our SAS implementations.

8.3 RANDOM SAMPLING

We have presented the macro RandomSample(), which extracts a random sample from a population dataset. However, in almost all data mining models the analyst needs at least two *disjoint* partitions or samples: a training partition and a validation partition. The simplest method of extracting these two partitions from the mining view is to use simple random sampling. The macro RandomSample() can do this job. However, what it does not do is ensure that these two partitions are not overlapping. This is a critical feature of training and validation partitions, without which the integrity of the model validation procedure is compromised. We present here a simple macro implementation that can extract two nonoverlapping partitions obtained at random from a dataset. However, before we present the macro we discuss the consistency conditions for random samples.

8.3.1 CONSTRAINTS ON SAMPLE SIZE

Because the training and validation partitions must always be disjoint, it is important to make sure that we have enough records to satisfy the requirements of each partition. Checking that the available number of records is enough for extracting the required samples is a simple task in the case of random samples. The case of balanced samples is a little more involved, as is presented in the next section.

Given a population dataset S with a total of N records, two nonoverlapping samples, S_1 and S_2, each with N_1 and N_2 records, respectively, the following inequality must be satisfied:

$$N \geq N_1 + N_2, \tag{8.1}$$

for all such samples S_1 and S_2.

In the case of random samples, this is the only constraint we have to check, which is in most cases a trivial task.

8.3.2 SAS IMPLEMENTATION

The steps to obtain two nonoverlapping random samples can be summarized as follows.

1. Calculate the number of records in the population (N).

2. Check the consistency constraint.

3. Draw the first sample S_1 with size N_1.

4. Append the dataset S_1 with a new variable to indicate that these records have already been sampled. Give this new field a value of 1.

5. Match-merge the dataset S_1 with the population S using the row ID. Store the resulting dataset in a temporary dataset, TEMP.

6. Draw the second sample S_2, with size N_2, from TEMP under the condition that the record selection indicator added in Step 4 is *not* 1.

There are many ways to implement this algorithm. In our implementation we opted for the following preferences:

- We used PROC SQL to perform simple record counting operations using the syntax: SELECT COUNT(*) FROM....

- We used PROC SURVEYSELECT to perform the actual sampling, which automatically adds two fields for the estimated selection probability and the record weight. Since these values are based on the assumption that only one sample is drawn from the population, we removed these two fields from the final samples.

- As mentioned, we assumed that for the purpose of sampling we would only operate on the row ID.

The implementation is included in the macro R2Samples(), for which the description follows.

Table 8.1   Parameters of macro R2samples().

Header	R2samples(S,IDVar,S1,N1,S2,N2,M_St);
Parameter	Description
S	Population dataset
IDVar	Row ID variable
S1	First random partition
N1	Size of first random partition
S2	Second random partition
N2	Size of second random partition
M_ST	Textual message to report errors and confirm result of data limitation constraint check

Step 1
Calculate the size of the population.

```
proc sql noprint;
  select count(*)into : N from &S;
  run;
quit;
```

Step 2

Check the data limitation constraint. If it is not satisfied, set the message variable and exit the macro without sampling.

```
%let Nx=%eval(&N1 + &N2);
%if &Nx > &N %then %do;
%let &M_st = Not enough records in population to
                 generate samples. Sampling canceled. ;
%goto Exit;
                          %end;
/* Otherwise, OK */
%let &M_St=OK;
```

Step 3

Draw the first sample, S1, with size N1.

```
proc surveyselect noprint
     data =&S
     method = srs
     n= &N1
     out=&S1;
run;
```

Step 4

Append S1 with the selection indicator.

```
data &S1;
 set &S1;
  selected =1;
  keep &IDVar Selected;
run;
```

Step 5

Merge S1 with the population into TEMP.

```
proc sort data=&S;
 by &IDVar;
run;
proc sort data=&S1;
 by &IDVar;
run;
Data temp;
 merge &S &S1;
 by &IDvar;
  keep &IDVar Selected;
run;
```

Step 6
Draw the second sample, S2, with size N2 from unselected records in TEMP.

```
proc surveyselect noprint
     data =temp
     method = srs
     n=&N2
     out=&S2;
     where Selected NE 1;
run;
```

Step 7
Clean the workspace, S1 and S2.

```
Data &S1;
 set &S1;
 keep &IDvar;
run;
Data &S2;
 set &S2;
 keep &IDVar;
run;
proc datasets library=work nodetails;
 delete temp;
run;
quit;
```

Step 8
Finish the macro.

```
%exit: ;
%mend;
```

8.4 BALANCED SAMPLING

In balanced sampling, we attempt to draw two samples from a population but with the composition of the dependent variable (DV) in each sample being different from that in the original population. For example, in a population of 100,000 banking customers, only 8% responded to a previous random campaign inviting them to open a new type of a savings account. This means that we have 8,000 responders (DV = 1) in this population dataset.

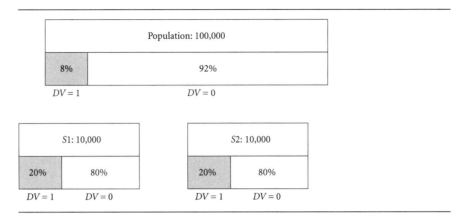

Figure 8.1   Balanced sampling.

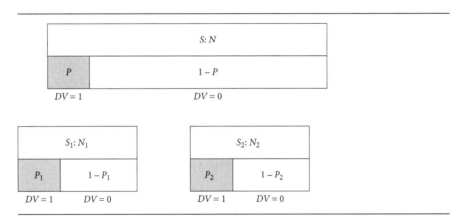

Figure 8.2   Data consistency constraints.

An example of balanced partitioning is when we draw two samples, of 10,000 records each, and with a response rate of 20%. This is illustrated in Figure 8.1.

8.4.1 CONSTRAINTS ON SAMPLE SIZE

We now turn our attention to the problem of the size of each of the samples in balanced sampling. Given a population dataset S with a total of N records and a dependent variable with a proportion P of $DV = 1$. We seek two nonoverlapping balanced partitions S_1 and S_2 with N_1 and N_2 records, and P_1 and P_2 proportions of $DV = 1$, as shown in Figure 8.2.

In this case, the partitions must satisfy the following inequalities:

$$N_1 + N_2 \leq N,$$
$$N_1 \bullet P_1 + N_2 \bullet P_2 \leq N \bullet P, \qquad (8.2)$$
$$N_1(1 - P_2) + N_2(1 - P_2) \leq N(1 - P).$$

It is easy to show that the first condition in Equation 8.3 is merely the summation of the second and third.

The first condition guarantees that the two samples do not contain more records than the original dataset. The second and third conditions guarantee that the two samples do not contain more records than the original dataset for each of the categories of the dependent variable. The three inequalities apply to the case of a dependent variable with two categories only, but they can be easily generalized to cases with more categories. We do not present these cases because the majority of classification models have binary dependent variables.

8.4.2 SAS IMPLEMENTATION

The implementation is included in the macro B2Samples(), as follows.

Table 8.2   Parameters of macro B2samples().

Header	B2samples(S,IDVar,DV,S1,N1,P1,S2,N2,P2,M_St);
Parameter	*Description*
S	Population dataset
IDVar	Row ID variable
S1	First balanced partition
N1	Size of first random partition
P1	Percentage of DV in S1
S2	Second balanced partition
N2	Size of second partition
P2	Percentage of DV in S2
M_ST	Textual message to report errors and confirm result of data limitation constraint check

Step 1
Calculate N, P for the population.

```
proc sql noprint;
 select count(*)into : N from &S; /* Population size */
 select count(*) into : NP
                from &S where &DV=1; /* Count of "1" */
```

```
 run;
quit;
%let NPc=%eval(&N - &NP);  /* Count of "0" (compliment)*/
```

Step 2
Check the consistency conditions.

```
%let Nx=%eval(&N1 + &N2);
%if &Nx > &N %then %do;
%let &M_st = Not enough records in population to generate
                samples. Sampling canceled. ;
%goto Exit;
 %end;
/* N1 P1 + N2 P2 <= N P */
%let Nx = %sysevalf((&N1*&P1+ &N2 * &P2), integer);
%if &Nx >&NP %then %do;
    %let &M_st = Count of DV=1 in requested samples
                    exceeds total count in population.
        Sampling canceled.;
 %goto Exit;
  %end;
/* N1(1-P1) + N2(1-P2) <= N(1-P)*/
%let Nx = %sysevalf((&N1*(1-&P1)+&N2*(1-&P2)),integer);
%if &Nx > &NPc %then %do;
    %let &M_st = Count of DV=0 in requested samples
                    exceeds total count in population.
                    Sampling canceled.;
 %goto Exit;
  %end;
/* Otherwise, OK */
%let &M_St=OK;
```

Step 3
Sort the population using the DV in ascending order.

```
proc sort data=&S;
by &DV;
run;
```

Step 4
Draw the sample S1 with size N1 and number of records N1P1, N1(1 − P1) in the strata 1,0 of the DV:

```
%let Nx1=%Sysevalf( (&N1*&P1),integer);
%let Nx0=%eval(&N1 - &Nx1);
proc surveyselect noprint
     data =&S
     method = srs
```

```
        n=( &Nx0 &Nx1)
        out=&S1;
        strata &DV;
run;
```

Step 5
Add a new field to S1—call it (Selected)—and give it a value of 1.

```
data &S1;
 set &S1;
   selected =1;
   keep &IDVar &DV Selected;
run;
```

Step 6
Merge S1 with the population S to find the already selected fields.

```
proc sort data=&S;
by &IDVar;
run;
proc sort data=&S1;
by &IDVar;
run;
Data temp;
 merge &S &S1;
 by &IDvar;
   keep &IDVar &DV Selected;
run;
```

Step 7
Draw the sample S2 with size N2 and number of records N2P2, $N2(1 - P2)$ in the strata 1,0 of the DV, under the condition that Selected is *not* 1.

```
proc sort data=temp;
by &DV;
run;
%let Nx1=%Sysevalf( (&N2*&P2),integer);
%let Nx0=%eval(&N2 - &Nx1);
proc surveyselect noprint
     data =temp
        method = srs
     n=( &Nx0 &Nx1)
out=&S2;
strata &DV;
where Selected NE 1;
run;
```

Step 8
Clean the workspace, S1 and S2, and finish the macro.

```
Data &S1;
 set &S1;
 keep &IDvar &DV;
run;

Data &S2;
 set &S2;
 keep &IDVar &DV;
run;

proc datasets library=work nodetails;
 delete temp;
run;
quit;

/*Label Exit: do nothing, end the macro)*/
  %exit: ;
  %mend;
```

Let us try to use the macro B2Samples() to extract two samples out of a population dataset. The first section of the code generates a population dataset of $100,000$ records with a DV (conveniently called DV); then it implements the macro to extract two balanced partitions.

The variable DV in the population has a percentage of 10% of the category 1. On the other hand, the two requested samples will each have a total of $5,000$ records and a DV=1 with a percentage of 50%.

```
/* First generate the population dataset */
   Data Population;
     do ID=1 to 100000;
       if ID <=10000 then DV=1;
           else DV=0;
     output;
     end;
     run;

/* Set the parameters needed to call the macro */
   %let S=Population;
   %let IDVar=ID;
   %let DV=DV;
   %let S1=Training;
   %let N1=5000;
   %let P1=0.50;
   %let S2=Validation;
```

```
%let N2=5000;
%let P2=0.50;
%let Status=;

/* call the macro */
    %B2samples(&S,&IDVar,&DV,&S1,&N1,&P1,&S2,&N2,&P2,Status);

/* Display the status variable in the SAS log. */
%put &status;
```

8.5 Minimum Sample Size

How large should the sample be? This is one of the most difficult questions in data mining, and one of the most asked! There are many anecdotal answers to that question, such as: *The sample size should be at least 10% of the population.* Unfortunately, these quick recipes do not withstand rigorous scrutiny. The answer is a bit more complicated than that.

Most real datasets used in data mining applications involve a combination, very often large, of nominal, ordinal, and continuous variables. A typical banking or retail dataset can contain many millions of records and hundreds of variables. Theoretical formulas providing rigorous answers to the sample size question, on the other hand, are available for very simplified cases. These formulas are mainly concerned with finding the minimum sample size such that the mean or the proportion of a variable is the same as that of the population with a specific confidence level. The use of these formulas in data mining is limited because real datasets are more complicated than the cases that have a theoretical estimate of the minimum sample size.

In the following, we present a summary of these simple cases. They can be used to check the validity of the sampling assumptions considering one variable at a time. Combining the results to check on the assumptions regarding the complete dataset is not possible without additional assumptions about the joint distribution of the variables. In most practical cases, it is not possible to infer much about the joint distribution of the variables.

We will summarize the formulas giving the minimum sample size for the different situations without proof. The complete discussion of these formulas can be found in Levy and Lemeshow (1999).

8.5.1 Continuous and Binary Variables

The following are two interesting situations where simple formulas exist for the calculation of sample size.

1. The average of a continuous variable. For example, the average age of the customers of a direct marketing company.

2. A value representing a proportion. This is typically the case of binary variables—for example, the default rate among credit card customers on their monthly payments.

Now let us introduce some notations. We denote the variable being sampled by x, and the proportion of a certain event in binary variables, say the proportion of the ones, by P_y.

The minimum sample size for estimating the mean of the population is given by

$$n \geq \frac{z^2 N V_x^2}{z^2 V_x^2 + (N-1)\varepsilon^2},$$ (8.3)

where

    n is the sample size

    N is the population size

    V_x is the coefficient of variation of the continuous variable x defined as $V_x = \sigma_x^2 / \bar{X}^2$, with $\bar{X}$ and σ_x the mean and the standard deviation of the population, respectively

    z is the *reliability coefficient,* defined as the normalized z-value for the normal distribution function

    ε is the maximum acceptable percentage difference between the population average and the sample average

In the case of estimating the proportion of a binary variable, the minimum sample size is given by

$$n \geq \frac{z^2 N P_y(1 - P_y)}{(N-1)\varepsilon^2 P_y^2 + z^2 P_y(1 - P_y)}.$$ (8.4)

Let us demonstrate the use of the formulas using simple examples.

EXAMPLE 8.1 The customer population of a telephone company is 10,000,000, for which we are building a cross-selling marketing campaign. We would like to calculate the minimum sample size on the basis of the monthly revenue per customer. We would like to keep a reliability level of 3.0, 99.87%, and accept a deviation of 5%. The average monthly revenue per customer in the entire population has been calculated to be $20.00, with a standard deviation of $6.50.

Using the preceding formulas, we have

$$V_x = \frac{\sigma_x^2}{\bar{X}^2} = \frac{6.5^2}{20^2} = 0.1056$$

$$n \geq \frac{z^2 N V_x^2}{z^2 V_x^2 + (N-1)\varepsilon^2} = \frac{(3)^2(10^7)(0.1056)^2}{(3)^2(0.1056)^2 + (10^7-1)(0.05)^2} \approx 41.$$

(The symbol "$\approx$" indicates that the result was rounded to nearest integer.)

This number represents the minimum possible sample that would preserve the average value of the monthly revenue per customer. For most typical data mining, applications, this number would be too small because of the interactions among the many variables in the analysis.

◆

EXAMPLE 8.2 For the population of the previous example, the average churn rate in the 10,000,000 customers was observed in the past and known to be an average of 4.5% per month. Using a similar reliability level of 3.0, 99.87%, and accepting a deviation of 5%, the minimum sample size to preserve the churn rate indicator would be calculated as follows:

$$n \geq \frac{3^2 10^7 (0.045)(1-0.045)}{(10^7-1)(0.05)^2(0.045)^2 + 3^2(0.045)(1-0.045)} \approx 75,821.$$

The result is *not* trivial.

◆

8.5.2 SAMPLE SIZE FOR A NOMINAL VARIABLE

The case of nominal variables with more than two categories can be handled as a general form of the case of binary variables. In this case we treat each of the categories as the event being sampled and calculate the minimum sample size. We then take the maximum of these sizes.

Note that this approach is based on transforming this nominal variable using 1 to N transformation and then using the resulting independent variables to calculate each minimum sample size. The 1 to N mapping is explained in detail in Chapter 9.

Let us demonstrate this process with an example.

EXAMPLE 8.3 Consider again the telephone company with 10 million customer records. And assume further that the marital status variable of the customers has the categories and distributions shown in Table 8.3.

Table 8.3   Distribution of marital status categories.

Category	Percentage (%)
Single	22
Married	24
Divorced/separated	18
Widowed	10
Unknown	26

We can then define five new dummy variables for each category to calculate the equivalent sample size for each one using Equation 8.4. Using the same assumptions of a reliability of 99.87% and an acceptance error of 5%, the results would be as follows:

$$n_{Single} \approx 12{,}748$$
$$n_{Married} \approx 11{,}388$$
$$n_{Divorced/separated} \approx 16{,}374$$
$$n_{Widowed} \approx 32{,}296$$
$$n_{Unknown} \approx 10{,}236$$

The *minimum* sample size to have all the categories would be 32,296 records—again, a *nontrivial* result.

◆

8.6 CHECKING VALIDITY OF SAMPLES

There are several considerations relating to the independent variables (IVs) and dependent variables (DVs) that should be taken into account when selecting a sample. These include:

■ *IV range and categories:* Continuous IVs in the sample should have the same range as that of the population, and nominal IVs should have the same categories.

■ *IV distribution:* The distribution of the values and categories of the IVs in the sample should be the same as (or at least close to that of) the population. This will not be true of a balanced sample because of the selective nature of the balanced sampling process.

■ *DV categories:* The DV in the sample should have all the categories represented in the population. For example, if the DV is a risk indicator with three levels—low, medium, and high—then the sample should also have these three categories.

- *Stratification:* Sometimes it is necessary, or desirable, to divide the population into separate strata to allow for the effect of some measure that is believed to segment the population naturally into distinct groups. In this case, the usual measures to segment the population into such strata are geography, product ownership, customer value (based on simple measures such as total sales or product usage), and similar simple attributes.

- *Missing values:* The main issue with missing values is to guarantee that the frequency of occurrence of missing values in the different variables in the sample matches that of the population.

With the exception of selecting the sample through the different strata, the criteria for sample selection can be tested only after drawing the sample. It is therefore expected that the sampling process might have to be repeated several times before an acceptable sample is reached.

CHAPTER 9

DATA TRANSFORMATIONS

9.1 RAW AND ANALYTICAL VARIABLES

Data transformation is perhaps the most important step in the data preparation process for the development and deployment of data mining models. Proper transformations can make the difference between powerful and useless models. In almost all practical cases, it is necessary to perform some transformations on extracted data before it can be used in modeling. Data transformation has two objectives.

1. Generate new variables, called analytical variables.

2. Fix any potential problems such as missing values and skewed variable distributions.

The mining view, which is extracted from a database or a data warehouse, usually contains *raw variables*. Raw variables are those that have a direct business meaning and exist in the same format and have the same content as in the original operational system. In most cases, these variables do not suffice to render the best predictive models. Therefore, a set of data manipulation steps is used to transform some or all of these variables into new variables with better predictive power, or better behavior with respect to the model formulations. The new variables are usually called *modeling variables* or *analytical variables*. An important feature of analytical variables is that some of them may not have a clear business meaning. Let us illustrate this point with a simple example.

When the database contains the data field of Date Of Birth, we can use this field as the raw variable in the mining view. However, using dates is not convenient because of the complexity of their arithmetic. Therefore, it is more appropriate to create a new field representing Age instead. Note that Age is a transformation on the date, which is calculated by subtracting the actual raw Date Of Birth from a reference date, which is given the default value of the current date. The value representing the number of years in the result is what we use as Age. However, further investigations into the modeling process may indicate that it is better to use the logarithm of Age instead of the raw value. This simple transformation usually spreads the histogram of a variable into a more favorable form, as detailed later in this chapter. The new analytical variable Log(Age) does not really have an easy-to-explain business meaning. For example, a customer with an age of 26 will have a Log(Age) of 3.258 (using natural logarithms). This is not a common way to represent a person's age.

In contrast, many transformations can yield analytical variables that have a clear meaningful and even useful business use. The following are examples of such variables commonly used in marketing and credit risk scoring applications.

- Average transaction value over a certain period (month, quarter, year)

- Average number of transactions over a certain period (month, week, etc.)

- Ratio of purchases from a specific product or product category to total purchases

- Ratio of total purchases in a time period to available credit in the same period

- Ratio of each purchase to the cost of shipment (specially when shipping costs are paid by the customer)

- Ratio of number/value of purchased products to size of household

- Ratio of price of most expensive product to least expensive product

- Ratio of largest to smallest purchase in a time period

- Ratio of total household debt to total household annual income

- Ratio of largest income in a household to total household income

- Ratio of available credit to household income

- Average annual income per household member

- Ratio of debt to available credit

- Average percentage of used portion of credit over a certain period

9.2 SCOPE OF DATA TRANSFORMATIONS

The number of possible data transformations is indeed large and limited only by imagination. In this book, we focus on the most common and useful transformations that can be easily implemented and automated using SAS. However, before we start exploring some of these transformations, it is necessary to note the following general principles that need to be considered when deciding on implementing certain data transformations.

1. *Efficiency of Transformations and Data Size*

   We need to take into consideration the size of the data to avoid creating a bottleneck in the data preparation process. This is particularly important in the case of using a transformation during the scoring process. One should always try to avoid computationally demanding transformations unless absolutely necessary. For example, in a credit scoring model one may normalize a payment amount by the maximum payment within a subgroup of the data. This requires the calculation of the maximum payment within the subgroups, then the normalization of the payment amounts by these values for the different groups. When both the number of subgroups and the number of records are large, this type of transformation becomes computationally demanding.

2. *Scope of Modeling and Scoring Datasets*

   Some, and in rare cases all, of the analytical variables resulting from data transformations are used in the construction of the data mining model. Because the resulting model depends on these variables, the raw variables must also be subjected to the same transformations at the time of scoring. This fact should always be remembered to make sure that any transformation performed during modeling, and its result being used in the construction of the model, should also be *possible* during scoring. Sometimes this can be tricky. For example, assume that we have the seven values of income (in dollars) shown in Table 9.1.

   One can normalize these values to make them take values between 0 and 1, as shown in Table 9.2. In doing so, we used the maximum and minimum values and used the simple formula:

$$\text{Normalized value} = (x - x_{\min})/(x_{\max} - x_{\min}), \tag{9.1}$$

   where, x, $x_{\min}$, and $x_{\max}$ are income, minimum income, and maximum income, respectively.

   The problem with such efficient, but naive, transformation is that we *cannot* assume that it will lead to values between 0 and 1 at the time of scoring. There

Table 9.1   Seven income values.

15,000	56,000	22,000	26,000	34,000	44,000	46,000

Table 9.2   Normalized income values.

0	1.00	0.17	0.27	0.46	0.71	0.76

could be records with income values higher than \$56,000 or lower than \$15,000. Also, we should not attempt to find the new maximum and minimum using the scoring data and then use them to apply the transformation because the model would have already been constructed on the basis of the minimum and maximum found in the modeling data. The only solution in this case, if we really want to use this transformation, is to keep in mind that this variable can take values outside the 0–1 range at the time of scoring.

3. *Modes of Scoring*
   There are two modes of scoring: batch scoring and real-time scoring. In the case of batch scoring, the scoring view is prepared with all the required transformations and then the model is used to score the entire set of records at one time. On the other hand, in the case of real-time scoring the scoring view contains only one record. The transformations are performed on that record; then the resulting values are fed to the model to render the score. Therefore, any data transformations that require information about other records may not be possible or technically allowable in terms of the time required to perform them. Realistically, at least at the time of writing this book, the majority of data mining model deployment scenarios employ batch scoring. However, with the increasing power of Internet-based applications and distributed databases, it is anticipated that the number of data mining models used in real-time scoring will increase significantly.

4. *Interpretation of Results*
   In many cases, the resulting scores of models need to be interpreted in terms of the variables used in developing them. A typical example is credit scoring. In this case, consumers in many countries have the right to know the justification behind their credit scores. This in turn requires that these variables themselves be meaningful in terms of the business problem being modeled. However, it is sometimes hard to explain the meaning of some of the transformations that prove to result in variables leading to good models.

   For example, it is difficult to assign an easy meaning, or even a label, to a variable that has the following definition:

$$\text{Variable}\,X = (T * B_6)^{1.6} / \log(\text{TCC6} * \text{IRate}), \tag{9.2}$$

where T is customer tenure, B_6 is the average balance of the checking account in the last six months, TCC6 is the number of transactions on the customer's credit card in the last month, and IRate is the maximum of a constant of ten or the average interest paid by the customer in the last three months.

Although the variable X, as defined, may be a good predictor of a certain behavior, and therefore can be used in the model, it is challenging to attempt to provide an easy-to-understand explanation for it.

The remaining sections of this chapter discuss the implementation of the most common variable transformation methods:

- Creation of new variables

- Mapping of categorical variables

- Reduction of cardinality for categorical variables

- Normalization of continuous variables

- Binning of continuous variables

- Changing the variable distribution

9.3 Creation of New Variables

The most obvious type of data transformation is the creation of new variables by combining raw variables using different mathematical formulas. There are two main methods of generating these formulas: (1) business-related formulas and (2) pure mathematical expressions.

The first approach relies on the analyst's understanding of the business problem, where the new variables would represent meaningful, or potentially meaningful, quantities that can be deduced from the raw variables. These quantities are usually based on using averages, sums, ratios, or other similar simple formulas. This category of variables has two advantages.

1. They are usually derived using simple formulas that can be easily programmed and implemented at both the modeling and the scoring stage.

2. They have definite business interpretations that can give an insight into the meaning of the results of the model.

The second method that can be used to create new variables relies on use of mathematical expressions that do not necessarily have a certain interpretation, but may prove beneficial to the model. The challenge with this type of variable is finding the appropriate mathematical expressions to define it. Experience with the data plays a significant role in helping the analyst to select appropriate candidate formulas. However, there exist many methods to generate these variables by relying on some heuristic that generates a large number of potentially useful transformations, then reduces this set of candidates into a much smaller set. The reduction is performed by the selection of those leading to a better model. The different algorithms implementing this heuristic share the following aspects.

1. They implement a predefined set of allowable forms to generate the new variables. Each algorithm offers the use of a set of equation forms, such as polynomials, products and divisions of database variables, and so on.

2. They adopt a criterion, or several of them, to filter the newly generated variables. Such criteria include correlation coefficients, entropy variance, the Pearson Chi-squared statistic, and the Gini variance, among others. The filtering criteria are used to formulate a merit function to score each of the new variables. The merit function could simply be the raw value of the filtering criteria, such as the correlation coefficient, or a complex function of several of them.

3. They use mechanism for reducing the variables using the merit function. One approach is to generate *all* the possible variables, then calculate their merit function value and select the best ones. Variations on this approach include the setup of a critical cutoff value for the merit function below which a variable would be dropped. The reduction phase of the analytical variables can also include the raw variables as candidates for reduction. The reduction procedures implement several iterative or stepwise reduction phases. For example, the correlation coefficient may be used to remove some variables in the first round; then the Gini variance could be used in a second run. Other heuristics attempt to *group* the variables in subsets that are either correlated to each other or have been derived from the same set of raw variables. Then the reduction process operates on the best variable from each group.

The last step of the algorithm, dealing with the reduction of automatically generated analytical variables, can be postponed until all the other analytical variables have been generated through other transformations, or it can be applied twice. The first time is when new variables are created to reduce their numbers and the second time when all the other transformations have been completed.

9.3.1 RENAMING VARIABLES

In order to develop a good implementation of variable generation and selection, it is usually easier to work with a set of *normalized* variable names. By that we mean that the variable names are mapped from their original values, such as age, income, and *TXC*, to a simple sequence of symbols such as X_1, X_2, and X_3. The use of such sets of normalized variable names in the generation of new variables allows us to implement a simple coding convention for new variables. Table 9.3 shows a simple coding scheme for naming new variables using the different operations.

The use of variables with the normalized names X_1, X_2, $\cdots$ in such a scheme is obviously easier than using the original raw names and will result in a SAS code that is smaller and less error prone. The following is a description of two macros that do this mapping and store the mapping scheme in a dataset. The first macro extracts the variable names from a list and generates a list of normalized names. It also saves the mapping scheme in a dataset. The second macro uses the mapping scheme to rename the variables in a new dataset, which is useful at the time of scoring (see Table 9.4).

Table 9.3   A convention for naming new variables.

Operation	Coding scheme	Example	Meaning
Log	L_Var	L_X_1	Log of variable x_1
To power y	P_y_Var	P_255_X1	$x_1^{(2.55)}$
Division	D_Var1_Var2	D_X1_X2	x_1/x_2
Multiplication	M_Var1_Var2	M_X1_X2	$x_1 * x_2$
Addition	A_Var1_Var2	A_X1_X2	$x_1 + x_2$

Table 9.4   Parameters of macro NorList().

Header	NorList(ListIn, VPrefix, M_ListOut, MapDS);
Parameter	*Description*
ListIn	Input list of original variable names
VPrefix	Prefix used to generate the normalized variable names
M_ListOut	Output list of normalized variable names
MapDs	Dataset of old and new variables (mapping scheme)

Step 1
We decompose the input list to the variable names and store them in a dataset. We use the macro ListToCol(), included in this book's appendix, which converts a list of variable names to the rows of a string variable in a dataset. We store the results in a temporary dataset, Temp_Vars.

```
%ListToCol(&ListIn, Temp_Vars, OldVarName, VIndex);
```

Step 2
Using a simple loop on this dataset, we create the mapping dataset and generate the new normalized variable names using the given prefix.

```
data &MapDS;
set Temp_Vars;
NewVarName=compress("&VPrefix" ||'_'|| VIndex);
run;
```

Step 3
Finally, we extract the new names into the output list. This step is only for checking the integrity of the results because we already know the names of the new variables,

and we could have simply written them in such a list. But this way we will guarantee that we have completed the mapping properly.

```
Data _Null_;
  set &MapDS;
    call symput ("x_" || left(_N_), NewVarName);
    call symput ("N" , _N_);
  run;
%let LOut=;
%do i=1 %to &N;
  %let LOut=&lOut &&x_&i;
%end;
%let &M_ListOut=&Lout;
```

Step 4
Clean the workspace and finish the macro.

```
proc datasets library=work nolist;
 delete temp_vars;
quit;
%mend;
```

The following code segment shows how to use the preceding macro.

```
%let Listin=a b c d e X1 X2 X45 Y8 H99 Age;
%let ListOut=;
%let MapDs=MapVars;

%NorList(&ListIn, Y, ListOut, &MapDS);
%put Output List = &ListOut;
proc print data=MapVars;
run;
```

Now the next macro implements the name-map dataset generated by the previous macro to normalize variable names in an input dataset.

Table 9.5   Parameters of macro NorVars().

Header	NorVars(DSin, MapDS, DSout);
Parameter	*Description*
DSin	Input dataset with the original variable names
MapDS	Dataset with name map generated by macro NorList above
DSout	Output dataset with normalized variable names

Step 1

Extract the old and new variable names from the name-map dataset to the macro variables.

```
Data _Null_;
  set &MapDS;
    call symput ("N_" || left(_N_), NewVarName);
    call symput ("O_" || left(_N_), OldVarName);
    call symput ("N" , _N_);
  run;
```

Step 2

Compile a variable-name list for use in a (RENAME) statement to generate the final dataset.

```
%let RenList=;
%do i=1 %to &N;
  %let RenList=&RenList %left(&&O_&i) = %left(&&N_&i);
%end;
```

Step 3

Apply the new name changes to a new dataset using the RENAME option of a simple DATA step, which does nothing other than store the output dataset with the new variable names.

```
DATA &DSout;
  SET &DSin  (RENAME=(&RenList));
RUN;
```

Step 4

Finish the macro.

```
%mend;
```

The next code shows the use of the macro to rename the variables Age and Income in the following simple dataset to Y_1 and Y_2, respectively.

```
Data Test;
 input CustName$ Age Income;
Datalines;
 Tom    20 53000
 Al     30 40000
 Jane   35 60000
;
run;
```

```
%let DSin=Test;
%let DSout=test_Nor;
%let ListIn=Age Income;
%let ListOut=;
%let MapDS=MapVar;

%NorList(&ListIn, Y, ListOut, &MapDS);
%NorVars(&DSin, &MapDS, &DSout);

proc print data=Test_Nor;
run;
```

9.3.2 AUTOMATIC GENERATION OF SIMPLE ANALYTICAL VARIABLES

Automatic generation of new analytical variables is a powerful technique that can be used when the required mathematical form is known. For example, the use of *interaction terms* is popular in regression analysis because it allows the introduction of nonlinear effects in the modeling data in a simple but effective way. Similarly, but less popular, the introduction of *ratio terms* between variables could also reveal non-linearities. However, with the ratio terms extra care should be taken because of the possibility of dividing by zero. Other forms that can be introduced include taking the logarithm of continuous variables to spread their histogram.

We now provide the details of the macro that will generate automatic variables to provide the interaction terms of a list of variables.

Table 9.6 Parameters of macro AutoInter().

Header	AutoInter(ListIn, DSin, M_ListInter, DSout, DSMap);
Parameter	*Description*
ListIn	Input list of variables to be used in the generation of interaction terms
DSin	Input dataset
M_ListInter	Output list of new variables
DSOut	Output dataset with interaction terms
DSMap	Dataset with mapping rules

Step 1
Begin by decomposing the input dataset using the utility macro ListToCol().

```
%ListToCol(&ListIn, Temp_Vars, BaseVars, VIndex);
```

Step 2

Extract the names of the variables from the dataset Temp_vars to a set of macro variables, $x_1, x_2, \dots$.

```
Data _Null_;
  set Temp_Vars;
   call symput ("x_" || left(_N_), BaseVars);
   call symput ("N", _N_);
 run;
```

Step 3

Create the dataset DSMap to hold the variables and their transformations. Start by storing the raw variables and their names. In the same dataset, generate the new variables and the formulas used to generate them. In this case, the formulas describe the interaction terms of the variables in the list.

```
Data &DSMap;
 format VarName $80.;
 format Expression $200.;
/* the first base ones are simply themselves */
 %do i=1 %to &N;
   VarName = "&&x_&i";
   Expression = VarName;
   Output;
 %end;
/* Generate the new variable transformation equations
   using the following two loops:  */
%do i=1 %to %eval(&N-1);    /* first loop: variable i */
  %do j=%eval(&i+1) %to &N;    /* Second loop: variable j */
   /* compose the new variable name */

VarName = "%sysfunc(compress(M_ &&x_&i _ &&x_&j))" ;

   /* Compose the equation LHS */
   %let RHS_&i._&j= &&x_&i * &&x_&j ;
   Expression = compress("&&RHS_&i._&j");
   output;
  %end;
 %end;
run;
```

Step 4

Finally, apply these transformations and create the new variables in the output dataset.

```
Data &DSout;
 set &DSin;
%do i=1 %to %eval(&N-1);    /* Loop: variable i */
```

```
%do j=%eval(&i+1) %to &N; /* Loop: variable j */
/* the new variable equation */
%sysfunc(compress(M_ &&x_&i _ &&x_&j)) = &&RHS_&i._&j;
 %end;
 %end;
run;
```

Step 5
Clean the workspace and end the macro.

```
proc datasets library = work nolist;
 delete temp_vars;
quit;
%mend;
```

The following code shows how to implement the preceding macro for an input dataset.

```
Data Test;
 input ID x1 x2 X3 TCmx;
 Datalines;
1 4 4 5  6.6
2 8 9 9  2.0
3 1 3 4  3.1
4 2 9 3 -1.8
5 3 3 4 -2.8
;
run;

%let ListIn=x1 x2 x3 TCmx;
%let DSin=Test;
%let ListInter=;
%let DSout=test_Inter;
%let DSMap=MapVar;

%AutoInter(&ListIn, &DSin, ListInter, &DSout, &DSMap);
```

9.4 MAPPING OF NOMINAL VARIABLES

By mapping, we mean the generation of a set of *indicator*, or *dummy*, variables to represent the different values of a categorical variable. For example, suppose we have a variable representing the type of customer residence, taking the values Rent (R), Own (O), Live with family (WF), Shared accommodation (SA), and Unknown (U). One could generate five indicator variables that take a value of either 1 or 0, depending on the value of the original variable, as shown in Table 9.7.

Table 9.7   Mapping of residence types.

Residence type	R	O	WF	SA	U
Rent	1	0	0	0	0
Own	0	1	0	0	0
With family	0	0	1	0	0
Shared accommodation	0	0	0	1	0
Unknown	0	0	0	0	1

The mapping in Table 9.7 is known as 1-to-N mapping, which means that one variable resulted in N new indicator variables, with N being the total number of categories of the original variable. The number of categories in a variable, N, is known as its *cardinality*.

A closer examination of the values reveals that we could infer the value of one of the new indicator variables by knowing the values of the others. In mathematical jargon, these variables are linearly dependent. Therefore, one of these variables can be dropped without loss of information. This is known as 1-to-$N-1$ mapping. In this case, one of the values is dropped and a total of $N-1$ indicator variables are generated in place of the original variable. The dropped value could be either the last new indicator variable, say alphabetically, or the one equivalent to the category with the lowest frequency.

A word of warning about mapping nominal variables: This should not be performed for variables with *high cardinality*. Attempting to do so will result in a large number of indicator variables, which in turn will lead to overly sparse data. Such sparse datasets very often lead to numerical and performance problems with many modeling algorithms. Therefore, mapping nominal variables with the macros described next should be performed only after reducing the cardinality of target variables to acceptable limits.

There are no scientific rules for determining an acceptable value for the maximum number of categories. We can only suggest, as a rule of thumb derived from experience, that categorical variables with a cardinality higher than about 10 to 12 are good candidates for cardinality reduction algorithms. These algorithms are discussed in Section 10.2.

As in the case of continuous variables, where we recommended mapping their names to a set of normalized names, it is recommended that the mapped nominal variables be given names using a systematic procedure. One such scheme is to append the variable name with the category index or with the value of the category itself. In the following SAS implementation, we allow for both methods. Of course, before deciding to map a nominal variable, we recommend that the different categories and their frequencies be first calculated and examined. Therefore, we start with the macro CalcCats(), which finds the categories and their frequencies, as shown in Table 9.8. The macro is a simple wrapper to PROC FREQ and is self-explanatory.

Table 9.8   Parameters of macro `CalcCats()`.

Header	`CalcCats(DSin, Var, DSCats);`
Parameter	*Description*
`DSin`	Input dataset
`Var`	Variable to calculate categories for
`DSCats`	Output dataset with the variable categories

```
%macro CalcCats(DSin, Var, DSCats);
proc freq data=&DSin noprint;
tables &Var /missing out=&DSCats;
run;
%mend;
```

The next macro is `MappCats()`, which does the actual mapping and uses PROC FREQ as one of its steps to calculate the different categories and their frequencies.

Table 9.9   Parameters of macro `MappCats()`.

Header	`MappCats(DSin, var, Method, DSout, DSCats);`
Parameter	*Description*
`DSin`	Input dataset
`Var`	Variable to calculate categories for
`Method`	Method of extending the variable name: Method =1 uses the index of categories, Method ≠ 1 uses the value of the category
`DSout`	The output dataset with the mapped variables
`DSCats`	Dataset with the variable categories

Step 1
Start by finding the different categories of the variable and their frequencies and store them in the dataset `DSCats`.

```
proc freq data=&dsin noprint;
tables &var /missing out=&DSCats;
run;
```

Step 2

Convert the categories to macro variables in order to use them, or their indexes, in the generation of the new indicator variables. Note that if the values of the categories are to be appended to the variable names, the resulting variable names must constitute valid SAS variable names. Furthermore, they should not contain special characters, such as +, -, and &, or spaces and will be within the permissible length of SAS variables. Missing values are assumed to have been replaced with some other value to allow such appending.

```
data &DSCats;
 set &DSCats;
 call symput("y"||left(_n_),&var);
 CatNo=_N_;
run;
```

Step 3

Count the categories and use a loop to generate the new variables in the output dataset, using either of the methods given in the macro parameter Method.

```
proc sql noprint;
 select count(*) into :Nc from &dscats;
run;
quit;

data &dsout;
 set &dsin;
  %do i=1 %to &Nc;

%if &Method=1 %then %do;
IF &var = left("&&y&i") then &var._&i=1;
ELSE    &var._&i=0;
%end;
                %else %do;
  IF &Var = left("&&y&i")  then &Var._&&y&i =1;
  ELSE    &Var._&&y&i =0;
                %end;

  %end;
run;
```

Step 4

Finish the macro.

```
%mend;
```

Let us demonstrate the use of the macro through a simple example. The following code generates the dataset Test and maps the variable X to new dummy variables.

```
data Test;
 input X $ y $;
datalines;
 A B
 C A
 A A
 B B
 B .
 B B
 D A
 ;
 RUN;

%let dsin=test;
%let var=X;
%let dsout=test_m;
%let dscats=Test_cats;

%MappCats(&dsin, &var,2, &dsout, &dscats);
```

The macro MappCats() performs 1-to-N mapping. If 1-to-$N-1$ mapping is required, we need only change step 3 where we limit the loop to only $N-1$ of the categories. Another option is to decide which category to remove by inspecting the results of the frequency distribution and remove, say, the category with the smallest frequency. This can be easily performed by doing a 1-to-N mapping and then dropping the unnecessary dummy variable.

9.5 NORMALIZATION OF CONTINUOUS VARIABLES

Normalization of continuous variables is performed by rescaling the values such that the variables have a mean value of zero and a standard deviation of one. This is usually termed *standard normalization*. There are two possible situations where the normalization of continuous variables is beneficial in the data mining process.

The first situation arises in several modeling algorithms that need the variables to be properly scaled in order to avoid numerical ill conditions. This is particularly true in the cases of linear and logistic regression, principal component analysis, and factor analysis. On the other hand, the implementation of these algorithms in most modern software packages, such as SAS, includes this normalization behind the scene.

The other situation is that of a business meaning of the normalized variable, especially when the values of the variable in the normalized form will be used for comparison and interpretation. In this case, rescaling does not necessarily create a mean of zero and a standard deviation of one. A typical example is to normalize the credit risk of a customer between zero and 1000. In such cases, the values are scaled such that they fall into a certain range. This type of normalization is termed *mid-range normalization.*

PROC STDIZE allows the user to standardize a set of variables using several criteria, including the mid-range normalization.

As for range standardization, the implementation only requires the computation of the minimum and maximum values and uses the following simple equation:

$$y = y_{\min} + R\left(\frac{x - x_{\min}}{x_{\max} - x_{\min}}\right), \tag{9.3}$$

where,

x	The current value
y	The new standardized value
$x_{\min}, x_{\max}$	Minimum and maximum original values
$y_{\min}$	Minimum value for the standardized range
R	The width of the standardized range

The SAS implementation of the transformation is straightforward.

9.6 CHANGING THE VARIABLE DISTRIBUTION

Changing the distribution of a variable, independent or dependent, can result in a significant change in model performance. This may reveal relationships that were masked by the variable distribution. This section discusses three methods for transforming the distribution of a continuous variable.

The first one is based on the variable ranks, and we show how the ranks could lead to the transformation of the variable to an almost normal distribution. The second method, using the set of transformations known as *Box–Cox transformations*, also attempts to transform the variable to a normally distributed one. The last method is based on the idea of spreading the histogram to expose the details of the variable distribution.

9.6.1 RANK TRANSFORMATIONS

The simplest method, which is valid only for continuous variables, is to replace the values with their *ranks*. The ranks are easily calculated using PROC RANK. Let us demonstrate this through an example. The following code creates the dataset T with the variable X having 50 observations.

```
data T;
input X @@;
datalines;
597.38  882.30  285.47  462.36  958.77
339.72  741.44  808.50   37.99  503.89
232.78  568.02  476.57  308.69  420.15
418.09  302.45  630.27  827.49   94.21
141.66  989.73  100.90   25.19  215.44
 73.71  910.78  181.60  632.28  387.84
608.17   85.20  706.30  834.28  435.41
 51.97  993.29  797.13  718.52   52.36
630.37  289.68  814.71  794.85  315.43
314.37  156.37  486.23  430.90  286.54
;
run;
```

We invoke PROC RANK as follows:

```
PROC RANK DATA = T OUT=TRanks;
        VAR X;
     RANKS X_Rank;
RUN;
```

This will create a new dataset, TRanks, and the ranks of the variable X are stored in the new variable X_Rank. The ranks are represented by integer values in ascending order from 1 to 50 (the total number of observations).

We can then transform these ranks into their normal scores (i.e., their probabilities on the normal distribution by spreading these values on the bell curve) using the simple transformation:

$$y_i = \Phi^{-1}\left(\frac{r_i - \frac{3}{8}}{n + \frac{1}{4}}\right), \tag{9.4}$$

with r_i being the rank of observation i, n being the number of observations, and Φ^{-1} being the inverse cumulative normal (PROBIT) function. The transformation will give a new variable that is very close to the normal distribution. The implementation of this transformation is very easy, as shown in the following code.

```
data TNormals;
 set Tranks nobs=nn;
 X_Normal=probit((X_Rank-0.375)/(nn+0.25));
run;
```

Furthermore, PROC RANK itself can provide this transformation directly by using the option NORMAL=BLOM in the PROC RANK statement.

```
PROC RANK DATA = T NORMAL=BLOM OUT=TRanks;
      VAR X;
    RANKS X_Normal;
RUN;
```

The modification will create the variable X_Normal directly.

The preceding method looks like a very easy approach to transform any variable to a normally distributed one. However, the difficulty in using this process is that it is possible to do it with the training data. At the time of scoring, the basis of ranking the training data is no longer available. Therefore, we are not able to deduce the equivalent transformation for the scoring values, and any model developed with a variable that was normalized using this method is not usable for scoring purposes.

We recommend that this approach be used only for cases where scores are not to be produced using a dataset other than the one used for training the model. Such cases exist in exploratory data analysis and in cases of cluster analysis when all the data is used to build the model. Another option is to normalize the variable in the entire population before sampling for the mining view.

9.6.2 BOX–COX TRANSFORMATIONS

The difficulty in selecting the optimal transformation for a variable lies in the fact that it is not possible to know in advance the best transformation to improve the model's performance. One of the most common transformations is the Box–Cox transformation, which attempts to transform a continuous variable into an *almost* normal distribution. This is achieved by mapping the values using the following set of transformations:

$$y = \begin{cases} x^{\lambda-1}/\lambda & \lambda \neq 0 \\ \log(x) & \lambda = 0 \end{cases}. \tag{9.5}$$

Linear, square root, inverse, quadratic, cubic, and similar transformations are all special cases of Box–Cox formulations. Because of the use of power and log relationships, the values of the variable x must all be positive. In order to handle the possibilities of negative values, we use the following more general form:

$$y = \begin{cases} (x+c)^{\lambda-1}/g\lambda & \lambda \neq 0 \\ \log(x+c)/g & \lambda = 0 \end{cases}. \tag{9.6}$$

The parameter c is used to appropriately offset negative values, and the parameter g is used to scale the resulting values. Parameter g is often taken as the *geometric mean* of the data. The procedure of finding the optimal value of the parameter λ simply iterates through different values, from the range of -3.0 to 3.0 in small steps, until the resulting transformed variable is as close as possible to the normal distribution.

The following implementation of the Box–Cox transformation attempts to maximize the likelihood function by testing different values of the parameter λ until the maximum is attained. The likelihood function is defined in Johnson and Wichern (2001):

$$L(\lambda) = -\frac{n}{2} \ln \left[\frac{1}{n} \sum_{j=1}^{n} (y_j - \bar{y})^2 \right] + (\lambda - 1) \sum_{j=1}^{n} \ln x_j, \qquad (9.7)$$

with y_j being the transformation of the observation x_j according to Equation 9.5. The average term $\bar{y}$ refers to the mean value of the transformed values, or

$$\bar{y} = \frac{1}{n} \sum_{j=1}^{n} y_j. \qquad (9.8)$$

Note that the term in the square brackets in Equation 9.7 is the biased variance of the transformed value. This fact makes the calculation of the likelihood function much easier.

Typically, λ lies between -3.0 and 3.0. The implementation allows the user to specify the width of the search step to adjust the accuracy of the deduced parameter. The code is divided into two macros; the first one calculates the likelihood function $L(\lambda)$, as in Equation 9.7, and the main macro loops over the values of λ and finds the maximum value of the likelihood. Once the maximum value of the likelihood is found, the equivalent λ is used to transform the variable and write the results into an output dataset.

We first present the likelihood function calculation, then the main macro.

Table 9.10   Parameters of macro `CalcLL()`.

Header	`CalcLL(DS,N,L,X,M_LL);`	
Parameter	*Description*	
DS	Input dataset	
N	Number of observations in DS	
L	Test value of parameter λ	
X	Name of variable	
M_LL	Likelihood function defined in Equation 9.7	

Step 1

Calculate the transformed values according to Equation 9.5. In doing so, we also calculate the logarithm of the variable to use it in the likelihood function expression.

```
data temp;
 set &ds;
  %if %sysevalf(&L=0) %then %do;
y_temp=log(&x);
```

```
%end;
  %else %do;
y_Temp=((&x.**&L)-1)/&L;
%end;
  lx_Temp=log(&x);
run;
```

Step 2

Use the variance function, VAR, to calculate the first term of the likelihood function and the sum of the Log transform of the raw values of the second term.

```
proc sql noprint;
select var(y_Temp)*(&N-1)/&N,
       sum(lx_Temp) into :vy, :slx from temp;
quit;
%let &M_LL = %sysevalf(
                  -&N * %sysfunc(log(&vy))/2
                  + (&L-1)*&slx);
```

Step 3

Finish the macro.

```
%mend;
```

The second part of the implementation presents the macro, which loops over the different values of the λ and finds the optimal one.

Table 9.11   Parameters of macro BoxCox().

Header	BoxCox(DSin, XVar, XVarT, DSout, W, M_Lambda, M_LL, M_C)
Parameter	*Description*
DSin	Input dataset
XVar	Name of variable to be transformed
XVarT	Name of variable after transformation
DSout	Output dataset
W	Value used as increment in the evaluation of λ
M_Lambda	Value of optimal λ
M_LL	Value of likelihood function at optimal Λ
M_C	Value of needed offset to make all raw values positive

Step 1

Evaluate the value of the offset parameter C needed to make all values positive.

```
proc sql noprint;
 select max(&Xvar) into :C from &dsin;
 select count(&Xvar) into :N from &dsin;
quit;
%if %sysevalf(&C <1e-8) %then
%let C=%sysevalf(-&C + 1e-8);
%else %Let C=0;
```

Step 2

Create a dataset with the transformed positive values.

```
data &dsout;
 set &dsin;
  &Xvar = &Xvar + &C;
run;
```

Step 3

Start the optimization loop of the likelihood function starting with a λ value of 3.0 and decrementing it to a minimum of -3.0 with steps of the given parameter W. To guarantee that each step increases the likelihood function, start with a current maximum of a large negative value, -1×10^{50}.

```
%let L_best =3;
%let LL_Max=-1e50;

%do i=1 %to %sysevalf(6/&W+1);
 %let L=%sysevalf(3-(&i-1)*&W);
```

Step 4

In each iteration, evaluate the likelihood function by calling the macro CalcLL.

```
%let LL_Now=;
%CalcLL(&dsout,&N,&L,&XVar,LL_Now);
```

Step 5

If the current value is higher than the previous maximum, exchange the values until the last increment (end of the loop).

```
%if %sysevalf(&LL_Now > &LL_max) %then %do;
     %let LL_max=&LL_now;
  %let L_best=&L;
```

```
   %end;
  /* Loop */
%end;
```

Step 6
Now set the values of the optimal λ and the likelihood function.

```
%let &mLL=&LL_Max;
%let &mLambda=&L_best;
%let &mC=&C;
```

Step 7
Finally, apply the optimal transformation and finish the macro.

```
data &dsout;
 set &dsout;
  %if %sysevalf(&L_Best=0) %then %do;
&XVarT=log(&XVar);
%end;
  %else %do;
&XVarT=((&XVar.**&L_best)-1)/&L_best;
%end;
 run;
%mend;
```

To demonstrate the use of the macro BoxCox(), we generate a dataset with a variable that is *not* normally distributed and apply the transformation on it. The following code generates the dataset Test with such properties.

```
data Test;
 do x = 1 to 10 by 0.01;
   y = x*x+exp(x + normal(0));
   output;
 end;
run;
```

By calling the macro BoxCox(), we generate a new dataset Test_BC with the variable Ty being *close to* normal.

```
%let dsin=Test;
%let Xvar=y;
%let XvarT=Ty;
%let dsout=Test_BC;
%let W=0.2;
%let Lambda=;
%let LL=;
%let C=;
```

```
%BoxCox(&dsin, &Xvar, &XVarT, &dsout, &W, Lambda, LL,  C);
%put &Lambda &LL &C;
```

We may examine the distribution of the resulting variable Ty in comparison to the original Y by using the equal width binning macro: BinEqW() (see Section 10.3.1). The results are displayed in Figure 9.1, which shows that the distribution of the transformed values resemble that of a normal distribution more than the original data.

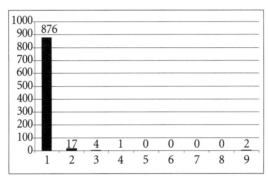

Before transformation (*Y*)

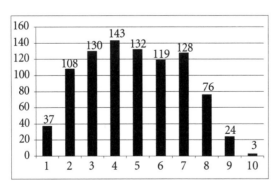

After transformation (*TY*)

Figure 9.1   Effect of Box–Cox transformation.

9.6.3 SPREADING THE HISTOGRAM

Spreading the histogram can be considered a special case of Box–Cox transformations. As Figure 9.1 shows, the Box–Cox transformation does spread the histogram. However, in other cases we may not be interested in actually converting the distribution to a normal one but merely in spreading it to allow the variable to exhibit some variance and thus be useful for modeling. This can be achieved by using two special cases of Box–Cox transformations.

The first transformation is using the logarithm of the variable (after adding a positive constant if necessary). This has the effect of spreading the distribution to the *right* side of the histogram. For example, using the same TEST dataset as in the case of the Box–Cox example just described, we create a new dataset with the transformed variable Log_Y as follows:

```
DATA Test_T;
 SET Test;
  Log_Y=LOG(y);
RUN;
```

Using equal-width histograms, Figure 9.2 shows the distribution of the variable Y before and after the transformations.

The opposite effect, that is, spreading the histogram to the *left*, can be achieved using a simple power transformation. This is displayed in Figure 9.3, which shows

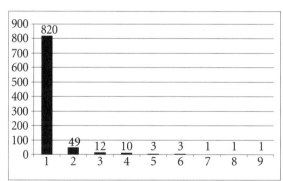

Before transformation (*Y*)

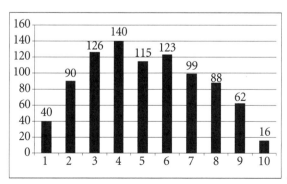

After transformation (*Log*(*Y*))

Figure 9.2   Effect of Log transformation.

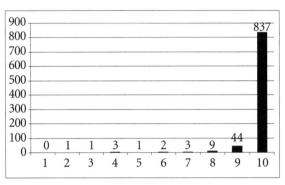

Before transformation (Z)

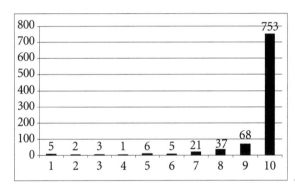

After transformation (Z⁴)

Figure 9.3   Effect of power transformation.

that the power transformation, a fourth order in this case, does spread the histogram, but not as successfully as the Log transformation.

Other similar and popular transformations are summarized in Table 9.12.

Table 9.12   Useful Transformations.

Original scale	Transformed scale
Counts, y	$\sqrt{y}$
Proportion, p	$\text{logit}(p) = \frac{1}{2}\log\left(\frac{p}{1+p}\right)$
Correlation, r	Fisher's $z(r) = \frac{1}{2}\log\left(\frac{1+r}{1-r}\right)$

CHAPTER **10**

BINNING AND REDUCTION OF CARDINALITY

10.1 INTRODUCTION

Binning is the process of converting a continuous variable into a set of ranges and then treating these ranges as categories, with the option of imposing order on them. We say *option* because sometimes it may not be necessary, or even desirable, to keep the order relationship of the ranges. For example, if we bin the variable representing the age of a customer into ranges of 10 years (0–10, 11–20, 21–30, . . . , etc.), a further analysis of the business problem may reveal that customers in the ranges 0 to 10 and 81 to 90 have similar behavior with respect to a certain issue, such as the cost of health services, and may be combined into a single group. Therefore, keeping the strict order of the bins is not always necessary. Similarly, classical scorecards built using regression models, in credit risk and marketing applications, employ binning to convert continuous variables to a set of indicator variables. The use of these variables in a regression model results in easy-to-interpret and easy-to-use scorecards.

Cardinality reduction of nominal and ordinal variables is the process of combining two or more categories into one new category. Nominal variables with high cardinality are a definite source of problems. If we attempted to map all their values to indicator variables, we would end up with a large number of variables, many of them almost full of zeros. On the other hand, if we do not convert them to indicator variables and use them with algorithms that can tolerate this problem, such as decision tree algorithms, we run into the problem of overfitting the model. Therefore, whenever possible one must consider reducing the number of categories of such variables.

Binning of continuous variables and cardinality reduction of nominal variables are two common transformations used to achieve two objectives:

1. Reduce the complexity of independent, and possibly (but less frequently) dependent, variables. For example, in the case of a variable representing the

balance of a checking account, instead of having a very large number of distinct values, we may bin the balance into, say, ranges of $500.00.

2. Improve the predictive power of the variable. By careful binning and grouping of categories, we can increase the predictive power of a variable with respect to a dependent variable for both estimation and classification problems. This is done by the selection of the binning and grouping scheme that will increase a certain measure of association between the DV and the variable at hand.

Binning and cardinality reduction are very similar procedures. They differ only in the fact that in the case of binning the order of the values is taken into account.

Methods of binning and cardinality reduction range from simple ad hoc methods based on the understanding of the data and the experience of the analyst to more sophisticated methods relying on mathematical criteria to assess the goodness of the grouping scheme. This chapter presents some of these methods. We start with the methods of cardinality reduction, and we will show later that cardinality reduction is the general case of binning.

10.2 CARDINALITY REDUCTION

10.2.1 THE MAIN QUESTIONS

The following are the three main questions that guide exposition of this subject.

1. What is the maximum acceptable number of categories?
2. How do we reduce the number of categories?
3. What are the potential issues at deployment time?

The answer to the first question is again based only on experience and can be the subject of debate. It also depends on the nature of the data and the meaning of the categories themselves.

For example, when considering the categories of a variable that represent marital status, it may be logical to group the category of Single together with those of Divorced and Separated. This is based on the understanding of the meaning of the values and assigning new groups on that basis. A general rule of thumb is that a nominal variable with more than about a *dozen* categories should be considered for cardinality reduction.

As for the second question, there are two main strategies for reducing the number of categories. The first approach, which is the easiest and most tempting, is to ignore some of the categories with small frequencies. However, this simplistic approach does not take into account the multivariate nature of all real-life datasets; that is, we are *not* dealing only with *this* variable, but rather with a large number of variables with interaction relationships. Therefore, the simple removal of some records may make it easier to handle this particular variable, but it will definitely affect the distribution of the other variables too, with unknown results.

The second approach is to devise some scheme to group the categories into a smaller set of new *super* categories. The grouping, or cardinality reduction, scheme could be based on investigating the contents of each category and grouping them on the basis of their meaning with respect to the current problem being modeled. This is the best and most recommended option. The SAS implementation of these grouping schemes is straightforward through the use of IF–THEN–ELSE statements, as illustrated using the following example.

EXAMPLE 10.1 Consider the following dataset with the two variables Age and Marital_Status.

```
DATA Test;
 FORMAT Marital_Status $10.;
 INPUT ID Age Marital_Status $ @@;

CARDS;
   1 24 Unknown     2 29 Single
   3 24 Divorced    4 29 Divorced
   5 30 Single      6 30 Separated
   7 39 Unknown     8 35 Divorced
   9 42 Separated  10 41 Separated
  11 44 Separated  12 47 Unknown
  13 45 Divorced   14 47 Married
  15 48 Widow      16 49 Married
  17 51 Single     18 54 Single
  19 53 Divorced   20 55 Single
  21 55 Married    22 56 Divorced
  23 56 Single     24 60 Widow
  25 59 Married    26 62 Widow
  27 61 Widow      28 68 Unknown
  29 66 Married    30 69 Married
;
run;
```

We now apply a set of ad hoc rules to reduce the cardinality of the variable Marital_Status to two categories, A and B, as follows:

```
Data Grouped;
  set Test;
   if  Marital_Status="Separated"
     OR Marital_Status="Widow"
     OR Marital_Status="Unknown" THEN Marital_Status="A";
   if  Marital_Status="Single"
     OR Marital_Status="Divorced"
     OR Marital_Status="Married" THEN Marital_Status="B";
run;
PROC FREQ DATA=Grouped;
  tables Marital_Status;
run;
```

The use of PROC FREQ should confirm that there are only two categories. The purpose of this almost trivial example is to show how programming this type of transformation is easy and problem dependent.

◆

However, it is not always possible to do that, especially when the number of categories is large, say 50, and there is no meaningful way of combining them. In this case, we have to combine the categories such that we increase the overall contribution of the variable in question to the model. This approach is the basis of decision tree models. In this case, the tree splits are designed such that different categories are grouped in order to increase the predictability of the dependent variable in terms of the current independent variable.

Methods based on decision trees splits in cardinality reduction are called *structured grouping methods*. We devote the next section to these methods and their implementation in SAS.

The last question with regard to cardianlity reduction is related to deployment procedures. Reducing the cardinality of a nominal variable leads to the definition of a new variable with new categories based on the grouping of the original categories. The mapping between the old and the new categories should be done efficiently in anticipation of preparation of the scoring view. One of the efficient statements in SAS is the IF-THEN statement. Therefore, in our implementation, we will make sure that the final output of the cardinality reduction macros is a set of IF-THEN statements.

10.2.2   STRUCTURED GROUPING METHODS

These methods are based on using decision tree splits to find the optimal grouping of the categories of a nominal variable into a smaller number of categories. Note that these methods also work for continuous and ordinal variables, in which case we seek to reduce the variable into a smaller number of bins.

10.2.3   SPLITTING A DATASET

The idea of grouping some categories together relies on the concept of finding a dataset split into subgroups. Figure 10.1 shows such a split with a root node and three child nodes on a nominal variable X. In this split, the variable X has been grouped into three nodes containing categories A; B,C; and D,E. The splitting algorithm determines these groups such that the total information gained about a certain dependent variable Y is maximized after the split. The term *information* is used to denote some measure of the desired property of the dependent variable Y. If we use $I(\cdot)$ to denote such an information function, then we say that the required split is the one that maximizes the expression

$$\sum_{j=1}^{m} I(C_j) - I(P), \qquad (10.1)$$

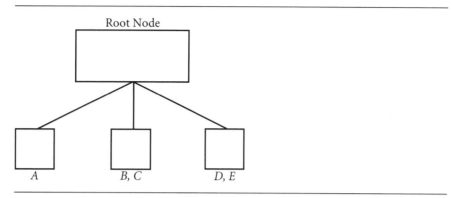

Figure 10.1   A dataset split.

where P denotes the parent node, and C_j, $j = 1, \cdots, m$ are the m child splits. By restricting the splits to binary, the right side of Expression 10.1 becomes

$$I(C_r) + I(C_l) - I(P), \qquad (10.2)$$

where C_r and C_l are the left and right child splits, respectively. Although Expression 10.2 is useful, it is more appropriate to represent the power of a split using the percentage increase of the information. This is defined as

$$\hat{I} = [I(C_r) + I(C_l) - I(P)]/I(P). \qquad (10.3)$$

Structured cardinality reduction algorithms are based on Equation 10.3. Various algorithms differ only in the definition of the information function $I(\cdot)$. The following are three common definitions of the information function.

- Entropy variance

- χ^2 test

- Gini measure of diversity

We will implement the algorithm that uses the Gini measure as an example.

10.2.4 THE MAIN ALGORITHM

Figure 10.2 shows how the main algorithm works. The algorithm starts with a root node, which is split into two nodes: 1 and 2, as shown in Figure 10.2(a). Now that we have a tree to work with, we focus only on the terminal nodes, which are nodes 1 and 2 in this case. Then we attempt to split each of these terminal nodes, as in Figure 10.2(b). We use the appropriate definition of the information function to find the best split. In the case of the displayed tree, it was better to split node 1, as in Figure 10.2(c).

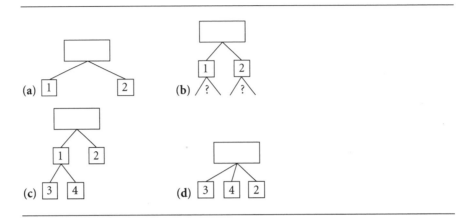

Figure 10.2   Splitting algorithm.

Now that we have a new list of terminal nodes (3, 4, 2), we can delete node 1 and replace it with its two children 3, 4, as shown in Figure 10.2(d). The procedure is then repeated until one of two conditions is satisfied: (1) The number of terminal nodes (new groups) reaches the required maximum number of categories, or (2) we cannot split any of the terminal nodes because the information function could not be increased by a significant amount. The limit on the significance of the information function and the maximum number of final groups are the two parameters that control the final result.

Note that the procedure is only a heuristic approach to solving the optimization problem at hand. It is not guaranteed to find the *best* grouping. However, it is guaranteed that the resulting grouping has a higher information content, with respect to the designated dependent variable, than the starting set of categories in the original dataset. This *theoretical* limitation is an unsolved issue in *standard* implementations of splitting algorithms. We say standard because some research has been done to find splitting algorithms that will find the global maximum information gain, but these methods are outside the scope of this book.

The algorithm just described can be formally stated as follows.

1. Start with an empty list of terminal nodes.

2. Find a split. This will generate right and left nodes R and L.

3. Store these nodes in the terminal node list.

4. The list now holds n terminal nodes.

5. If n is equal to the maximum required number of categories, stop.

6. Else, loop over *all* n nodes in the terminal node list.

7. Attempt to split each node and measure the information gained from that split.

8. Find the best split among the n candidate splits. Call this node C_x.

9. If the information gain is less than the minimum required gain for a split, then stop.

10. Else, split node C_x into right and left nodes R and L. Delete C_x from the terminal node list and add R and L.

11. Set $n = n + 1$.

12. Go to step 5.

The exact mathematical expression for the information function depends on three factors:

- The type of the information function, that is, Gini, Entropy or χ^2-based

- The nature of the independent variable being binned or reduced: nominal, ordinal, or continuous

- The nature of the dependent variable used to guide the splitting: nominal or continuous

10.2.5 REDUCTION OF CARDINALITY USING GINI MEASURE

This section presents an algorithm for the reduction of cardinality of a nominal (independent) variable with the aid of another nominal dependent variable using the Gini diversity measure. As mentioned in Chapter 2, most data mining projects involve a classification task with the dependent variable being binary. In our implementation we represent the dependent variable using a strict binary representation, either 0 or 1.

Figure 10.3 shows the details of a split of a binary dependent variable into a total of m splits. In addition to Figure 10.3, we will adopt the notation shown in Table 10.1.

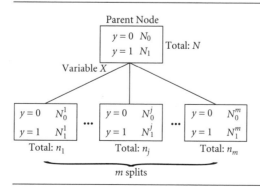

Figure 10.3   Details of binary DV splits.

Table 10.1   Notation of splits with binary DV.

Symbol	Description
y	Dependent variable (DV)
N	Total number of records in the dataset
X	The independent variable
N_1, N_0	Number of records for the categories 1 and 0 of y
N_1^j, N_0^j	Number of records in the jth child node with $y = 1$ and $y = 0$, respectively
n_j	Total number of records in the jth child node
m	Number of splits of the variable X

It is easy to confirm the following relationships:

$$n_j = N_1^j + N_0^j, \quad j = 1, \cdots, m. \tag{10.4}$$

$$N_k = \sum_{j=1}^{m} N_k^j, \quad k = 0, 1, \tag{10.5}$$

$$N = \sum_{k=0}^{1} N_k = \sum_{j=1}^{m} n_j. \tag{10.6}$$

We define the Gini measure of the parent node as follows:

$$G_p = 1 - \frac{\sum_{k=0}^{1} N_k^2}{N^2}. \tag{10.7}$$

We define the Gini measure for the jth child node as

$$G_j = 1 - \frac{\sum_{k=0}^{1} (N_k^j)^2}{(n_j)^2}. \tag{10.8}$$

The weighted Gini measure, $\hat{G}$, for the current split on X is then given by

$$\hat{G} = \sum_{j=1}^{m} \frac{n_j}{N} G_j. \tag{10.9}$$

Finally, the Gini ratio is defined as

$$G_r = 1 - \frac{\hat{G}}{G_p}. \tag{10.10}$$

The value of the Gini ratio, G_r, represents the percentage increase in the information function defined in Equation 10.3 using Gini diversity measure. This function is the basis of our implementation of the algorithm described in Section 10.2.4.

Our SAS implementation is divided into three macros.

1. GSplit() returns the best split among a set of terminal nodes that are candidates for further splitting.

2. GRedCats() is the main macro. It creates the list of terminal nodes and calls GSplit to iteratively split them into more binary splits until the termination condition is reached. The result of the splits is stored in a mapping dataset. The mapping dataset contains the mapping rules for the generation of the new categories.

3. AppCatRed() is used to apply the mapping rules to new datasets, either at the time of modeling or during scoring.

We start with the main macro: GRedCats (see Table 10.2).

Table 10.2   Parameters of macro GRedCats().

Header	GRedCats(DSin, IVVar, DVVar, Mmax, DSGroups, DSVarMap);
Parameter	*Description*
DSin	Input dataset
IVVar	Variable to be recategorized
DVVar	Dependent variable
MMax	Maximum number of categories
DSGroups	Dataset to store the new groups of categories
DSVarMap	Dataset to store the new group maps

Step 1

Determine the distinct categories of the X variable. This is achieved using the service macro CalCats. The results are stored in a temporary dataset, Temp_cats.

```
%CalcCats(&DSin, &IVVar, Temp_Cats);
```

Step 2

Convert the categories and their frequencies into macro variables using a simple DATA step.

```
Data _null_;
set Temp_Cats;
call symput ("C_" || left(_N_), compress(&IVVar));
call symput ("n_" || left(_N_), left(count));
call symput ("M", left(_N_));
Run;
```

Step 3

Calculate the count and percentages of $y = 1$ and $y = 0$ for each category using PROC SQL and store the results in a temporary dataset, Temp_Freqs.

```
proc sql noprint;
create table Temp_Freqs
 (Category char(100), DV1 num,
  DV0 num, Ni num, P1 num );
    %do i=1 %to &M;
select count(&IVVar) into :n1 from &DSin
where &IVVar = "&&C_&i" and &DVVar=1;
select count(&IVVar) into :n0 from &DSin
where &IVVar = "&&C_&i" and &DVVar=0;
%let p=%sysevalf(&n1 / &&n_&i);
insert into Temp_Freqs
values("&&C_&i", &n1, &n0, &&n_&i, &p);
   %end;
quit;
```

Step 4

Sort the categories according to the percentage of $y = 1$ and store this order into a set of macro variables.

```
proc sort data=temp_Freqs;
 by p1;
run;

data _Null_;
set temp_Freqs;
call symput("Cat_"||left(_N_), compress(Category));
run;
```

Step 5

Create a dataset to store the terminal nodes and the list of categories in each of them. This dataset is Temp_TERM. To initialize this dataset we insert *all* the categories. The number of terminal nodes now is only 1, which is the root node.

```
data Temp_TERM;
length node $1000;

Node=";
 %do j=1 %to &M;
   Node = Node ||" &&C_&j";
 %end;
run;
%let NNodes=1;
```

Step 6

Start the splitting loop. Convert all the rows of the dataset Temp_TERM, which are equivalent to terminal nodes, into macro variables representing the list categories to attempt to split in each node.

```
%DO %WHILE (&NNodes <&MMax);
Data _Null_;
set Temp_TERM;
call symput ("L_" || left(_N_), Node );
run;
```

Step 7

Loop on all these terminal nodes, attempt to split them by calling the macro GSplit(.), and find the best split by maximizing the largest Gini measure (BestRatio).

```
%let BestRatio =0;
%DO inode=1 %to &NNodes;
 %let List_L=; %let List_R=; %Let GiniRatio=;
%GSplit(&&L_&inode, Temp_Freqs, List_L,
List_R, GiniRatio);
%if %sysevalf(&GiniRatio > &BestRatio)
%then %do;
%let BestRatio=&GiniRatio;
%let BestLeft=&List_L;
%let BestRight=&List_R;
%let BestNode=&Inode;
     %end;
%End;
```

Step 8

Add this best split to the list of terminal nodes Temp_TERM by adding its right and left children and by removing it from the list. Also increment the node count by +1. This completes the main splitting loop.

```
Data Temp_TERM;
  Set Temp_TERM;
    if _N_ = &BestNode Then delete;
run;
proc sql noprint;
 insert into Temp_TERM values ("&BestLeft");
   insert into Temp_TERM values ("&BestRight");
quit;

 %let NNodes=%Eval(&NNodes +1);
%END;   /* End of the splitting loop */
```

Step 9

We should now have a set of groups of categories that we need to map to the original ones. We will adopt a simple method for generating new names for the categories by subscripting the variable name by _1, _2, and so on. These new names will be stored in the output dataset DSGroups.

```
data &DSGroups;
set Temp_TERM (REname=(Node=OldCategory));
length NewCategory $40;
NewCategory="&IVVar._"||left(_N_);
run;
```

Step 10

We are now in a position to create the mapping dataset. The mapping dataset (DSVarMap) contains simply two columns, the old category name and the new name. This is done in two steps.

First convert the list of terminal nodes and the categories listed in them into a set of macro variables.

```
data _NULL_;
Set Temp_TERM;
call symput("List_"||left(_N_), Node);
call symput("NSplits",compress(_N_));
run;
```

Then create the table DSVarMap and loop on each of the macro variables, representing the list of categories in terminal nodes. Decompose each list and register the entries in the dataset DSVarMap. The decomposition of the list is performed using the service macro Decompose(.).

```
proc sql noprint;
create table &DSVarMap
(OldCategory char(30), NewCategory char(30));
quit;
%DO ix=1 %to &NSplits;
  /* decompose each list */
%Decompose(&&List_&ix, Temp_list);
  /* convert the new list dataset to macro variables */
data _Null_;
set Temp_list;
call symput("CC_"||left(_N_),compress(Category));
call symput("CM", compress(_N_));
run;
/* insert all these values into the mapping dataset */
proc sql noprint;
%do j=1 %to &CM;
  insert into &DSVarMap values
        ("&&CC_&j", "&IVVar._&ix");
```

```
%end;
quit;
%END;
```

Step 11
Clean up and finish the macro.

```
proc datasets library = work nolist;
  delete temp_cats Temp_freqs Temp_term
         temp_list temp_gcats;
run;quit;
%mend;
```

The second macro, GSplit(), performs the actual splitting using the Gini measure (See Table 10.3).

Table 10.3   Parameters of macro GSplit().

Header	GSplit(Listin, DSFreqs, M_ListL, M_ListR, M_GiniRatio);
Parameter	*Description*
Listin	Input list of categories
DSFreqs	Dataset containing frequencies of categories
M_ListL	List of categories in the *left* child node
M_ListR	List of categories in the *right* child node
M_GiniRatio	Resulting Gini ratio of this split

Step 1
Decompose the list into the categories and put them in a temporary dataset Temp_GCats, using the macro Decompose(.). Then store these categories in a set of macro variables.

```
%Decompose(&Listin, Temp_GCats);
data _null_;
set Temp_GCats;
call symput("M",compress(_N_));
call symput("C_"||left(_N_), compress(Category));
run;
```

Step 2
Start a loop to go over the categories in the list and calculate the Gini term for the parent node.

```
proc sql noprint;
%let NL=0; %let N1=0; %let N0=0;
%do j=1 %to &M;
```

```
%let NL=%Eval(&NL+&&Ni_&j);
%let N1=%eval(&N1+&&DV1_&j);
%let N0=%eval(&N0+&&DV0_&j);
%end;
%let GL = %sysevalf(1 - (&N1 * &N1 + &N0 * &N0)
/(&NL * &NL));
quit;
```

Step 3

Loop on each possible split, calculate the Gini ratio for that split, and monitor the maximum value and the split representing that current best split. This will be used later as the best split for this list (terminal node).

```
%let MaxRatio=0;
%let BestSplit=0;
%do Split=1 %to %eval(&M-1);
/* the left node contains nodes from 1 to Split */
%let DV1_L=0;
%let DV0_L=0;
%let N_L=0;
%do i=1 %to &Split;
%let DV1_L = %eval(&DV1_L + &&DV1_&i);
%let DV0_L = %eval(&DV0_L + &&DV0_&i);
%let N_L = %eval(&N_L + &&Ni_&i);
%end;
/* The right node contains nodes from Split+1 to M */
%let DV1_R=0;
%let DV0_R=0;
%let N_R=0;
%do i=%eval(&Split+1) %to &M;
%let DV1_R = %eval(&DV1_R + &&DV1_&i);
%let DV0_R = %eval(&DV0_R + &&DV0_&i);
%let N_R = %eval(&N_R + &&Ni_&i);
%end;
%let G_L  = %sysevalf(1 - (&DV1_L*&DV1_L+&DV0_L*&DV0_L)
/(&N_L*&N_L));
%let G_R = %sysevalf(1 - (&DV1_R*&DV1_R+&DV0_R*&DV0_R)
/(&N_R*&N_R));
%let G_s= %sysevalf( (&N_L * &G_L + &N_R * &G_R)/&NL);

%let GRatio = %sysevalf(1-&G_s/&GL);
%if %sysevalf(&GRatio >&MaxRatio)
%then %do;
%let BestSplit = &Split;
%let MaxRatio= &Gratio;
%end;
    %end;
```

Step 4
Now that we know the location of the split, we compose the right and left lists of categories.

```
/* The left list is: */
 %let ListL =;
%do i=1 %to &BestSplit;
  %let ListL = &ListL &&C_&i;
 %end;
 /* and the right list is: */
%let ListR=;
%do i=%eval(&BestSplit+1) %to &M;
  %let ListR = &ListR &&C_&i;
 %end;
```

Step 5
Store the results in the output macro variables and finish the macro.

```
/* return the output values */
%let &M_GiniRatio=&MaxRatio;
%let &M_ListL=&ListL;
%let &M_ListR = &ListR;
%mend;
```

The final macro, AppCatRed(.), is used to apply the mapping rules to a dataset. This macro would be invoked on both the mining and scoring views (see Table 10.4).

Table 10.4   Parameters of macro AppCatRed().

Header	AppCatRed(DSin, Xvar, DSVarMap, XTVar, DSout);
Parameter	*Description*
DSin	Input dataset
XVar	Variable to be recategorized
DSVarMap	Mapping rules dataset obtained by macro GRedCats(.)
XTVar	New name of transformed variable
DSout	Output dataset with the new grouped categories

Step 1
Extract the old and new categories into macro variables.

```
Data _NULL_;
set &DSVarMap;
call symput ("OldC_"||left(_N_), compress(OldCategory));
call symput ("NewC_"||left(_N_), compress(NewCategory));
```

```
call symput ("Nc", compress(_N_));
run;
```

Step 2
Generate the rules and create the output dataset with the transformed variable. Finish the macro.

```
DATA &DSout;
length &XTVar $40;
set &DSin;
%do i=1 %to &Nc;
    IF &XVar = "&&OldC_&i" THEN &XTVar = "&&NewC_&i" ;
%end;
RUN;
%mend;
```

10.2.6 LIMITATIONS AND MODIFICATIONS

In the SAS code of the previous subsection, we implemented the algorithm to reduce the number of categories using a nominal dependent variable using the Gini measure. The implementation is subject to the following limitations.

DV Type

The SAS code included the calculations only for the case of a binary dependent variable. We can extend this code to include the use of two more types: nominal dependent variables with more than two categories and continuous DVs.

In the first case, more than two categories, there are two modifications to the algorithms. The first one deals with the extension of the equations defining the Gini ratio to more than two categories. The Gini term for the parent node is defined as

$$G_l = 1 - \frac{\sum_{k=1}^{c} N_k^2}{N^2},$$

(10.11)

with c being the number of categories of the DV. The Gini measure for the jth node is then given as

$$G_j = 1 - \frac{\sum_{k=1}^{c} (N_j^k)^2}{(n_j)^2}.$$

(10.12)

The weighted Gini measure, $\hat{G}$, for the current split on X is similarly defined as

$$\hat{G} = \sum_{j=1}^{m} \frac{n_j}{N} G_j.$$

(10.13)

Finally, the Gini ratio is calculated as

$$G_r = 1 - \frac{\hat{G}}{G_l}. \tag{10.14}$$

The second modification is the search for the split point in the list of ordered categories according to the content of the DV categories. In the case of a binary DV, we sorted the categories using their percentage of the category $y = 1$. In the case of a multicategory DV, we need to perform this search for each category. Therefore, we would be working with several lists simultaneously, each representing one of the categories being equivalent to the binary case of $y = 1$. Although it is straightforward to modify the SAS implementation to accommodate this situation, in most practical applications the DV is binary.

In the case of using a continuous DV, we will have to convert the definition of the information function to use the average value of the DV instead of the count of one of the categories. This is detailed in the next section.

Type of Information Function

So far, we have defined the information function using the Gini diversity measure. However, we can also define the information function using χ^2 or the Entropy variance.

The extension of the presented code to account for the type of dependent variable, and of the information functions, should be straightforward by modifying the relevant section of the code.

10.3 BINNING OF CONTINUOUS VARIABLES

The main issue in binning is the method used to assign the bounds on the bins. These bounds can be assigned by dividing the range of the variable into an equal number of ranges; thus the bins are simply bins of equal width. This method is called *equal-width binning*. Other binning methods involve more sophisticated criteria to set the boundaries of such bins. In this section, we present three methods: *equal-width*, *equal-height*, and *optimal binning*.

10.3.1 EQUAL-WIDTH BINNING

Equal-width binning is implemented using the following steps.

1. Calculate the range of the variable to be binned.

2. Using the specified number of bins, calculate the boundary values for each bin.

3. Using the specified boundaries, assign a bin number to each record.

These steps are implemented in the macro BinEqW2(). This macro generates a new variable with the postfix _Bin containing the bin number. It also stores the mapping scheme in a dataset. A simpler version of the macro is BinEqW(), which does not store the binning scheme (see Table 10.5). As discussed, storing the binning scheme is important to allow the use of the same bin limits during scoring.

Table 10.5   Parameters of macro BinEqW2().

Header	BinEqW2(DSin, Var, Nb, DSOut, Map);
Parameter	*Description*
DSin	Input dataset
Var	Variable to be binned
Nb	Number of bins
DSOut	Output dataset
Map	Dataset to store the binning maps

Step 1

Calculate the maximum and minimum of the variable Var, and store these values in the macro variables Vmax and Vmin. Then calcluate the bin size BS.

```
/* Get max and min values */
proc sql  noprint;
 select  max(&var) into :Vmax from &dsin;
 select  min(&Var) into :Vmin from &dsin;
run;
quit;

 /* calcualte the bin size */
%let Bs = %sysevalf((&Vmax - &Vmin)/&Nb);
```

Step 2

Loop on each value, using a DATA step, and assign the appropriate bin number to the new variable &Var._Bin, that is, the original variable name postfixed Bin.

```
/* Now, loop on each of the values and create the bin
    limits and count the number of values in each bin
*/
data &dsout;
 set &dsin;
  %do i=1 %to &Nb;
  %let Bin_U=%sysevalf(&Vmin+&i*&Bs);
  %let Bin_L=%sysevalf(&Bin_U - &Bs);
  %if &i=1 %then  %do;
```

```
IF &var >= &Bin_L and &var <= &Bin_U THEN &var._Bin=&i;
  %end;
  %else %if &i>1 %then %do;
IF &var > &Bin_L and &var <= &Bin_U THEN &var._Bin=&i;
 %end;
  %end;
run;
```

Step 3

Finally, create a dataset to store the bin limits to use later to bin scoring views or other datasets using the same strategy.

```
/* Create the &Map dataset to store the bin limits */
proc sql noprint;
 create table &Map (BinMin num, BinMax num, BinNo num);
  %do i=1 %to &Nb;
  %let Bin_U=%sysevalf(&Vmin+&i*&Bs);
  %let Bin_L=%sysevalf(&Bin_U - &Bs);
  insert into &Map values(&Bin_L, &Bin_U, &i);
  %end;
quit;
```

Step 4

Finish the macro.

```
%mend;
```

The only remaining issue in equal-width binning is how to assign the values if they happen to be exactly equal to the boundary value of the bins. This issue becomes a real problem in cases where the values of the variable take integer values and the binning boundaries are also integers. Consider a bin with upper and lower limits of b_u and b_l, respectively. We can set the rule to assign the value x to this bin using one of two rules:

A. Assign x to bin b if $b_l < x \le b_u$.

B. Assign x to bin b if $b_l \le x < b_u$.

Rule A will cause a problem only at the minimum value, and rule B will cause a problem at the maximum value. Intermediate integer values that coincide with b_l and b_u will be assigned to different bins depending on the rule we use. This can sometimes dramatically change the resulting distribution of the binned variable. One solution for values on the boundaries is to divide their frequencies to the two bins. However, this results in the counterintuitive noninteger frequency counts.

There is no standard solution to this problem. Different vendors of commercial analysis software use different methods for assigning records to the different bins.

10.3.2 EQUAL-HEIGHT BINNING

In equal-height binning, we attempt to select the upper and lower limits of each bin such that the final histogram is as close to uniform as possible. Let us demonstrate this concept by a simple example.

Assume we have the following 20 values for a variable, x, which is sorted in ascending order: 20, 22, 23, 24, 25, 25, 25, 25, 25, 27, 28, 28, 29, 30, 32, 40, 42, 44, 48, 70. Assume further that we wish to bin this variable into 5 bins of equal height. In the case of equal-width binning, we find the bin size as

$$\text{Bin size} = (70 - 20)/5 = 10 \qquad (10.15)$$

and the frequencies for each bin would be as shown in Table 10.6. (Note that in Table 10.6 the use of brackets follows the convention: ("(" means *larger than*, and "]", means *less then or equal to*).

Table 10.6   Equal-width bins.

Bin	Bin limits	Frequency
1	[20 , 30]	14
2	(30 , 40]	2
3	(40 , 50]	3
4	(50 , 60]	0
5	(60 , 70]	1

If we decided to change the bin limits such that each bin would contain more or less the same number of records, we would simply attempt to assign about 4 observations to each bin. This can be done using the scheme shown in Table 10.7.

Table 10.7   Equal-height bins.

Bin	Bin limits	Frequency
1	[20 , 24]	4
2	(24 , 25]	5
3	(25 , 28]	4
4	(28 , 42]	4
5	(42 , 70]	3

The frequency distribution of the new bins is almost uniform. However, the bins do not have exactly equal size but are more or less of equal height.

The algorithm adopted to set the values in equal height is a simple one. It works as follows:

1. Determine the approximate number of observations to be allocated to each bin. This number is calculated from the simple formula:

$$N_b = N/B, \tag{10.16}$$

   where

   N_b = Number of observations per bin

   N = Total number of observations

   B = Number of bins

   The calculation is rounded to the nearest integer.

2. Sort the values in ascending order.

3. Start with the first bin: Allocate the first Nb values to the first bin.

4. If repeated values fall on the bin boundary, there could be two types of solutions for this bin count: (1) we could carry the repeated values over to the next bin and leave this bin with less than the average frequency, or (2) we could allow the bin to have more than average frequency by taking all the repeated values into the current bin. We always take the option that would result in the minimum deviation from the required frequency.

5. Calculate the accumulated error in terms of the accumulated frequency of the bins compared with the expected cumulative frequency.

6. We may attempt to correct for this error immediately in the next bin or attempt to spread the correction over some or all of the remaining bins.

The implementation of this algorithm is straightforward, with the exception of the last step, which may lead to complications. The simplest method to handle the last step is to attempt to compensate for the accumulated error immediately in the very next bin.

The algorithm is implemented in the following macro.

Step 1
Find the unique values and their frequencies using PROC FREQ. Also calculate the cumulative frequencies (see Table 10.8).

```
proc freq data = &dsin noprint;
 tables &var / out=&var._Freqs outcum;
run;

/* Get sum of frequencies */
proc sql  noprint;
 select  max(cum_freq) into :SumFreq from &Var._Freqs;
```

Table 10.8   Parameters of macro BinEqH().

Header	BinEqH(DSin, Var, Nb, DSOut, Map);
Parameter	*Description*
DSin	Input dataset
Var	Variable to be binned
Nb	Number of bins
DSOut	Output dataset
Map	Dataset to store the binning maps

```
run;
quit;
```

Step 2
Calculate the average bin size.

```
 /* calculate the bin size */
%let Bs = %sysevalf(&SumFreq/&Nb);
```

Step 3
Assign the bin number for each unique value by adjusting the width of the bins to account for possible spillovers.

```
data &Var._Freqs;
 set &var._freqs;

/* starting values */
retain bin 1 used 0 past 0 spill 0 binSize &Bs;

/* If a spillover occurred in the last iteration
   then increment the bin number, adjust the bin width,
   and save the used frequencies as "past" */
if spill=1 then do;
past = used;
BinSize=(&sumFreq-used)/(&Nb-bin);
Bin=Bin+1;
Spill=0;
end;
used = used + count;

/* check if this results in a spillover */
if used >= past +BinSize then spill =1;
else spill=0;

run;
```

Step 4

Find the upper and lower limits and the frequency in each bin.

```
proc sort data=&Var._Freqs;
 by bin;
run;

data &Var._Freqs;
 set &Var._Freqs;
  by bin;
  retain i 1;
  if first.bin then call symput ("Bin_L" || left(i), &var);
  if last.bin then do;
call symput ("Bin_U" || Left (i), &var);
i=i+1;
  end;
run;

/* Check the actual number of bins and get
   the frequency within each bin */
proc sql noprint;
 select max(bin) into :Nb from &Var._Freqs;
 %do i=1 %to &Nb;
   select sum(count) into :Bc&i from &Var._Freqs
                               where bin=&i;
 %end;
 run;
quit;
```

Step 5

Add the bin number to the data and store the bin limits in the Map dataset.

```
data &dsout;
 set &dsin;
  %do i=1 %to &Nb;
IF &var >= &&Bin_L&i and &var <= &&Bin_U&i
   THEN &var._Bin=&i;
  %end;
run;

/* and the binning limits to the dataset VarBins */

data &Map;
 do BinNo=1 to &Nb;
   &var._Lower_Limit=symget("Bin_L" || left(BinNo));
   &var._Upper_Limit=symget("Bin_U" || left(BinNO));
```

```
    Frequency = 1.* symget("Bc" || left(BinNo));
    output;
  end;
run;
```

Step 6
Clean the workspace and finish the macro.

```
/* clean workspace */
proc datasets library=work nolist;
delete &Var._Freqs;
quit;

%mend;
```

10.3.3 OPTIMAL BINNING

Equal-height binning attempts to make the frequencies of the records in the new bins equal as much as possible. Another way to look at it is that it attempts to *minimize* the difference between the frequencies of the new categories (bin numbers). Therefore, we consider it a special case of *optimal binning*.

However, in this section, we use the term *optimal* to mean that the new categories will be the *best* set of binning strategies so that the variable has the *highest predictive power* with respect to a specific dependent variable. This is similar to the case of reducing the cardinality of categorical variables, discussed earlier in this chapter, using structured grouping methods.

In fact, the method presented here depends on transforming the continuous variable to a large number of categories, using simple equal-width binning, and then using the Gini measure category reduction method to reduce these bins into the required number of bins. That is the reason we stated in Section 10.1 that binning could be treated as a special case of cardinality reduction.

The method described in the previous paragraph is actually the basis of decision tree algorithms with a continuous independent variable. As with cardinality reduction, we could have employed a number of alternative splitting criteria to find the optimal grouping, such as the Entropy variance, or χ^2, of the resulting grouping.

The macro GBinBDV() is the SAS implementation using the Gini measure, which assumes that the dependent variable is binary (1/0). (See Table 10.9)

The parameter NW is used to initially divide the range of the variable IVVar to NW equal divisions before grouping them to the final bins. The larger this number, the more accurate the binning, but the more it becomes demanding in terms of computing time. Also note that this macro does not result in an output dataset with the bin numbers assigned to the records. We will implement this separately in an another macro.

The implementation assumes the following.

- The dependent variable is binary (1/0).

- The variable to be binned is continuous. If it contains only integer values, the resulting bin limits may not be integers.

- No missing values are accounted for in either the dependent variable or the binning variable.

The macro is very similar to that used to reduce the cardinality of nominal variables, GRedCats(), with the exception of the initial binning, using the equal-width method, and the calculation of the generated mapping rules.

Table 10.9   Parameters of macro GBinBDV().

Header	GBinBDV(DSin, IVVar, DVVar, NW, Mmax, DSGroups, DSVarMap);
Parameter	*Description*
DSin	Input dataset
IVVar	Continuous variable to be binned
DVVar	Dependent variable used to bin IVVar
NW	Number of divisions used for initial equal-width binning
MMax	Maximum number of bins
DSGroups	Dataset with final groups of bins (splits)
DSVarMap	Dataset with mapping rules

Step 1
Start by binning the variable IVVar into a total of NW equal-width bins using the macro BinEqW2(). But first copy the IVVar and the DVVar into a temporary dataset to make sure that the original dataset is not disturbed.

```
Data Temp_D;
  set &DSin (rename=(&IVVar=IV &DVVAR=DV));
  keep IV DV;
run;
```

```
%BinEqW2(Temp_D, IV, &NW, Temp_B, Temp_BMap);
```

Step 2
Determine the count of each bin and the percentage of the DV=1 and DV=0 in each of them. We know that the bin numbers are from 1 to NW, but some bins may be empty. Therefore, we use macro CalcCats() to get the count of only those in the Temp_GB dataset.

```
%CalcCats(TEMP_B, IV_Bin, Temp_Cats);
```

Step 3
Next, sort Temp_Cats using IV_Bin and convert the bins to macro variables.

```
proc sort data=Temp_Cats;
   by IV_Bin;
 run;

Data _null_;
  set Temp_Cats;
      call symput ("C_" || left(_N_), compress(IV_Bin));
        call symput ("n_" || left(_N_), left(count));
      call symput ("M", left(_N_));
   Run;
```

Step 4
Calculate the count (and percentage) of DV=1 and DV=0 in each category using PROC SQL and store the results values in the dataset Temp_Freqs.

```
proc sql noprint;
   create table Temp_Freqs (Category char(50),
                            DV1 num, DV0 num,
                            Ni num,  P1 num );

%do i=1 %to &M;
  select count(IV) into :n1 from Temp_B
                where IV_Bin = &&C_&i and DV=1;
  select count(IV) into :n0 from Temp_B
                where IV_Bin = &&C_&i and DV=0;
  %let p=%sysevalf(&n1 / &&n_&i);
  insert into Temp_Freqs
              values("&&C_&i", &n1, &n0, &&n_&i, &p);
%end;
quit;
```

Step 5
Create the TERM dataset to keep the terminal nodes and their category list, and initialize the node counter. Store all the categories as a starting point.

```
data Temp_TERM;
  length node $1000;

  Node=";
 %do j=1 %to &M;
   Node = Node ||" &&C_&j";
 %end;
run;
```

Step 6
Start the splitting loop.

```
%let NNodes=1;

%DO %WHILE (&NNodes <&MMax);
/* Convert all the rows of the splits to macro variables,
   we should have exactly NNodes of them. */
   Data _Null_;
      set Temp_TERM;
       call symput ("L_" || left(_N_), Node );
   run;
/* Loop on each of these lists, generate possible splits
   of terminal nodes, and select the best split using
   the GiniRatio. */
%let BestRatio =0;

%DO inode=1 %to &NNodes;
/* The current node list is &&L_&i
   Using this list, get the LEFT and RIGHT categories
   representing the current best split, and the
   Gini measure of these children. */
   %let List_L=; %let List_R=; %Let GiniRatio=;
%GSplit(&&L_&inode, Temp_Freqs, List_L, List_R, GiniRatio);

 /* Compare the GiniRatio, if this one is better,
    and keep a record of it. */
%if %sysevalf(&GiniRatio > &BestRatio) %then %do;
%let BestRatio=&GiniRatio;
%let BestLeft=&List_L;
%let BestRight=&List_R;
%let BestNode=&Inode;
    %end;

%End; /* end of the current node list */

/* Add this split to the Temp_TERM by removing the
   current node, and adding two new nodes. The contents of the new
   nodes are the right and left parts of the current node. */
Data Temp_TERM;
  Set Temp_TERM;
    if _N_ = &BestNode Then delete;
run;
proc sql noprint;
 insert into Temp_TERM values ("&BestLeft");
   insert into Temp_TERM values ("&BestRight");
quit;
```

```
/* increment NNodes */
%let NNodes=%Eval(&NNodes +1);

%END;   /* End of the splitting loop */
```

Step 7

Now we should have a set of bin groups, which we need to map to a new set of ranges
for final output and transformation of the input dataset. These new ranges will be
obtained by getting the lower and upper bounds on the smallest and largest bins in
each node. The results are stored in the output dataset DSVarMap.

```
/* we get all the final lists from the splits */
data _NULL_;
 Set Temp_TERM;
   call symput("List_"||left(_N_), Node);
   call symput("NSplits",compress(_N_));
run;

/* And we create the new explicit mapping dataset */
proc sql noprint;
 create table &DSVarMap (BinMin num, BinMax num,
                         BinNo num);
quit;
%DO ix=1 %to &NSplits;
/* Get the first and last bin number from each list. */
 %let First_bin=;%let Last_bin=;
 %FirstLast(&&List_&ix, First_bin, Last_bin);

 /* get the outer limits  (minimum first, maximum last)
    for these bins */
 proc sql noprint;
   select BinMin into :Bmin_F from Temp_BMap
                     where BinNo=&First_bin;
   select BinMax into :Bmax_L from Temp_BMap
                     where BinNo=&Last_bin;

   /* Store these values in DSVarMap under the
      new bin number: ix */
   insert into &DSVarMap values (&Bmin_F, &Bmax_L, &ix);
 quit;
%END;
/* Generate DSGroups */
 data Temp_TERM;
     set Temp_TERM;
first=input(scan(Node,1),F10.0);
 run;
 proc sort data=Temp_TERM;
```

```
  by first;
 run;

 Data &DSGroups;
  set Temp_TERM (Rename=(Node=OldBin));
  NewBin=_N_;
  drop first;
 run;

     /* Because the split number is not representative
        of any specific order, we should sort them on
        the basis of their values */
     proc sort data=&DSVarMap;
      by BinMin;
     run;
     /* and regenerate the values of BinNo accordingly. */
     data &DSVarMap;
      Set &DsVarMap;
       BinNo=_N_;
     run;
```

Step 8
Clean the workspace and finish the macro.

```
/* clean up and finish */
 proc datasets library = work nolist;
  delete temp_b Temp_bmap Temp_cats temp_d
        temp_freqs temp_gcats temp_Term;
    run;quit;

%mend;
```

To apply the determined bins, we present the following macro, which reads the bin limits from the maps dataset and generates the new bin number in the input dataset (see Table 10.10).

The macro is implemented in two steps.

Step 1
The binning conditions are extracted.

```
%macro AppBins(DSin, XVar, DSVarMap, XTVar, DSout);

/* extract the conditions */
data _Null_;
 set &DSVarMap;
  call symput ("Cmin_"||left(_N_), compress(BinMin));
```

Table 10.10 Parameters of macro AppBins().

Header	AppBins(DSin, XVar, DSVarMap, XTVar, DSout);
Parameter	*Description*
DSin	Input dataset
XVar	Continuous variable to be binned
DSVarMap	Dataset with mapping rules
XTVar	The new transformed variable (bin numbers)
DSOut	Output dataset

```
  call symput ("Cmax_"||left(_N_), compress(Binmax));
  call symput ("M", compress(_N_));
run;
```

Step 2

Then the new transformed variable is added to the output dataset.

```
/* now we generate the output dataset */
Data &DSout;
  SET &DSin;
  /* The condition loop */
  IF &Xvar <= &Cmax_1  THEN  &XTVar = 1;
  %do i=2 %to %eval(&M-1);
    IF &XVar > &&Cmin_&i AND &XVar <= &&Cmax_&i
    THEN  &XTVar = &i ;
  %end;
  IF &Xvar > &&Cmin_&M  THEN  &XTVar = &M;
  run;

%mend;
```

CHAPTER 11

TREATMENT OF MISSING VALUES

11.1 INTRODUCTION

Missing values exist in abundance in databases, and procedures for treating them are by far the most recurring theme in data mining modeling. Therefore, I allowed this chapter to be the longest in the book!

One may ask two questions regarding missing values: (1) What do they mean, and (2) where do they come from? To answer these questions, we have to trace the origins of missing values. A missing data may represent, or be a product of, any of the following.

- An unknown value. For example, during surveys, responders may not answer certain questions.

- A result of the design of the operational system, such as the activation date of a credit card. Before the card is activated, the activation date is NULL—a missing value.

- An error while transforming data from different platforms and systems. For example, while porting data from a flat file to a relational database, we may attempt to feed a numeric field in a table with string values. In most cases, this raises an error and a missing value is generated.

- An undefined value resulting from mathematical operations either on other missing values or as a result of prohibited mathematical operations, such as division by zero or taking the log of a nonpositive number. The result of such ill-defined operations depends strongly on the data processing engine. For example, in SAS operations on missing values return missing values, in most cases without an error message (only a note in the SAS Log).

The first two cases in the list represent situations where the missing value has some specific business meanings, and the last two represent suppressed or ignored errors.

171

The problem is that the analyst is usually confronted with the mining view as an extract from the database and may not know the reason for the missing values. It is, therefore, advisable to attempt to know, as much as technically and economically feasible, the source of missing values before embarking on replacing them or dealing with them using one of the techniques described in this chapter.

The next important questions are: Do we need to do anything? Can we use the variables with the missing values? In other words, when should we resort to replacing missing values with something else *at all?* To answer this question, we need to know the meaning of the missing values, that is, are they errors that need correction or do they have a business meaning? If they have a meaning, then we have to make sure that any scheme used to replace these values will retain or properly represent this meaning. In view of this, the most difficult situation is when some missing values of a certain variable have a meaning while some are just errors that need correction.

The last factor to consider when attempting to treat missing values is to examine the specific requirements of the data mining technique to be used with the data, as well as the implementation software. Some data mining algorithms tolerate missing values and can treat them as a separate category, such as decision trees. Other methods need to have all the values represented by numeric values, such as neural networks, regression models, and clustering algorithms. In addition, some software implementations allow the user to treat missing values at the time of modeling, thus making the task of explicitly replacing or imputing them seem redundant or unnecessary. However, explicit treatment of missing values provides the analyst with better control over the results and ensures that the same procedures and values used in modeling are applied at the time of scoring. In addition, using cleaner variables in the final mining view with any modeling package allows the analyst to focus on taking advantage of their features in the modeling phase by solving the data problems beforehand.

The following are three basic strategies to treat missing values.

1. *Ignore the Record*

   In this case, we elect to remove the record that contains the missing value from the mining view. The advantage of this option is that we will use a record only when it is complete and therefore the model will be based on actual data and not on guessed values. There are two disadvantages to this method. First, most real datasets are so sparse that only a relatively small proportion of records is free of missing values. This small proportion may not be adequate to describe the behavior the model is supposed to capture and represent. The second reason is that the scoring data will also contain missing values. Therefore, if the model is based on the assumption that the values of all variables are known, those records with missing values will not be scored correctly, or perhaps not scored at all.

   Hence, this approach is recommended when the proportion of the data containing missing values is relatively small in both the training and the scoring datasets. It can be effectively used, however, in cases where the data collection procedures should not allow missing values as an option. For example, in scientific and engineering applications of data mining, such as weather prediction and industrial process control, the data is gathered from measurement equipment that does not normally result in missing values. When records do contain missing values, it is an indication that something went wrong with the data collection equipment or software, and these records should not be used at all.

2. *Substitute a Value*

   In this strategy, we substitute missing values with some value of our choosing. This value could be based on the general characteristics of the variable, such as the mode or the mean, or on a user-defined value, such as zero or any given value. In this scheme, the following options are typically used.

   - Nominal variables

     – The mode: most occurring value
     – Any of the categories (user-defined value)
     – A new category to indicate a missing value

   - Ordinal and continuous variables

     – The mean (only continuous)
     – The median
     – The mode
     – Maximum value
     – Minimum value
     – Zero or any other user-defined value

   In all these options, we must be aware that we are creating a *bias* in the data toward the selected value (i.e., mode, mean, etc). In the case of continuous variables, using the median usually creates less bias than does using the mean.

   One advantage of this approach is that the implementation of the substitution routines is simple and straightforward. Also, the justification for selecting the specific replacement option is often easy. For example, in the case of nominal variables, the mode represents the most probable value.

   We will provide two macros, one for nominal variables and another for continuous variables, for the replacement of missing values with the preceding options.

3. *Impute the Values*

   In this case, we attempt to *re-create* the data and simulate the process of data generation by fitting the data to some model and using the results of that model to predict the values that appeared as missing. Therefore, we use the nonmissing values of some variables to predict the missing values in other variables. The Multiple Imputation (MI) procedure of SAS/STAT implements several methods to impute missing values for continuous, ordinal, and nominal variables. Imputation algorithms depend on the *pattern* of missing values. We will elaborate more on this subject shortly and show how to identify what we call the *missingness* pattern and how to select the appropriate algorithm. Because PROC MI contains all the procedures needed for imputing missing values, our exposition focuses on understanding the background of the subject matter, writing macros that allow us to use PROC MI properly by identifying the missingness pattern, and wrapping up the procedure with an easy-to-use macro.

11.2 SIMPLE REPLACEMENT

11.2.1 NOMINAL VARIABLES

We will assume that nominal variables are defined in SAS datasets as string variables. Accordingly, the following macro calculates the nonmissing value of the mode of a string variable in a dataset. We exclude the possibility of the mode being the missing value because we plan to use this macro to substitute for the missing values themselves. The macro relies on PROC FREQ to calculate the frequencies of the categories of the variable XVar in the dataset DSin and selects the largest value as the output M_Mode.

```
%macro ModeCat(DSin, Xvar, M_Mode);
/* Finding the mode of a string variable in a dataset */
%local _mode;
proc freq data=&DSin noprint order=freq;
 tables &Xvar/out=Temp_Freqs;
run;
/* Remove the missing category if found */
data Temp_freqs;
 set Temp_freqs;
  if &Xvar='' then delete;
run;
/* Set the value of the macro variable _mode */
data Temp_Freqs;
 set Temp_Freqs;
if _N_=1 then call symput('_mode',trim(&xvar));
run;

  /* Set the output variable M_mode and clean the workspace */
%let &M_Mode=&_mode;

proc datasets library=work nodetails nolist;
 delete Temp_Freqs;
quit;

%mend;
```

The next macro provides three methods for the substitution of missing values in a string variable: (1) the mode, (2) a user-defined value, or (3) deletion of the record. To calculate the mode, we use the macro ModCat().

```
%macro SubCat(DSin, Xvar, Method, Value, DSout);
/*
Substitution of missing values in a nominal (String) variable
DSin:   input dataset
Xvar:   the string variable
Method: Method to be used:
1=Substitute mode
2=Substitute Value
3=Delete the record
Value:  Used with Method
DSout:  output dataset with the variable Xvar free of missing
        values
*/
/* Option 1: Substitute the Mode */
%if &Method=1 %then %do;
  /* calculate the mode using macro ModeCat */
      %let mode=;
%ModeCat(&DSin, &Xvar, Mode);
 /* substitute the mode whenever Xvar=missing */
 Data &DSout;
  Set &DSin;
   if &Xvar='' Then &Xvar="&mode";
  run;
    %end;
/* Option 2: Substitute a user-defined value */
%else %if &Method=2 %then %do;
 /* substitute the Value whenever Xvar=missing */
 Data &DSout;
  Set &DSin;
   if &Xvar='' Then &Xvar="&Value";
  run;
     %end;

/* Option 3: (anything else) delete the record */
%else %do;
 /* Delete record whenever Xvar=missing */
 Data &DSout;
  Set &DSin;
   if &Xvar='' Then delete;
  run;
   %end;
%mend;
```

The following sample code shows how to use the three methods.

```
data WithMiss;
length Gender $6.;
input ID Age Gender $ @@;
datalines;
```

```
 1    . Male      2  28 Male
 3   35 Male      4  27 Male
 5   41 Male      6  21 Female
 7   30 .         8   . Male
 9   28 Female   10  32 Male
11   38 Female   12  42 .
13   37 .        14  28 Female
15   38 Male     16  18 Male
17   46 Female   18   . Female
19   32 Male     20  27 Female
;
run;

/* Substitute the mode */
%let Dsin=WithMiss;
%let Xvar=Gender;
%let Method=1;
%let Value=;
%let DSout=Full_Mode;
%SubCat(&DSin, &Xvar, &Method, &Value, &DSout);

/* Substitute the value "Miss" */
%let Dsin=WithMiss;
%let Xvar=Gender;
%let Method=2;
%let Value=Miss;
%let DSout=Full_Value;
%SubCat(&DSin, &Xvar, &Method, &Value, &DSout);

/* Delete the record */
%let Dsin=WithMiss;
%let Xvar=Gender;
%let Method=3;
%let Value=;
%let DSout=Full_Del;
%SubCat(&DSin, &Xvar, &Method, &Value, &DSout);
```

11.2.2 CONTINUOUS AND ORDINAL VARIABLES

In the case of continuous variables, the options for substituting missing values are more than those for nominal variables. In this case the following are the options.

- The mean (only continuous)

- The median

- The mode

- Maximum value

- Minimum value

- Zero or any other user-defined value

Section 6.5 presented macro VarUnivar1(), which calculates all the univariate statistics of a continuous variable in a dataset. We will use this macro to calculate these statistics, and then use them to substitute for the missing values. In addition to the list of possible values, the macro allows the use of the values of the standard deviation, P1, P5, P10, P90, P95, P99, and it allows deletion of the record. All these options are accessible by defining the value of the parameter Method.

```
%macro SubCont(DSin, Xvar, Method, Value, DSout);
/* Calculate the univariate measures */
 %VarUnivar1(&DSin, &Xvar, Temp_univ);
/* Convert them into macro variables */
data _null_;
 set Temp_univ;
    Call symput('Mean'  ,Vmean);
Call symput('min'   ,VMin);
Call symput('max'   ,VMax);
Call symput('STD'   ,VStd);
Call symput('mode'  ,Vmode);
Call symput('median',Vmedian);
Call symput('P1'    ,VP1);
Call symput('P5'    ,VP5);
Call symput('P10'   ,VP10);
Call symput('P90'   ,VP90);
Call symput('P95'   ,VP95);
Call symput('P99'   ,VP99);
run;


/* Substitute the appropriate value using the
   specified option in the parameter 'Method' */
Data &DSout;
 set &DSin;
%if %upcase(&Method)=DELETE %then %do;
 if &Xvar=. then Delete;
  %end;
%else %do;
 if &Xvar=. then &Xvar=
   %if %upcase(&Method)=MEAN %then &mean;
   %if %upcase(&Method)=MIN %then &min;
   %if %upcase(&Method)=MAX %then &max;
   %if %upcase(&Method)=STD %then &std;
   %if %upcase(&Method)=MODE %then &mode;
   %if %upcase(&Method)=MEDIAN %then &median;
   %if %upcase(&Method)=P1 %then &p1;
   %if %upcase(&Method)=P5 %then &P5;
   %if %upcase(&Method)=P10 %then &P10;
```

```
    %if %upcase(&Method)=P90 %then &P90;
    %if %upcase(&Method)=P95 %then &P95;
    %if %upcase(&Method)=P99 %then &P99;
    %if %upcase(&Method)=VALUE %then &Value;
%end;
run;

/* Finally, clean the workspace */
proc datasets library=work nolist nodetails;
 delete temp_univ;
run; quit;
%mend;
```

The following code demonstrates the use of the macro with few options using the last dataset, WithMiss, for the continuous variable Age.

```
/* Use the mean */
%let DSin=WithMiss;
%let Xvar=Age;
%let Method=mean;
%let value=;
%let DSout=Full_mean;
%SubCont(&DSin, &Xvar, &Method,&value, &DSout);

/* Use the median */
%let DSin=WithMiss;
%let Xvar=Age;
%let Method=median;
%let value=;
%let DSout=Full_median;
%SubCont(&DSin, &Xvar, &Method,&value, &DSout);

/* Use a user-defined value */
%let DSin=WithMiss;
%let Xvar=Age;
%let Method=value;
%let value=25.8;
%let DSout=Full_value;
%SubCont(&DSin, &Xvar, &Method,&value, &DSout);

/* Delete the record */
%let DSin=WithMiss;
%let Xvar=Age;
%let Method=delete;
%let value=-560;
%let DSout=Full_del;
%SubCont(&DSin, &Xvar, &Method,&value, &DSout);
```

11.3 IMPUTING MISSING VALUES

We start this section by examining the most used method for data imputation: the regression method. Assume that we have five continuous variables: x_1, x_2, x_3, x_4, and x_5. Assume further that the variables x_1, x_2, x_3, and x_4 are all made of complete observations, that is, they do not contain missing values. Only variable x_5 contains some missing values. Additionally, we have business reasons to believe that there is a correlation between the variable x_5 and all the other variables x_1, x_2, x_3, x_4. An obvious way of inferring the missing values is to fit a regression model using x_5 as a dependent variable and the variables x_1, x_2, x_3, x_4 as independent variables, using all the nonmissing observations of the dataset. We then apply this model to the observations where x_5 is missing and predict those missing values. This process will yield one fitted value for each observation where x_5 is missing.

11.3.1 BASIC ISSUES IN MULTIPLE IMPUTATION

Multiple imputation methods add a twist on the preceding procedure. Instead of fitting only one regression model, we could generate several models by allowing the model parameters themselves to follow some probability distribution and add some random error to the fitted value. In this way, we *re-create* the original distribution from which the values of the variable x_5 were drawn. Therefore, we end up with *multiple imputed* values for each missing value of x_5. The number of these imputed values need not be large. In fact, it can be shown that only a small number of imputed values can lead to accurate results (Rubin 1987). In practice the number of imputed values is taken between 3 and 10.

Multiple imputation theory also provides the methods to perform statistical inference regarding the imputed variable, x_5 in our example, by combining the imputed values with the original nonmissing records.

The main features of multiple imputation can be summarized as follows.

- The imputation process is divided into three steps: (1) fitting a set of models that represent the nonmissing values of the variable in question, (2) using these models to impute several values for each missing value, and (3) combining these values to produce statistical inferences about the imputed variables.

- The final result of the imputation procedure is not one *best* or *better* estimate of the missing value, but rather a set of values representing the distribution from which this value was drawn.

- The focus of the procedure is to provide better estimates of the statistical properties of the variables with missing values.

The last feature strikes at the heart of the problem.

In data mining, we have two distinct procedures: modeling and scoring. During both of these procedures, we encounter missing values that we need to replace with something. Although the procedures MI and MIANALYZE of SAT/STAT do a good job of fitting the imputation models and combining them, the multiple imputation procedure just described leaves us with the following tasks and questions.

- We need to devise a method to combine the imputed values into *one appropriate* value to use.

- If we fit an imputation model using the modeling data, how do we replicate that model for the scoring data? Do we use the same fitted imputation models to score the scoring data and produce the imputed values, and then combine them? Or do we use the scoring data to fit new models, and use those instead to calculate the imputed values? And if the latter is the choice, does that mean that the relationship among variables in the scoring data is different from that among variables in the modeling data? Is that allowed?

- Some imputation models require the data to have a certain distribution of their missing values, their *missingness pattern*. How do we guarantee that this pattern will be the same in both the modeling and scoring datasets?

Now that we have asked the difficult questions, let us address the easy ones: What models are there in PROC MI? What are their assumptions? How do we make the best of them? Let us start with some background about the patterns of missing values, or *missingness patterns*.

11.3.2   PATTERNS OF MISSINGNESS

There are three types of missing data patterns: (1) monotone missing data pattern, (2) non-monotone missing data pattern, and (3) arbitrary missing data pattern.

Consider a set of variables, $V_1, V_2, \ldots, V_n$, with some missing values across the different records. If we consider the variables in this strict order $(V_1, \ldots, V_n)$, then these variables are said to have a *monotone missing data pattern* if, in all records where the value of the variable V_i is missing, the values of the variables V_j, $j > i$ are all missing. If this condition does not apply, the pattern of missing data is called *non-monotone*. Finally, if we do not observe or we ignore the pattern of the missing data, we say that the dataset has an *arbitrary* missing data pattern. Note that the term *data with an arbitrary missing pattern* refers to a position taken by the analyst and not an actual state of the data.

Let us demonstrate these definitions using an example of the five variables $x_1, \cdots, x_5$. The values of these five variables are shown in Table 11.1, which shows that the fourth record contains missing values for variables x_1, x_2, and x_3 but nonmissing values for both x_4 and x_5. Therefore, this dataset has a non-monotone missing data pattern. However, we can reorder the variables, as shown in Table 11.2, where the data has a monotone missing pattern.

When working with PROC MI of SAS/STAT, one has more flexibility in selecting the imputation method. Therefore, starting with a dataset with a non-monotone missing pattern, it is desirable to attempt to convert it to have a monotone pattern. This may

Table 11.1   Five variables with missing values.

Record	x_1	x_2	x_3	x_4	x_5
1	.	.	.	.	.
2	13	10	18	12	13
3	18	16	12	12	11
4	.	.	.	12	4
5	18	7	5	16	11
6	1	17	6	19	4
7	.	.	.	.	7
8	.	8	.	13	11
9	14	8	.	16	18
10	.	.	.	9	7

Table 11.2   Reordered five variables with missing values.

Record	x_5	x_4	x_2	x_1	x_3
1	.	.	.	.	.
2	13	12	10	13	18
3	11	12	16	18	12
4	4	12	.	.	.
5	11	16	7	18	5
6	4	19	17	1	6
7	7	.	.	.	.
8	11	13	8	.	.
9	18	16	8	14	.
10	7	9	.	.	.

be possible by simply reordering the variables, but this is not always guaranteed to succeed. In this case, we can impute just enough values to make the missing pattern monotone, and then apply one of the methods of monotone pattern. We will adopt this two-stage methodology to impute missing values.

11.4 IMPUTATION METHODS AND STRATEGY

We now take a look at the imputation methods available in PROC MI of SAS/STAT (version 9.1). The methods that PROC MI offers depend on the type of the imputed variable as well as on the pattern of missing values. Table 11.3 summarizes these methods.

Table 11.3 shows that when the missing pattern is monotone, PROC MI offers more flexibility in the choice of algorithm to use, especially for imputing continuous variables. We do not go into the details of the theory behind different methods because the SAS online documentation covers them in full. Additional details on algorithms of multiple imputation can also be found in Rubin (1987) and Schafer (1997).

Table 11.3 Imputation methods available in PROC MI.

Pattern of missingness	Type of imputed variable	Recommended methods
Monotone	Continuous	Regression Predicted mean matching Propensity score
Monotone	Ordinal	Logistic regression
Monotone	Nominal	Discriminant function method
Arbitrary	Continuous	MCMC full-data imputation MCMC monotone-data imputation

Before presenting our imputation scheme, we make the following comments:

- The MCMC (Markov Chain Monte Carlo) method can impute missing values for continuous variables to make the pattern monotone. There is no similar option for either nominal or ordinal variables at the moment in PROC MI. Therefore, when the pattern of missing data in a set of nominal variables is not monotone, we can only attempt to either reorder the variables, in hopes that this would reveal that they are monotone, or replace some values with known values (such as the mode) and test the missingness pattern again.

- The default method for imputing a continuous variable is regression.

- When imputing continuous variables, we can specify several interaction or nonlinear terms to be used during the imputation process. This is a big advantage that often leads to better results. Although the exact nonlinear form that will lead to such improvement is not known in advance, typical interaction and second-order terms of continuous variables usually lead to some improvement.

Now, our general imputation strategy is to attempt to make the missing pattern monotone by rearranging the variables. If that does not work, we resort to the MCMC method to impute enough observations to make the pattern monotone. But, as shown in Table 11.3, this option is available only for continuous variables. Therefore, when the rearranged variables contain ordinal or nominal variables and the missing pattern is not monotone, we have to deal with ordinal and nominal variables separately. We can summarize this process in the following steps.

1. Given the list of variables that are believed to be related to each other and that contain missing values, we first identify the pattern of missingness with the current order of variables.

2. If the missingness pattern is not monotone, we attempt to arrange the variables to make it monotone.

3. If the rearranged variables still do not have a monotone missing pattern, we separate the continuous variables from the others and use MCMC to make them follow a monotone pattern, and then we use one of the methods of continuous variable imputation to impute *all* the continuous variables and combine the imputed variables to form *one* set with *nonmissing* continuous variables.

4. Now that all the continuous variables have nonmissing values, we add the nominal and ordinal variables and check again whether we could arrange the variables to form a set with a monotone missing pattern.

5. If the resulting set still does not have a monotone pattern, we treat each group of nominal or ordinal variables using a separate imputation model.

Figure 11.1 shows schematically these steps as a comprehensive process that could be adopted to impute the missing values.

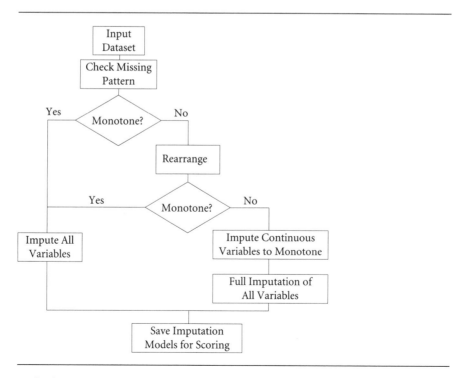

Figure 11.1   Multiple imputation strategy.

Implementing this process with a large number of variables is not a trivial task. However, in most practical cases with large number of variables, we are usually able to divide the variables into a number of smaller groups of variables. Each group usually contains 5 to 10 variables. The groups are usually formed by considering the meaning of the variables and the likely interdependence or correlation between them. In cases where we do not have enough insight into the problem domain, we may resort to calculating the correlation matrix among all the variables and using its entries to divide the variables into smaller sets of correlated variables. The application of the preceding process to each of these groups then becomes a much easier task.

The last issue we need to consider in planning our imputation strategy is how to deal with the fact that we are dealing with not one but at least two datasets: the modeling and scoring views. This setting poses an important question: If we impute the values of the modeling view, how do we use the same set of models to impute similar values for the scoring view?

To address this issue, we have to make the following assumption: The missing data pattern observed in the modeling dataset is identical to that in the scoring dataset.

Using this assumption, we have all the freedom to find the most suitable arrangement to impute the missing values in the modeling dataset. We then translate that into a simple model to use for replacing the missing values in the scoring dataset. This approach is very practical because most real-life scoring datasets have a large number of records; therefore, they require simple and efficient algorithms. We will use a logistic regression model to impute values of nominal and ordinal variables and a linear regression model to impute values of continuous variables.

Considering the previously listed steps of implementing multiple imputation, we note that we need macros to achieve the following tasks.

1. A macro to extract the pattern of missing values given a dataset and a list of variables in a certain order.

2. A macro to rearrange a list of variables such that their pattern of missing values becomes either monotone or as close as possible to monotone pattern. The inputs to this macro will be the initial order of these variables and their initial missing data pattern.

3. A macro to check that a given pattern of missing values is monotone.

4. A macro to apply the MCMC method to a set of continuous variables to impute just enough values to give them a monotone missing pattern.

5. A macro to impute a set of continuous variables with a monotone missing pattern.

6. A macro to combine the results of imputation of a set of continuous variables into one complete dataset.

7. A macro to apply the logistic regression method to impute one nominal or ordinal variable using a set of nonmissing variables (of any type).

8. A macro to combine the imputed values of ordinal or nominal variables.

9. A macro to use the results of imputation of a modeling view to extract a model that can be used to substitute missing values for a scoring dataset. This model will be a simple linear regression model for continuous variables and a logistic regression model for ordinal and nominal variables.

11.5 SAS MACROS FOR MULTIPLE IMPUTATION

11.5.1 EXTRACTING THE PATTERN OF MISSING VALUES

The first macro we present extracts the pattern of missing values of a set of variables in a dataset. The variables are given as an ordered list. We should note that PROC MI extracts such a pattern, but it does not provide an easy way to output that pattern into a dataset for further processing.

The macro works by counting the number of variables in the list and generating all missing patterns that could be present in a list of such length (see Table 11.4). It then tests the presence of all of these patterns and eliminates all but those that prove to be present in the data. The number of such combinations increases rapidly with the number of variables in the list. The exact number of these combinations is 2^n where n is the number of variables in the list. For example, if we have a list of 10 variables, we would be testing 1028 patterns. However, the implementation is a simple set of IF-THEN rules, which makes it fast for most practical cases with 10 to 15 variables in one list.

Table 11.4   Parameters of macro MissPatt().

Header	MissPatt(DSin, VarList, MissPat);	
Parameter	*Description*	
DSin	Input dataset	
VarList	List of variables in the given order	
MissPat	Output dataset with the pattern of missing values	

Step 1
First count the variables and store their names in macro variables.

```
%let i=1;
%let condition = 0;
%do %until (&condition =1);
   %let Var&i=%scan(&VarList,&i);
   %if "&&Var&i" ="" %then %let condition =1;
   %else     %let i = %Eval(&i+1);
%end;
%let Nvars=%eval(&i-1);
```

Step 2

Read one observation at a time, obtain the variable types, and store them in the macro variables T1, ... TNvars.

```
Data _Null_;
 set &DSin (Obs=1);
 %do i=1 %to &Nvars;
  call symput("T&i", VType(&&Var&i));
 %end;
run;
```

Step 3

Now that we have Nvars variables, the number of possible patterns is 2^{Nvars}. Therefore, construct a dataset to contain these patterns. This dataset will be the output of the macro MissPatt(). Create it first using PROC SQL.

```
proc sql noprint;
 create table &MissPat ( %do i=1 %to &Nvars;
                           &&Var&i  num,
                         %end;
                         PatNo num);
quit;
```

Step 4

To facilitate finding the patterns, enumerate the 2^{Nvars} patterns such that they all fit into just one loop. First generate all possible patterns, store them in a dataset, use them to build testing conditions, and then search for these conditions in the input dataset.

To generate the patterns, observe that for the first variable, we need two rows: a row with all 1's and a second row with a 0 in the first variable. For the second variable, we need to copy the two rows of the first variable and replace the 1 for the second variable with 0. We then repeat this process for all the other variables. Therefore, for variable *i*, we insert $2^{(i-1)}$ rows and replace the ith location with 0 for the variable *i*. In the implementaton, we use the variable PatNo as temporary storage for the variable index i for replacement.

```
proc SQL noprint;
/* first row, insert all X's and PatNo=0 */
 insert into &MissPat values (%do i=1 %to &Nvars;
                               1,
                              %end;
                               0);
quit;
```

```
/* then start the loop on the variables */
%do i=1 %to &Nvars;
  /* select all the rows to a temporary table,
  change Var&i to zero and set PatNo to i */
  data temp;
    set &MissPat;
    &&Var&i =0;
    PatNo=&i;
  run;

  /* Append &MissPat with the temp dataset */
  data &MissPat;
    set &MissPat temp;
  run;
%end;

/* finally, we renumber the patterns from 1 to 2^Nvars,
  and create a new field called Present */
data &MissPat;
 set &MissPat;
  PatNo= _N_;
  Present =0;
 run;
```

Step 5

Now confirm that these patterns really exist in the dataset DSin. Loop on these patterns, extract the equivalent condition of the missing pattern, and then mark that pattern as present in the data (in the Present field).

```
/* Number of patterns */
%let NPats=%sysevalf(2**&Nvars);

%do ipat=1 %to &Npats;
  /* extract the condition by extracting the values
     of the variables */
 proc sql noprint;
  select %do i=1 %to &Nvars;  &&Var&i , %end; PatNo
    into %do i=1 %to &Nvars; :V&i, %end; :P
          from &MissPat where PatNo=&ipat;
 quit;
```

Step 6

Compile the condition and shape it depending on the variable type N or C.

```
%let Cond=;
%do i=1 %to &Nvars;
 %if (&i>1) %then %let Cond=&Cond and;
   %if &&V&i=0 %then %do;
     %if &&T&i=C %then     /* String C */
           %let Cond=&Cond &&Var&i = '';
     %if &&T&i=N %then     /* Numeric N */
           %let Cond=&Cond &&Var&i=. ;
                       %end;
   %else %do;
     %if &&T&i=C %then
           %let Cond=&Cond &&Var&i ne '';
     %if &&T&i=N %then
           %let Cond=&Cond &&Var&i ne . ;
         %end;
   %end;
```

Step 7

Now, read the records from the dataset and check whether the condition exists. If it exists in the dataset, mark the record by setting Present=1. This concludes the pattern loop.

```
%let Nc=0;
  data _null_;
    set &Dsin;
      IF &Cond then do;
         call symput('Nc',1);
        stop;
                  end;
  run;

    %if &Nc=1 %then %do;
    proc sql noprint;
       update &MissPat set Present=1 where PatNo=&ipat;
    quit;
                  %end;

%end;  /* End of the pattern loop */
```

Step 8

Now that all the Present flags have been updated, remove all patterns but those with Present=1, and drop all PatNo and Present variables from the dataset MissPat.

```
data &MissPat;
 set &MissPat;
 if Present =0 then delete;
```

```
  drop Present PatNo;
run;
```

Step 9
Clean the workspace and finish the macro.

```
proc datasets library =work nodetails nolist;
 delete temp;
run; quit;

%mend;
```

The following code demonstrates the use of the macro MissPatt() in a simple case.

```
data test;
 input x1 x2 x3 x4$ x5;
 datalines;
 . 1  . Abc 1
 . 1  1 .   1
 1 .  1 B   .
 . 1  . C   1
 . 1  1 .   1
 1 .  1 D   1
 . 1  . E   1
 . 1  . .   1
 1 .  1 F   1
 . 1  . A   .
 . 1  1 .   1
 1 .  . A   1
 . 1  . A   1
 . 1  1 .   1
 1 .  . DD  .
 ;
run;

%let DSin=test;
%let VarList=x1 x2 x3 x4 x5;
%let MissPat=MP;
%MissPatt(&DSin, &VarList, &MissPat)

proc print data=mp;
run;
```

The SAS output window should display the contents of the dataset MP, as shown in Table 11.5, where each observation in the dataset now represents an existing missing data pattern. The table shows that this dataset has a non-monotone missing pattern.

Table 11.5   The dataset MP as calculated by macro `MissPatt()`.

Obs	x1	x2	x3	x4	x5
1	1	0	1	1	1
2	0	1	0	1	1
3	1	0	0	1	1
4	0	1	1	0	1
5	0	1	0	0	1
6	1	0	1	1	0
7	0	1	0	1	0
8	1	0	0	1	0

11.5.2   REORDERING VARIABLES

Given a list of variables in a certain order along with their missing patterns, this macro attempts to reorder these variables such that they have either a monotone missing pattern or as close to a monotone pattern as possible. This macro should be used before attempting to impute values to facilitate the use of the different methods for datasets with monotone missing patterns. It requires the invocation of the macro `MissPatt()` of Section 11.5.1 to calculate the missing pattern dataset.

The macro works by reordering the columns of the missing pattern dataset, and not the actual dataset, such that the resulting pattern is monotone. A monotone pattern will be achieved if the columns are such that their sum is in decreasing order from left to right. A true monotone pattern also has the sum of the rows in increasing order from top to bottom. And this is exactly the algorithm used in this macro (see Table 11.6). The macro, however, cannot guarantee that the resulting order would be a monotone missing pattern because such patterns may not exist.

Table 11.6   Parameters of macro `ReMissPat()`.

Header	ReMissPat(VListIn, MissIn, MissOut, M_VListOut);
Parameter	*Description*
VListIn	Input list of variables
MissIn	Input missing pattern dataset
MissOut	Output missing pattern dataset
M_VListOut	Output list of variables in the new order

Step 1

Start by extracting the variable names from the input variable list `VlistIn` and count their number.

```
%let i=1;
%let condition = 0;
%do %until (&condition =1);
  %let Var&i=%scan(&VListIn,&i);
  %if "&&Var&i" ="" %then %let condition =1;
  %else   %let i = %Eval(&i+1);
%end;
%let Nvars=%eval(&i-1);
```

Step 2

Now we have Nvars variables. Create the first sum of the missing pattern matrix in each record to use it later in sorting. Assume that the missing pattern dataset contains at least one variable. That simplifies the code and starts the summation loop from the index 2. Then use this summation variable to sort the rows in descending order.

```
/* create the summation variable _Total_V. */
data Temp_MP;
  set &MissIn;
   _Total_V=sum(&Var1
     %do i=2 %to &Nvars;
     , &&Var&i
     %end;);
run;
/* Sort using the row totals,
   and then drop the field _Total_V.*/
proc sort data=Temp_mp;
 by descending _total_v;
run;
Data Temp_MP;
 set Temp_MP;
 drop _Total_V;
run;
```

Step 3

Transpose the missing pattern to prepare for sorting using the column sum.

```
proc transpose data=Temp_mp out=Temp_mpt Prefix=P;
 run;
```

Step 4

Similar to the case of the rows, find the summation of the original columns and sort on that summation variable and then drop it.

```
data temp_mpt;
 set temp_mpt;
 _total_P=sum (P1 %do i=2 %to &Nvars; , p&i  %end; );
```

```
     _index=_N_;
run;

proc sort data=temp_mpt;
 by descending _total_p;
run;
data temp_MPT;
 set temP_MPT;
 drop _total_P;
run;
```

Step 5
In preparation for the final extraction of the new variable order, transpose the missing pattern to its original orientation again.

```
proc transpose data=temp_mpt out=temp_mptt prefix=v;
run;
```

Step 6
By now, the dataset temp_mptt should contain the closest pattern to a monotone as possible, with the last row containing the order of variables that leads to that pattern. Therefore, extract the new order from the variable names stored in the macro variables $v_1, \ldots, v_{Nvars}$ and compile the output list.

```
proc sql noprint;
 select v1
   %do i=1 %to &Nvars;
     , v&i
   %end;
   into     :P1
        %do i=1 %to &Nvars;
          , :P&i
        %end;
     from temp_mptt
       where _Name_ ='_index';
quit;
```

Step 7
In case some of the variables did not exist in the missing pattern, remove all rows containing missing values in the resulting new missing pattern. Also delete unnecessary rows that were used in the calculations.

```
data &MissOut;
  set temp_Mptt;
  if _Name_='_index' then delete;
/* delete missing rows */
  %do i=1 %to &Nvars;
```

```
      if v&i = . then delete;
   %end;
   drop _Name_;
run;
```

Step 8

We can now restore the names of the original variables and compile the output variable list in the new order.

```
data &MissOut (Rename =
                 (%do i=1 %to &Nvars;
                  %let j=&&P&i;
                  V&i=&&Var&j
                  %end;)
                           );
 set &Missout;
run;

%let ListOut=;
%do i=1 %to &Nvars;
  %let j=&&P&i;
  %let ListOut= &ListOut &&Var&j;
%end;
%let &M_VListOut=&ListOut;
```

Step 9

Clean the workspace and finish the macro.

```
proc datasets library=work nodetails nolist;
delete temp_mp temp_mpt temp_mptt;
quit;
%mend;
```

The following code continues from the sample code in Section 11.5.1 to demonstrate the use of the macro ReMisspat.

```
%let LOut=;
%let Lin= x1 x2 x3 x4 x5;
%let Missin=MP;
%let MissOut=Re_MP;

%ReMissPat(&Lin, &MissIn, &MissOut, Lout);
%put Output List = &Lout;
```

The %put statement at the end of the code will display the following line in the SAS Log:

```
Output List = x4 x5 x1 x3 x2
```

Table 11.7   The dataset Re_MP as calculated by macro ReMissPat().

Obs	x4	x5	x1	x3	x2
1	1	1	1	1	0
2	1	1	0	0	1
3	1	1	1	0	0
4	0	1	0	1	1
5	1	0	1	1	0
6	0	1	0	0	1
7	1	0	0	0	1
8	1	0	1	0	0

In addition, the new dataset representing the pattern of missing values, Re_MP, will be as shown in Table 11.7. The table shows that these variables are now closer to having a monotone missing pattern, but the dataset could not be made completely monotone.

11.5.3 CHECKING MISSING PATTERN STATUS

This macro checks whether a given missing pattern is monotone or not. We achieve that by applying the definition of a monotone missing pattern. Recall that for a missing pattern to be monotone, we require that, in any given observation, if a variable in the variable list is missing, then all subsequent variables in that list are also missing. To prove that a pattern is monotone is not a simple task. But to prove that it is *not* is relatively easy. All we need to find is *one* record that violates the definition. This is how this macro works.

We check the rows of the missing pattern dataset and loop over the variables in order. If any variable has a missing value in that pattern, then we check if any of the subsequent variables is *not* missing. When this condition is satisfied, the missing pattern is non-monotone. If we cannot find violations to the definition, the dataset is monotone.

The following are the details of macro Check Mono() (see Table 11.8).

Table 11.8   Parameters of macro CheckMono().

Header	CheckMono(MissPat, VarList, M_Result);
Parameter	*Description*
MissPat	Input missing pattern dataset
VarList	Input variable list
M_Result	Output result

Step 1

Load the variable names into macro variables, count them, and count the number of the missing patterns.

```
%let i=1;
%let condition = 0;
%do %until (&condition =1);
   %let Var&i=%scan(&VarList,&i);
   %if "&&Var&i" ="" %then %let condition =1;
   %else    %let i = %Eval(&i+1);
%end;
%let Nvars=%eval(&i-1);

/* add a pattern number variable
   and count the patterns. */
data temp_MP;
 set &MissPat;
 _PatNo=_N_;
 call symput ('Np', trim(_N_));
run;
```

Step 2

Assume that the pattern is monotone.

```
%let Mono=1;   /*  The default assumption */
```

Step 3

Loop over the patterns, extract the values of the pattern flags corresponding to each of the variables, and store them in macro variables.

```
/* Pattern loop */
%do ipat=1 %to &Np;
 proc sql noprint;
   select &Var1 %do i=2 %to &Nvars;
               , &&Var&i
               %end;
        INTO  :P1 %do i=2 %to &Nvars;
                     , :P&i
                %end;
     FROM temp_MP where _PatNo=&ipat;
  quit;
```

Step 4

Check the assumption of monotone missingness for each pattern by finding the first variable that has a zero in that pattern. If a zero is found, then attempt to find a subsequent variable with a one in the same pattern. If a one is found, then this pattern violates the monotone pattern assumption and we reset the status flag Mono.

```
/* Find the lowest index jmin
   with a zero in the pattern */
%let jmin=%eval(&Nvars+1);
%do i=1 %to &Nvars;
 %if (&&P&i = 0) %then %do;
     %if (&jmin > &i) %then %let jmin = &i;
                   %end;
%end;
/* jmin should be smaller than Nvars */
%if &jmin < &Nvars %then %do;
 /* Search for any value of 1 above this index */
  %do i=%eval(&jmin+1) %to &Nvars;
    %if (&&P&i =1) %then %let Mono=0; /* Violation */
  %end;
                   %end;
```

Step 5
Finish the pattern loop and store the result in the output macro parameter M_Result.

```
%end;/* end of pattern loop */
%let &M_Result=%trim(&mono);
```

Step 6
Clean the workspace and finish the macro.

```
proc datasets library=work nodetails nolist;
delete temp_mp;
quit;
%mend;
```

The following code shows how to use the macro CheckMono(). The output macro variable M_Result will return a value of one if the pattern is monotone and a value of zero otherwise. The code generates an artificial simple pattern for five variables.

```
data Miss;
input x1 x2 x3 x4 x5;
datalines;
0 0 0 0 0
1 1 1 1 0
1 1 1 1 1
1 0 0 0 0
1 1 0 0 0
1 1 1 0 0
```

```
;
run;

%let VarList=x1 x2 x3 x4 x5;
%let MissPat=Miss;
%let Result=;

%CheckMono(&MissPat, &VarList, Result);
%put &Result;
```

11.5.4 IMPUTING TO A MONOTONE MISSING PATTERN

This macro wraps PROC MI to implement the MCMC method to impute just enough missing values for the input dataset to have a monotone missing pattern. It is valid only for the imputation of continuous variables. Before we proceed to the implementation of the macro, we discuss two key parameters of PROC MI, namely, the number of imputed values for each missing value and the random seed.

The number of imputations performed by PROC MI is determined by the parameter NIMPUTE. Its default value is 5. For most datasets, the number of imputations should be between 3 and 10. If we denote the value of the NIMPUTE parameter by m, and the number of records in the original dataset by N, then the resulting dataset with the imputed values will have mN records. In cases of very large datasets, we may be forced to use lower values of NIMPUTE (e.g., 3); with smaller datasets we could use larger values (e.g., 10). In the following macro, we use the default value of 5.

In addition, PROC MI uses a random seed to implement the random variants in the different algorithms. One should always set the SEED parameter to a fixed value (e.g., 1000) to guarantee the repeatability of the results.

```
%macro MakeMono(DSin, VarList, DSout);
proc mi data=&DSin nimpute=5 seed=1000 out=&DSout noprint;
 mcmc impute=monotone;
 var &VarList;
 run;
%mend;
```

The output of the macro MakeMono() is the output dataset DSout containing five new imputed values for each missing value such that the new pattern of missing values is monotone. A variable, called _Imputation_, is added to the dataset, indicating the imputation index (from 1 to 5 in this case). Further invocation of PROC MI should include a BY statement, as follows:

```
BY _Imputation_;
```

This will guarantee that PROC MI uses all the imputed values to estimate the new final imputed values for the variables included in the variable list VarList.

11.5.5 IMPUTING CONTINUOUS VARIABLES

PROC MI offers the following four methods for imputing missing values of continuous variables.

1. Regression (monotone)

2. Predicted mean matching (monotone)

3. Propensity scores (monotone)

4. Markov Chain Monte Carlo (arbitrary)

The first three methods are available only for datasets with the monotone missing pattern, and the MCMC method is available for the arbitrary missing pattern. We have adopted the strategy of converting the missing pattern to a monotone pattern before the full imputation.

Implementing PROC MI to impute the missing values of a set of continuous variables is straightforward. Therefore, our macro is a wrapper of PROC MI. The only consideration is that, as discussed in Section 11.4, we need to keep in mind that we are not interested only in imputing the missing values (and combining them somehow to replace the missing values), but also in fitting a model that could be applied to the scoring data. The method that best meets these requirements is the regression method.

The regression method of PROC MI attempts to fit a linear model to predict the values of the variable in question in terms of the other variables with nonmissing values. Hence, it is subject to all the limitations of linear models and their assumptions. The linearity assumptions could be relaxed sometimes by the introduction of *interaction terms*. For example, if we attempt to fit the values of the variable y in terms of the variables x_1, x_2, x_3, x_4, the standard linear model would fit the following equation:

$$y = a_1 x_1 + a_2 x_2 + a_3 x_3 + a_4 x_4. \tag{11.1}$$

This model may not represent all possible nonlinear relationships between the variable y and x_1, x_2, x_3, x_4. Therefore, we attempt to improve the model by fitting the values of y to the following more complex form:

$$\begin{aligned} y = {} & a_1 x_1 + a_2 x_2 + a_3 x_3 + a_4 x_4 \\ & + b_1 x_1^2 + b_2 x_2^2 + b_3 x_3^2 + b_4 x_4^2 \\ & + c_{12} x_1 x_2 + c_{13} x_1 x_3 + c_{14} x_1 x_4 + c_{23} x_2 x_3 + c_{24} x_2 x_4 + c_{34} x_3 x_4. \end{aligned} \tag{11.2}$$

In this last model, the equation of y includes all possible second-order terms of the variables x_1, x_2, x_3, x_4. The term *interaction terms* is usually reserved for the terms on the third line of Equation 11.2.

Chapter 9 introduced a macro for the automatic generation of such interaction terms and for calculating them as new variables in a dataset. PROC MI allows the specification of such interaction terms *during modeling*. This means that the variables are not actually stored in a dataset, but generated on the fly while modeling. Although this approach saves the disk space used to store the additional variables in these datasets, we prefer to generate these interaction terms explicitly as new variables in an intermediate dataset and include them in the imputation model. This facilitates the imputation of missing values during scoring.

Adopting this approach for the generation of interaction terms makes the implementation of PROC MI a simple task. The following macro wraps PROC MI to impute a set of continuous variables with monotone missing pattern using the regression method. To use this macro for both cases of direct imputation, or imputation after making the dataset have a monotone missing pattern using partial imputation, implement a set of %if conditions. These conditions impute only one set of values using the (BY _Imputation_;) command in the case of a dataset that has been processed by macro MakeMono() of Section 11.5.4.

If the input variable IfMono is set to N, five imputed values will be generated for each missing value of the variable specified in the MonoCMD variable. The format of the MonoCMD command describes the MONOTONE statement of PROC MI, as in the following example:

```
MONOTONE REG (Y = X1 X2 X3 M_X1_X3);
```

In the preceding code, the variable Y will be imputed in terms of the variables X1, X2, X3, and M_X1_X3. The MonoCMD variable may contain many such commands separated by semicolons. For example, we can define the variable MonoCMD as follows:

```
%let MonoCMD= MONOTONE REG (Y1 = X1 X2 X3 M_X1_X3) %str(;)
MONOTONE REG (Y2 = X1 X2 X3 M_X1_X3) %str(;)
MONOTONE REG (Y3 = X1 X2 X3 M_X1_X3) %str(;) ;
```

The function %str() has been used to write a semicolon in the macro variable MonoCMD without terminating it prematurely. The command will generate three imputation models for the variables Y1, Y2, and Y3.

```
%macro ImpReg(DSin, VarList, MonoCMD, IFMono, NImp, DSout);
/*
 Imputing a set of variables using regression models.
 The variables are assumed to have a monotone missing pattern.
 The variable MonoCMD contains the details of the monotone
 command. The IFMono (Y/N) indicates whether the input
 dataset has been made monotone using the MCMC method before,
 and, therefore, contains the variable _Imputation_,
 which then should be used in the BY statement.
 Also, if the variable _Imputation_ exists, we impute
 only 1 value, and in this case the parameter Nimp is
 ignored (but must be specified in the macro call).
*/
 proc mi data=&DSin
        seed=1000  out=&DSout noprint
```

```
nimpute=%if %upcase(&IfMono)=Y %then 1;
        %else &Nimp   ;
   ;
&MonoCMD;
var &VarList;
%If %upcase(&IfMono)=Y %then by _Imputation_;;
 run;
%mend;
```

As in previous PROC MI implementations, we specified the seed, using SEED=1000, to guarantee the repeatability of the results of different runs. The specification of the seed number is arbitrary; any integer value could be used.

11.5.6   COMBINING IMPUTED VALUES OF CONTINUOUS VARIABLES

Now that we have imputed a few values for each missing value, we need to combine them into one dataset to use in either modeling or scoring. In the case of continuous variables, we could use the average of the imputed values as the estimate of the missing value. The imputed values for each missing value are labeled using the automatic variable _Imputation_. The following macro performs this averaging for one continuous variable in a dataset.

In this macro, the variable _Imputation_ is termed the *imputation index* variable because it defines the label for the imputation set. The macro requires the definition of a unique identification variable, IDVar. This should not be a problem because all datasets used in practical data mining applications have a unique identifier, as discussed in Section 1.3.

The macro AvgImp() works by rolling up the imputed values and finding the average value of the variable in question, as shown in Figure 11.2.

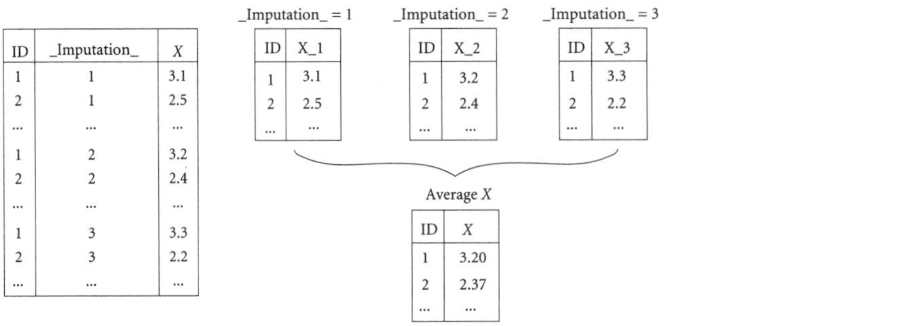

Figure 11.2   Combining imputed values for a continuous variable.

Table 11.9   Parameters of macro AvgImp().

Header	AvgImp(DSin, Nimp, IDVar, IDImp, Xvar, DSout)
Parameter	Description
DSin	Input dataset
Nimp	Number of imputed values
IDVar	Unique ID variable
IDImp	Variable used to label imputations
XVar	Imputed variable
DSout	Output dataset with the average of imputed values

Step 1
Roll up the different imputed values into separate datasets named Temp_1, Temp_2, and so on. Each of these datasets contains the imputed values of the variable XVar in a new variable using a suitable subscript. Sort each dataset by the unique data identifier IDVar.

```
%do i=1 %to &nimp;
Data temp_&i;
  set &dsin;
  if &IDImp=&i;
  x_&i=&Xvar;
  keep &Xvar._&i &IDvar;
run;
    proc sort data=temp_&i;
    by &IDvar;
    run;
%end;
```

Step 2
Merge the datasets Temp_1, Temp_2, ... to a single dataset using the ID variable IDVar.

```
    data temp_all;
     merge %do i=1 %to &Nimp; temp_&i %end; ;
by &IDvar;
    run;
```

Step 3
The output dataset should contain the average of all the imputed values merged from the rollup datasets.

```
  Data &DSout;
   set temp_all;
```

```
&Xvar =MEAN( x_1 %do i=2 %to &Nimp; , x_&i %end;) ;
keep &IDvar &Xvar;
   run;
```

Step 4

Clean the workspace and finish the macro.

```
proc datasets library=work nolist nodetails;
delete temp_all %do i=1 %to &Nimp; temp_&i %end; ;
run; quit;
%mend;
```

The following code shows how to use the preceding macro. The dataset Test simulates the imputed values by creating the variable _Imputation_ directly. As the macro syntax shows, we do not need to keep the default name of this variable, but it is recommended that we keep it unchanged because other SAS procedures, such as PROC MIANALYZE, use this variable for summary statistics.

```
data test;
 input _Imputation_  ID X;
 datalines;
1 1 2  1 2 3  1 3 5  1 4 7
2 1 3  2 2 5  2 3 5  2 4 7
3 1 4  3 2 9  3 3 5  3 4 7
;
run;
options mprint;
%let nimp=3;
%let dsin=test;
%let IDImp=_Imputation_;
%let IDVar=id;
%let Xvar=x;
%let DSout=out;
%AvgImp(&DSin, &Nimp, &IDvar, &IDImp, &xvar, &dsout);
```

Note on Using the Average

Could we have used a summary statistic other than the average—for example, the mode or the median? The answer comes from the theory of the imputation itself. The theory does not attempt to create *one* new value to replace the unknown missing value. It provides a set of values that represent the *distribution* from which the unknown value came. It is up to us to extract from this distribution what we need. Because we only need one value, we may use the average as the best unbiased estimate. In addition, in view of the small number of imputed values, fewer than 10 in general, there should not be a large difference between the average and the median. PROC MIANALYZE uses *all* the imputed values to accurately calculate univariate statistics of the *entire* dataset, with the imputed values included.

11.5.7 IMPUTING NOMINAL AND ORDINAL VARIABLES

Table 11.3 earlier in this chapter showed that PROC MI implements logistic regression for imputing ordinal variables. It also shows that imputing nominal variables could be achieved by the discriminant function method. In the case of binary nominal variables only, logistic regression could also be used for nominal variables. In both cases, PROC MI requires a CLASS statement with the variable(s) being modeled as nominal or ordinal variables. Also, in both cases, PROC MI requires a monotone missing values pattern.

It is known that logistic regression, as well as discriminant function, models perform better when all the predictors are continuous. In addition, our imputation strategy relies on imputing all the missing values of the continuous variables first. In view of this, we assume that all the predictors in the imputation of nominal and ordinal variables are continuous and have no missing values.

In this case, the imputation of ordinal and nominal variables is reduced to wrapping PROC MI, as in the following macro.

```
%macro NORDImp(DSin, Nimp, Method,CVar, VarList,DSout);
/* Imputing Nominal and Ordinal variables
  DSin:    input dataset.
  DSout:   output dataset.
  Nimp:    Number of imputations
  Method:  either Logistic or Discrim
  CVAr:    variable to be imputed. If CVar is ordinal,
           only logistic method could be used. If CVar is
           nominal and binary, both Logistic and Discrim
           methods could be used. If CVar is nominal and NOT
           binary, then only Discrim method could be used.
  VarList: list of NONMISSING variables to be used as
           predictors in the imputation models.
*/
proc mi data=&DSin out=&DSout nimpute=&Nimp seed=1000 noprint;
  class &CVar;
  monotone &Method (&Cvar);
  var &VarList &Cvar;
  run;
%mend;
```

11.5.8 COMBINING IMPUTED VALUES OF ORDINAL AND NOMINAL VARIABLES

Imputed values for *ordinal* variables could be combined in a similar fashion to that of continuous variables, that is, by taking averages. However, unlike continuous values, ordinal variables, although preserving order relationship, admit a certain finite set of values. Therefore, the use of the average is inappropriate, because it will render new values that may not exist in the original categories. We could select an existing value that is nearest to the computed mean value or select the *median* and require that the number of imputed values be odd to guarantee that the median value will always be one of the original values. The macro AvgImp(), described in Section 11.5.6, could be modified by changing the function in step 3 from MEAN to MEDIAN.

The case of *nominal* variables is a bit more complex. The logical option is to substitute the *mode*, the most frequent value, from the imputed values for each missing value. Writing a macro to find the mode of a set of values is straightforward. (Review Section 5.6.) Unfortunately, the computational cost of implementing such a scheme is not acceptable in most cases.

For example, consider the case where we have a scoring dataset of one million records with one nominal variable of which only 5% of the values are missing (i.e., 50,000 missing values). And assume that we imputed five values for each missing value. Then we will attempt to invoke the mode finding macro 50,000 times. Therefore, we may use this macro to calculate the mode and use it to combine the imputed values for a nominal variable only when the number of missing values is small. To overcome this difficulty with nominal variables, we may pursue one of the following two alternative strategies.

- During imputation, decide to impute only one value and use it to substitute for the missing value.

- Avoid multiple imputation altogether. This approach is explained in the last section of this chapter.

Finally, we would like stress that combining the values of nominal variables is not a theoretical difficulty, but rather a computational limitation imposed by the special needs of data mining procedures for working with large scoring datasets. If the computational time is not an issue, or if the analyst has access to powerful computers, then computing the mode should not be a problem.

11.6 PREDICTING MISSING VALUES

By *predicting* missing values, we mean that we develop a predictive model that describes the relationship between the variables that are correlated to the variable in question. For example, for each continuous variable with some missing values, we may develop a linear regression model in the other variables that are free of missing values. Similarly, we may develop a logistic regression for each binary nominal or ordinal variable in terms of a set of continuous variables free of missing values (or that have been completed through imputation).

The fundamental difference between this approach and that of multiple imputation is that by fitting a model, we do not attempt to generate the original distribution from which the variable is assumed to be drawn. We rather fit *one* value based on the dependence between the variable and other variables in the dataset.

The most appealing advantage to this approach is the ease of implementation, especially at the time of scoring. Fitting a logistic regression model using the non-missing training data, and then using it to substitute the missing values in both the training and scoring datasets, should be straightforward. What makes things even easier is that SAS implementation of both linear and logistic regression, PROC REG and PROC LOGISTIC, use only nonmissing observations by default.

Using PROC REG and PROC LOGISTIC is thoroughly documented in the SAS/STAT documentation and many textbooks on the subject. But for the purpose of completeness, we present the following example code.

We start with the dataset WithMiss.

```
Data WithMiss;
input x1 x2 x3 y$ @@;
datalines;
4   2   3   .   1   4   1   A
0   1   0   B   2   3   3   A
3   1   0   A   2   3   1   .
2   3   1   B   0   3   2   A
1   0   0   B   3   3   1   B
1   3   0   .   1   1   4   A
3   2   1   B   2   3   3   B
1   0   1   B   3   3   3   A
1   3   3   .   2   3   2   A
3   0   4   A   1   0   4   .
2   1   4   A   0   1   0   B
4   2   3   A   1   1   3   A
;
run;
```

We create a logistic regression model that fits the values of the variable y in terms of the nonmissing variables x1, x2, and x3.

```
proc logistic data=WithMiss outest=LogModel noprint;
model y (Event='A')= x1 x2 x3;
run;
```

Before we score the data, we label the missing observations with a new variable Miss. We also rename the variable y as y1.

```
data Modeling;
 set WithMiss;
 Y1=Y;
 if Y1 ='' then Miss=1;
 else Miss=0;
 drop Y;
 run;
```

PROC LOGISTIC offers the option of generating the scores from a saved model. But we will use PROC SCORE and substitute in the logit equation to explore the full details of the model. Therefore, we start by using PROC SCORE to substitute in the linear form needed for the logit function. It results in a new variable y.

```
proc score data=Modeling
           out=WithoutMiss1
           score=LogModel
           type=parms;
Var x1 x2 x3;
run;
```

Now we use the logit function formula to calculate the score of the variable. If the score is larger than 0.5, we score it A, otherwise B. We perform this scoring only for the missing observations marked with the variable Miss.

```
data WithoutMiss;
 set WithoutMiss1;
 if Miss=1 then do;
   PorbA=exp(-y)/(1+exp(-y));
    if ProbA>0.5 Then Y1='A';
else Y1='B';
end;
keep x1 x2 x3 Y1;
run;
```

The final dataset, WithoutMiss, should have all the missing values substituted by the appropriate score of the logistic regression model.

In the preceding code, we should keep the dataset LogModel to score the scoring dataset in a similar way and substitute for missing values of the variable y.

PREDICTIVE POWER AND VARIABLE REDUCTION I

12.1 INTRODUCTION

The reduction of the number of candidate independent variables of a predictive model is a good practice according to Occam's razor (Mitchell 1997). It states that the best solution is the one that is the simplest. In the case of predictive modeling, it would be the model with the fewest predictors, which is known as a *parsimonious* model. To achieve that, we need to do the following two things.

1. Remove all variables expected to have small or no contribution to the model.

2. For the remaining *good* predictors, *if possible,* find a set of transformations that will reduce their number but at the same time keep all, or most, of the information in them.

To achieve the first task, we need to define a *metric,* or set of metrics, to assess the *predictive power* of a variable. As for the second task, we will need to define another metric to measure the *information content* of a variable. These two concepts are somehow related because it is not acceptable to say, or worse to discover, that a variable with no information content has a high predictive power!

The definition of a metric of predictive power requires a dependent variable to define the predictive aspect of the question. Various measures of predictive power differ in how they weigh the different errors and how we plan to use the variable in the model. For example, the correlation coefficient between a continuous dependent variable and a candidate continuous predictor may be appropriate when we plan to use linear regression. This is because correlation measures the degree of linear association between continuous variables. Similarly, the Gini measure is more suitable with a decision tree model.

Defining the information content of one or more variables is more tricky. In the case of a set of continuous variables, the concept of information content is realized using the *covariance matrix*. In this case, keeping the information of a set of variables translates to keeping the variance in the data that is expressed by the covariance matrix. This is the basis of factor analysis and principal component analysis.

In addition, many predictive modeling algorithms have mechanisms for selection of variables. For example, linear and logistic regression models can be used to iteratively select the variables by inserting and removing the different possible predictors and testing the contribution of each variable. This is the basic idea of stepwise variable selection algorithms in regression models. However, it is recommended that before importing a large number of variables into the modeling software, the number of actual variables be reduced. This is particularly important when using a large training partition.

However, before we use the different metrics to measure the predictive power of the candidate variables, we should do some simple checks to eliminate those that are guaranteed to show low value. This step involves considering the removal of the following variables:

- Constant fields—that is, variables with a cardinality of one. These variables will certainly not contribute to any model.

- Variables with high content of *missing values* (say, more than 99%). These variables are almost identical to constant fields, except that the constant value in this case is the missing value.

- Categorical variables with high cardinality. These variables cannot be easily used in regular models because they result in overfitted models. A typical example of these variables is the postal (zip) code portion of an address. In order to use this type of variable, it is usually necessary to transform it into another form, such as the distance between two points on the map or the expected driving time/distance between two locations. Another option is to group the categories of the zip code to a higher level with a smaller cardinality.

In the remainder of this chapter, we discuss the methods and metrics used for variable reduction. However, we defer the bulk of the SAS implementation to Chapter 17, after all the details of the needed metrics and reduction methods have been presented in Chapters 13 through 16.

12.2 METRICS OF PREDICTIVE POWER

The definition of a metric of the predictive power for a variable assumes that we have a well-defined dependent variable. As mentioned in Chapter 2, in classification

Table 12.1   Common predictive power metrics.

Variable X	Variable Y		
	Nominal	*Ordinal*	*Continuous DV*
Nominal	X^2 G, E	r, r_s G, E	r, r_s F-test G, E
Ordinal		r, r_s G, E	r, r_s F-test G, E
Continuous			r, r_s F-test G, E

problems the dependent variable will be either categorical or binary, and in regression or estimation problems it will be continuous. All metrics used to define the predictive power of a variable depend on measuring the level of association between the dependent variable and the candidate predictor in question. Table 12.1 summarizes the most common metrics.

In the table, X^2 is the Pearson Chi-squared statistic, r is the Pearson correlation coefficient, r_s is the Spearman correlation coefficient, G is the Gini variance, and E is the Entropy variance. (We discuss these measures in full detail in Chapters 13 through 16). Furthermore, the table is symmetric. We display only the diagonal and off-diagonal elements.

The use of the correlation coefficients to measure the predictive power of a variable is probably the easiest and most tempting method. However, it has been shown that variables exhibiting low correlation could still play a significant role in the final model when combined with other variables. This interesting finding can be clearly demonstrated in the case of linear regression (Wickens 1995). Therefore, it is not recommended to rely solely on the calculation of the correlation coefficients, nor any other single metric, in the selection of the variables.

The conservative and recommended approach is to use several metrics to assess all the variables. Then we select *all* the variables that show significant contributions to the model, using *any* metric. In this way, we minimize the chance of erroneous elimination of a possibly useful variable.

12.3 METHODS OF VARIABLE REDUCTION

As mentioned in the introduction section, our plan is to reduce the variables over two stages. First, we remove the variables that do not show good prospects for contributing to the planned model. Second, we reduce the groups of good variables to smaller sets of new variables, without losing too much of the information content.

In the second stage, two methods are commonly used. They are (1) Principal Component Analysis and (2) Factor Analysis. Principal Component Analysis (PCA) aims at finding a set of linear transformations of a set of *continuous* variables such that the resulting set contains *most* of the *variance* in the original set within the first few terms. Factor Analysis (FA), on the other hand, attempts to find a smaller set of *hidden* variables, *factors*, such that performing a set of linear transformations on these factors would lead to the current set of variables.

PCA and FA are two sides of the same idea, finding a set of linear transformations. The difference is that the result of PCA, the principal components, is unique for any set of variables. FA, as detailed in Chapter 16, could result in different sets of factors depending on the criterion used to define these factors.

Furthermore, the factors resulting from FA could sometimes be given business interpretation. This was the original objective of developing factor analysis—to uncover hidden variables that govern the observed phenomena. For example, in banking applications, one could conduct factor analysis with the objective of uncovering a hidden factor that represents the *wealth* of each customer, their *willingness* to adopt new products, and so on. However, proper interpretation of factors is, in general, difficult. Therefore, we focus on using factor analysis for the task of data reduction.

12.4   VARIABLE REDUCTION: BEFORE OR DURING MODELING

Many modeling techniques, such as decision trees, regression analysis, and some implementations of neural networks, offer systematic methods for the reduction of variables while building the model. The reduction algorithms adopt a simple optimization heuristic by attempting to optimize some model performance metric, such as R^2 (coefficient of multiple determination) in regression, or *RMSE* (Root of Mean Square Error) in neural networks.

These methods could offer an alternative to systematic variable reduction, using the methods described in this chapter and in Chapter 17. In most real business applications, however, the number of variables in the final mining view is too large to effectively use the modeling features of variable reduction. Therefore, it is recommended that systematic variable reduction methods be adopted as part of the data preparation procedure, so that the modeling technique would focus on the final tuning and selection from the best set of variables.

CHAPTER 13

ANALYSIS OF NOMINAL AND ORDINAL VARIABLES

13.1 INTRODUCTION

This chapter presents association measures of nominal and ordinal variables. In this context, these measures are used to explore the relationship between the variables. They are also used in the variable reduction process. Throughout the presentation, we follow the notation and formulations given in Agresti (2002).

We first present the details of the main tool used in the analysis of nominal and ordinal variables: contingency tables. Then we present the different measures of association between the variables.

13.2 CONTINGENCY TABLES

A fundamental tool in the analysis of nominal and ordinal variables is what is known as contingency tables. The result of the analysis of contingency tables is a set of measures of the *association* between variables. Therefore, in the context of data preparation procedures, we can use these results in the following two areas.

- To reduce the number of independent variables by removing those that do not show reasonable association with the dependent variable.

- To compare the distribution of variables in two or more samples to make sure that the model training and validation partitions are not biased with respect to any of their variables. In other words, to make sure that the variables are *not* associated with the sampling process itself.

Table 13.1   Gender distribution of mailing campaign results.

Gender	Response status		Total
	Yes	*No*	*Total*
Female	587	18,540	19,127
Male	987	22,545	23,532
Total	1,574	411,085	42,659

Contingency tables are simply the *counts* of cross-tabulation of two or more nominal or ordinal variables. Therefore, when similar analysis is to be performed on continuous variables, binning may be necessary.

Table 13.1 shows the gender distribution of the response to a mail campaign. The purpose of the analysis is to investigate the level of association between the response behavior and gender. If the analysis reveals that gender does not play a significant role in deciding the response, then it may make sense to remove this variable from the mining view.

In Table 13.1, instead of the Gender variable, we could have used the two partitions used for training and validating a model. In this case, we could rephrase the question as: Do the two partitions represent the same population with respect to response rate? If the result of the analysis is No, then we have to reconsider our sampling approach.

We begin the analysis by setting the mathematical notation and the definition of the measures of association.

13.3 NOTATION AND DEFINITIONS

We denote the variable with the categories spanning the columns as the Y variable and that spanning the rows of the table as the X variable. Both variables are discrete (i.e., nominal or ordinal) and may have more than two categories. Table 13.2 shows the notation used for the number of records in each cell of the table. The table contains I rows (levels of variable X) and J columns (levels of variable Y).

As shown in Table 13.2, the total number of records in row i is denoted n_{i*}, and the total number of records in column j is n_{*j}. The total number of records in the dataset is n, which is also equal to the sum of the row totals, the column totals, or the cell totals, that is,

$$n = \sum_{i=1}^{I} n_{i*} = \sum_{j=1}^{J} n_{*j} = \sum_{i=1}^{I} \sum_{j=1}^{J} n_{ij}. \tag{13.1}$$

The cell proportion for the cell ij is defined as

$$p_{ij} = \frac{n_{ij}}{n}. \tag{13.2}$$

Table 13.2   Contingency table notation.

		Y			
X	y_1	$\cdots$	y_j	$\cdots$	y_J	$Total$
x_1	n_{11}	$\cdots$	n_{1j}	$\cdots$	n_{1J}	n_{1*}
$\vdots$						$\vdots$
x_i	n_{i1}	$\cdots$	n_{ij}	$\cdots$	n_{iJ}	n_{i*}
$\vdots$						$\vdots$
x_I	n_{I1}	$\cdots$	n_{Ij}	$\cdots$	n_{IJ}	n_{I*}
$Total$	n_{*1}	$\cdots$	n_{*j}	$\cdots$	n_{*J}	n

Next, we discuss a set of metrics for the association between the X and Y variables. We denote Y the *response* variable and X the *independent* variable. In addition, since the response variable Y, in most cases, has only two categories, we label one of these two categories *success* and the other *failure*. In cases where the term *success* has a clear business meaning, this definition will be most convenient. In all other cases, as will be shown later, it is immaterial which label is assigned to which category.

In addition to defining measures of association, sometimes it is important to make statistical inferences about that measure. This means that we would like to calculate the confidence intervals. The procedure in these cases is always the same. It consists of the following three steps.

1. Calculate the variance of the measure.

2. Determine the probability distribution that this measure should follow. In most cases, the cell counts (n_{ij}) follow either a binomial or Poisson distribution. When the response variable is binary and the total sample size is fixed, then the cell count follows a binomial distribution. On the other hand, when the X variable represents the count of an event, such as the number of times a customer uses a credit card per month, the cell count follows a Poisson distribution. In either case, when the sample size is large (> 30), both distributions approach that of the normal distribution. When examining measures that represent the ratio of two cell counts, the measure usually follows the χ^2 distribution.

3. The size of the confidence interval is calculated using the properties of the variable distribution and the standard deviation, which is sometimes called *standard error*.

Before introducing the different measures, we present a SAS macro that extracts the contingency table for any two variables in a dataset (see Table 13.3). The macro that follows is based on PROC FREQ, which is designed to do exactly that.

Table 13.3   Parameters of the macro `ContinMat()`.

Header	`ContinMat(DSin, Xvar, Yvar, ContTable);`
Parameter	*Description*
`DSin`	Input dataset
`XVar`	X variable
`YVar`	Y variable
`ContTable`	The output contingency table of X versus Y

```
%macro ContinMat(DSin, Xvar, Yvar, ContTable);
   proc freq data=&DSin noprint;
     tables &Xvar * &Yvar / out=&ContTable;
   run;
   Data &ContTable;
    set &ContTable;
    keep &Xvar &Yvar Count;
   run;
   %mend;
```

The code uses the output of PROC FREQ and stores it in the dataset ContTable the X and Y variables, as well as the count of their cells.

13.4 Contingency Tables for Binary Variables

We first present the analysis of contingency tables when both the X and Y variables have two levels, that is, binary variables, which is called *two-way contingency tables*. The following are typical examples of cases when both X and Y are binary.

- Response behavior (Yes/No) in two samples or partitions
- Response behavior(Yes/No) with respect to a possible binary predictor, such as the presence or absence of some attribute (having a credit card, purchased a particular product, or responded to a certain campaign)
- The possible association between two independent binary variables, with the intention of removing one of them if they are strongly associated

In the list we use the generic term *response* to denote either actual response or any similar binary status, such as the credit status (Good/Bad), and profit level (High/Low).

The following subsections present several measures of association and their SAS implementation. We should note that PROC FREQ calculates all these measures.

However, in our presentation, we calculate some of the values from their original expressions to clarify the concepts.

13.4.1 DIFFERENCE IN PROPORTION

Table 13.1 provides the response behavior versus gender for a marketing mailing campaign. In this case, it is easy to label the observations for which the response to the mailing campaign was positive as the success event. The ratio of success rate for both males and females can then be calculated, as shown in Table 13.4.

Table 13.4   Success rate for each gender.

Gender	Success rate
Female	0.0307
Male	0.0419

The table shows that the difference in success rate between males and females is $0.0419 - 0.0307 = 0.0113$. The question now is: How significant is this difference? Can one infer that the campaign success rate with males is different from that with females?

To answer this question, we need to calculate the standard deviation of the difference in proportion of success. We denote the proportion of success in each of the two categories of the variable X by p_1 and p_2, such that

$$p_1 = n_{11}/n_{1*}, \tag{13.3}$$

and

$$p_2 = n_{12}/n_{2*}. \tag{13.4}$$

Note that we use the index 1 in the Y variable for the success event. When the cell count in the two rows is two independent binomial samples, then the standard deviation of the difference in proportion $p1 - p$, denoted $\hat{\sigma}(p_1 - p_2)$, is given by

$$\hat{\sigma}(p_1 - p_2) = \sqrt{\frac{p_1(1 - p_1)}{n_{1*}} + \frac{p_2(1 - p_2)}{n_{2*}}}. \tag{13.5}$$

Equation 13.5 shows that the standard error (standard deviation) decreases as n_{1*} and n_{2*} increase. When both n_{1*} and n_{2*} are large, then the distribution of the standard error $\hat{\sigma}(p_1 - p_2)$ follows the normal distribution, and we calculate the $100(1-\alpha)\%$ confidence interval as

$$(p_1 - p_2) \pm z_{\alpha/2}\hat{\sigma}(p_1 - p_2), \tag{13.6}$$

where $z_{\alpha/2}$ denotes the standard normal percentile, having right-tail probability of $\alpha/2$. For example, a 95% confidence interval has an $\alpha = 0.05$ and $z_{\alpha/2} = 1.96$.

In the mailing campaign example, we did not really have two independent samples for each gender. However, it is reasonable to assume that we knew in advance the gender of each customer who received mail. Therefore, we can assume that when examining the results of the campaign, we have drawn two independent samples of 19,127 females and 23,532 males. By substitution in Expression 13.6, we obtain the 95% confidence interval for the difference in proportion of response rate in the two genders as

$$(0.0438 - 0.0317) \pm (1.96)\sqrt{\frac{0.0438(1 - 0.0438)}{23532} + \frac{0.0317(1 - 0.0317)}{19127}}.$$

The calculation gives the confidence interval between (0.0094) and (0.0131). Because both the upper and lower limits of the confidence interval are positive, we can infer that there *is* a significant difference between the rate of response in men and women. It is interesting to observe that the result is independent of our choice of the category of the variable Y as the success event. When we define the success event as Response=No, we obtain exactly the same result.

The SAS implementation of the preceding procedure assumes that we already have the contingency table, which could be obtained using the macro ContinMat() implemented in Section 13.3. The following macro, PropDiff(), calculates the upper and lower limit of the confidence interval for the difference in proportion (see Table 13.5).

Table 13.5   Parameters of macro PropDiff().

Header	PropDiff(ContTable, Xvar, Yvar, Alpha, M_Prop, M_Upper, M_Lower);
Parameter	*Description*
ContTable	Input contingency table
Xvar	X variable name
Yvar	Y variable name
Alpha	Used to determine the confidence level of $(1-\alpha/2)\%$
M_Prop	Difference in proportion (absolute value)
M_Upper	Resulting upper limit of the confidence interval
M_Lower	Resulting lower limit of the confidence interval

Step 1
Sort the contingency table using both the X and Y variables to guarantee the meaning of the different entries.

```
proc sort data=&ContTable;
 by &Xvar &Yvar;
run;
```

Step 2
Transform the entries of the contingency table into macro variables.

```
data _NULL_;
 set &ContTable;
 call symput ("n_"||left(_N_), COUNT);
run;
```

Step 3
Substitute into Equation 13.6.

```
%let N1star=%eval(&N_1+&N_2);
%let N2star=%eval(&N_3+&N_4);
%let P1=%sysevalf(&N_1/&N1star);
%let P2=%sysevalf(&N_3/&N2star);
%let P1P2=%sysfunc(abs(&p1-&P2));
%let sigma=%sysfunc(sqrt((((&P1*(1-&P1))/&N1star)
                        +((&P2*(1-&P2))/&N2star)));
%let &M_Prop = &P1P2;
%let &M_Upper=%sysevalf(&p1p2
            + &sigma * %sysfunc(probit(1-&alpha/2)));
%let &M_Lower=%sysevalf(&p1p2
            - &sigma * %sysfunc(probit(1-&alpha/2)));
%mend;
```

To demonstrate the use of the macro PropDiff(), we create a contingency table using the following DATA step:

```
DATA contingency;
 INPUT Count Gender $ Response $;
DATALINES;
18540 Female N
587   Female Y
22545 Male   N
987   Male   Y
;
RUN;
```

The following code shows how to call the macro and print the upper and lower limits to the SAS Log.

```
%let ContTable=Contingency;
%let Xvar=Gender;
%let Yvar=Response;
%let Alpha=0.05;
%let Prop=;
%let Upper=;
```

```
%let Lower=;
%PropDiff(&ContTable, &Xvar, &Yvar, &Alpha,
        Prop, Upper, Lower);
%put ********** Prop. Diff.= &Prop;
%put ********** Lower Limit= &Lower;
%put ********** Upper Limit= &Upper;
```

13.4.2 THE ODDS RATIO

Recall the results of the marketing campaign as shown in Table 13.6.

Table 13.6   Gender distribution of mailing campaign results.

	Response status		
Gender	*Yes*	*No*	*Total*
Female	587	18,540	19,127
Male	987	22,545	23,532
Total	1,574	411,085	42,659

We denote the *probability* of success of the marketing effort in the case of female customers given in the first row π_1. Similarly, we denote the probability of success for male customers, in the second row, π_2. We can determine the probability of *failure* for the first and second rows as $(1 - \pi_1)$ and $(1 - \pi_2)$, respectively. These probabilities are, in principal, unknown. However, we may estimate their values using the ratios p_1 and p_2, as in Equations 13.3 and 13.4.

The *odds* of success in the case of female customers is defined as the ratio of the probability of success to that of failure:

$$\text{Odds}_1 = \frac{\pi_1}{1 - \pi_1}. \tag{13.7}$$

Similarly, the odds of success with male customers is defined as

$$\text{Odds}_2 = \frac{\pi_2}{1 - \pi_2}. \tag{13.8}$$

The *odds ratio* is then defined as the ratio between these two quantities as

$$\theta = \frac{\text{Odds}_1}{\text{Odds}_2} = \frac{\pi_1/(1 - \pi_1)}{\pi_2/(1 - \pi_2)}. \tag{13.9}$$

Because the proportions are the sample *estimates* of the probabilities, we may write the odds ratio in terms of the proportions p_1 and p_2 as

$$\theta = \frac{p_1/(1-p_1)}{p_2/(1-p_2)} = \frac{n_{11}/n_{12}}{n_{21}/n_{22}} = \frac{n_{11}n_{22}}{n_{12}n_{21}}. \tag{13.10}$$

The odds ratio determines the odds of success in row 1 relative to those of row 2. It is always a positive number. Interchanging the rows of the contingency table results in the inverse value of the odds ratio; that is, it changes the value of θ to $1/\theta$. The farther the value of θ from 1.0, in either direction, the more association there is between the variables X and Y.

In the example of Table 13.6 of the campaign responses, the odds ratio is $\theta = 0.723$, which, as in the case of the difference of proportion, shows that there is an association between the response rate and the gender. It should be noted that although computer programs can calculate θ to many significant digits, there is no need to do so because we are using the sample proportions as approximations to the real unknown probabilities. Therefore, interpreting θ for up to, say, three significant digits is usually sufficient.

To calculate the confidence interval for the odds ratio, θ, it is more convenient to use its logarithm, $\log(\theta)$. Therefore, we calculate the confidence interval for the logarithm of the odds ratio, and then use the exponential function to find the actual range. In large samples, the distribution of the logarithm of the odds ratio is normal with a mean of $\log(\theta)$ and a standard deviation, known as the *asymptotic standard error*, denoted ASE, of

$$ASE(\log \theta) = \sqrt{\frac{1}{n_{11}} + \frac{1}{n_{12}} + \frac{1}{n_{21}} + \frac{1}{n_{22}}}. \tag{13.11}$$

Equation 13.11 shows, as expected, that the ASE decreases as the cell counts increase. The $(1-\alpha)\%$ confidence interval of the logarithm of the odds ratio is then given by

$$\log \theta \pm z_{\alpha/2} ASE(\log \theta), \tag{13.12}$$

with $z_{\alpha/2}$ being the standard normal percentile, having right-tail probability of $\alpha/2$.

In the example of the response to the marketing campaign, the bounds of the 95% confidence interval of the logarithm of the odds ratio are -0.428 and -0.219. Using the natural exponential function, the actual bounds on the odds ratio are 0.652 and 0.803. Since this range for θ *does not* contain the unity 1.0, we infer that the true odds for males and females *are* different with a confidence of 95%.

Equation 13.12 fails when one of the cell counts is 0. In this case, the odds ratio is either 0 or ∞. To account for this case, the formulas for θ and ASE are modified by adding $\frac{1}{2}$ to each n_{ij},

$$\tilde{\theta} = \frac{(n_{11} + \frac{1}{2})(n_{22} + \frac{1}{2})}{(n_{12} + \frac{1}{2})(n_{21} + \frac{1}{2})}, \tag{13.13}$$

and

$$\widetilde{ASE}(\log\theta) = \sqrt{\frac{1}{(n_{11} + \frac{1}{2})} + \frac{1}{(n_{12} + \frac{1}{2})} + \frac{1}{(n_{21} + \frac{1}{2})} + \frac{1}{(n_{22} + \frac{1}{2})}}. \qquad (13.14)$$

The modification does not change the values of either θ or ASE when the cell counts are large, as in our example of Table 13.6. The macro OddsRatio() calculates the odds ratio and its confidence interval using these modified formulas (see Table 13.7).

Table 13.7 Parameters of macro OddsRatio().

Header	OddsRatio(ContTable, Xvar, Yvar, Alpha, M_Theta, M_Upper, M_Lower);
Parameter	*Description*
ContTable	Input contingency table
Xvar	X variable name
Yvar	Y variable name
Alpha	Used to determine the confidence level of $(1-\alpha/2)\%$
M_Theta	Odds ratio
M_Upper	Resulting upper limit of the confidence interval
M_Lower	Resulting lower limit of the confidence interval

Step 1
Sort the contingency table by the categories of the X variable and the Y variable.

```
proc sort data=&ContTable;
 by &Xvar &Yvar;
run;
```

Step 2
Convert the count into macro variables that contain the cell counts.

```
data _NULL_;
 set &ContTable;
 call symput ("n_"||left(_N_), COUNT);
run;
```

Step 3
Calculate the odds ratio and the ASE using the modified ratio (just in case any of the cell counts is 0).

```
%let Theta=%sysevalf((&N_1+0.5)*(&N_4+0.5)/
                    ((&N_2+0.5)*(&N_3+0.5)));
%let ASE_log=%sysfunc(sqrt(1/(&N_1+0.5)+ 1/(&N_2+0.5)
                         +1/(&N_3+0.5)+ 1/(&N_4+0.5) ));
```

Step 4

Calculate the confidence interval for the log of the odds ratio, and use the exponential function to obtain the actual limits.

```
%let LogT=%sysfunc(log(&Theta));
%let LogU= %sysevalf(&LogT + &ASE_Log *
                    %sysfunc(probit(1-&alpha/2)));
%let LogL= %sysevalf(&LogT - &ASE_log *
                    %sysfunc(probit(1-&alpha/2)));
%let &M_Theta = &Theta;
%let &M_Upper = %sysfunc(exp(&LogU));
%let &M_Lower = %sysfunc(exp(&LogL));
%mend;
```

13.4.3 THE PEARSON STATISTIC

The *Pearson Chi-squared statistic* is another measure that tests the association between the variables X and Y, by comparing the actual cell counts with the *expected* counts, under the assumption of independence. When the resulting categories of the variable Y are independent of those of the variable X, then we expect that the cell counts reflect that, such that the probability of success in a row is independent of the row itself.

Let's demonstrate this idea using a simple example. Consider the data in Table 13.8, which shows the results of a marketing campaign in terms of the credit card type that the customer owns. Table 13.8 shows that the probability of response for the Visa card owners is $(8/100) = 8\%$ and for the MasterCard owners is $(40/200) = 20\%$. If the response behavior is independent of the credit card type, both rows should show equal response rate. This in turn would have translated to the cell count of the Yes category being proportional to the sample size for each card group.

Table 13.8   Response versus credit card type.

	Response status		
Credit card	Yes	No	Total
VISA	8	92	100
MasterCard	40	160	200
Total	48	252	300

Since we have a total of 48 Yes responders, they should be divided according to the ratio of the total count of each group of card owners, that is 16 for Visa owners and 32 for MasterCard owners. A similar argument could be made for the case of the No responders. These cell counts are the *expected* cell counts under the assumption of independence between response result and card type. Table 13.9 shows these counts in parentheses under the actual counts.

Table 13.9   Actual expected counts of response status versus credit card type.

	Response status		
Credit card	*Yes*	*No*	*Total*
Visa	8	92	100
	(16)	(84)	
MasterCard	40	160	200
	(32)	(168)	
Total	48	252	300

The expected count of the cell ij, denoted μ_{ij}, is in fact calculated as

$$\mu_{ij} = \frac{n_{i*}n_{*j}}{n}.$$ (13.15)

The Pearson Chi-squared statistic is defined as

$$X^2 = \sum \frac{(n_{ij} - \mu_{ij})^2}{\mu_{ij}},$$ (13.16)

with the summation being over all the cells of the contingency table. It is the sum of the squared difference between the actual and expected cell counts, normalized by the expected counts. For example, using the values in Table 13.9, we calculate X^2 as

$$X^2 = \frac{(8 - 16)^2}{16} + \frac{(92 - 84)^2}{84} + \frac{(40 - 32)^2}{32} + \frac{(160 - 168)^2}{168} = 7.143.$$

When the cell counts are large, the X^2 follows a χ^2 distribution with degrees of freedom (df) of $(J - 1)(I - 1)$. Therefore, in the case of contingency tables with two binary variables, $df = 1$. The assumption of large cell counts is usually considered valid for modest values, such as when $\mu_{ij} \geq 5$, which is almost the case in all real business data. We use the χ^2 distribution to find the probability of independence, such that

$$Pr(\text{independence}) = \chi^2(X^2, df).$$ (13.17)

The value of $Pr()$ could be calculated using the SAS function PROBCHI(.,.), which taks the values of X^2 and df as arguments. To implement the Pearson Chi-squared statistic and the confidence test, we could either program it using the original

Table 13.10   Parameters of meters of macro PearChi().

Header	PearChi(DSin, Xvar, Yvar, M_X2, M_pvalue);
Parameter	*Description*
DSin	Input dataset
Xvar	X variable name
Yvar	Y variable name
M_X2	Pearson Chi-squared statistic, X^2
M_pvalue	p-value of the χ^2 test of the Pearson statistic

formulas or use PROC FREQ, which calculates it along with other measures. The macro PearChi() uses PROC FREQ, and extracts from its results the probability (p-value) of the χ^2 test of the Pearson statistic (see Table 13.10).

```
%macro PearChi(DSin, Xvar, Yvar, M_X2, M_pvalue);
PROC FREQ data =&DSin NOPRINT;
 TABLES &Xvar * &Yvar/chisq;
 OUTPUT All out=temp_chi chisq;
RUN;

/* Extract the P-value of the Chi square test */
Data _Null_;
set Temp_chi;
call symput("Mpvalue", P_PCHI);
call symput("MX2",_PCHI_);
run;
%let &M_Pvalue=&Mpvalue;
%let &M_X2 =&MX2;
proc datasets library=work nolist;
  delete temp_chi;
quit;
%mend;
```

Let us demonstrate the use of the macro with a simple dataset. The following code generates a dataset with 100 records of two variables, Gender (Female/Male) and Response (Yes/No). The values of the categories of Gender and Response are assigned at random using the SAS uniform distribution random number generator function RanUni(.).

```
data test;
length Response $3. Gender $6. ;
 do i=1 to 100;
  if ranuni(0)>0.8 then Response='Yes';
     else Response ='No';
```

```
   if ranuni(0)>0.6 then Gender ='Male';
      else Gender ='Female';
  output;
  end;
  drop i;
run;
```

Finally, we call the macro and display the result of the test in the SAS Log using the following code:

```
%let DSin=test;
%let Xvar=Gender;
%let Yvar=Response;
%let X2=;
%let pvalue=;

%PearChi(&DSin, &XVar, &Yvar, x2, pvalue);
%put The Pearson chi-square Stat.= &X2;
%put Probability of Independence = &pvalue;
```

The small *p*-value indicates that the two variables *are* associated and the large *p*-value confirms their independence.

13.4.4   THE LIKELIHOOD RATIO STATISTIC

This statistic is similar to the Pearson Chi-squared statistic, except it is derived using the maximum likelihood method. The statistic is defined as

$$G^2 = 2 \sum n_{ij} \log \left(\frac{n_{ij}}{\mu_{ij}} \right), \tag{13.18}$$

with the summation taken over all the cells of the contingency table. The G^2 statistic also follows the χ^2 distribution, with $(J-1)(I-1)$ degrees of freedom, and is called the *likelihood ratio Chi-squared statistic*. The Pearson statistic and G^2 usually provide similar results for large datasets and result in the same conclusion.

The G^2 statistic and its Chi-squared test are also calculated by PROC FREQ. This will be the basis of our implementation of the macro LikeRatio(), the macro identical to that used to calculate the Pearson statistic test, with the exception that it extracts the likelihood ratio statistic and its *p*-value (see Table 13.11).

```
%macro LikeRatio(DSin, Xvar, Yvar, M_G2, M_pvalue);
proc freq data =&DSin noprint;
 tables &Xvar * &Yvar/chisq;
 output All out=temp_chi chisq;
run;
```

Table 13.11   Parameters of macro `LikeRatio()`.

Header	`LikeRatio(DSin, Xvar, Yvar, M_G2, M_pvalue);`
Parameter	*Description*
DSin	Input dataset
Xvar	*X* variable name
Yvar	*Y* variable name
M_G2	The likelihood ratio statisic, G^2
M_pvalue	*p*-value of the χ^2 test of the G^2 statistic

```
/* Extract the G2 and it sp-value */
Data _Null_;
set Temp_chi;
call symput("Mpvalue", P_LRCHI);
call symput("MG2", _LRCHI_);
run;
%let &M_Pvalue=&Mpvalue;
%let &M_G2 =&MG2;
proc datasets library=work nolist;
  delete temp_chi;
quit;
%mend;
```

Again, a small *p*-value indicates that the two variables are associated and the large value indicates their independence.

The two macros `PearChi()` and `LikeRatio()` could have been combined into one macro because the option `/CHISQ` of the `TABLES` statement of `PROC FREQ` calculates both statistics and their *p*-values. We implemented them separately only for clarity.

13.5 CONTINGENCY TABLES FOR MULTICATEGORY VARIABLES

The extension of the evaluation of the association methods among the variables of the contingency tables to the case of variables with several categories is straightforward. However, because there is no particular category of the *Y* variable that could be denoted as Success, we are restricted to the methods that do not depend on such a definition. Therefore, the difference in proportion and the odds ratio are not applicable.

Equations 13.16 and 13.18, defining the Pearson Chi-squared statistic and the likelihood ratio statistic, are valid for multicategory variables. Furthermore, the implementation of the two macros `PearChi()` and `LikeRatio()` also allows for either or both of the *X* and *Y* variables to have more than two categories.

Table 13.12   Parameters of macro ContnAna().

Header	ContnAna(DSin, VarX, VarY, ResDS);
Parameter	*Description*
DSin	Input dataset
VarX	*X* variable name
VarY	*Y* variable name
ResDS	Results dataset

Therefore, we do not need to provide separate implementations for the case of multicategory nominal variables. However, we present a macro that calculates *all* the measures of association with PROC FREQ and extract them with their description to a dataset (see Table 13.12). This macro should replace the macros PearChi() and LikeRatio().

In addition to the Pearson statistic and the likelihood ratio, this macro extracts three more statistics that measure association. They are the Mantel-Haenszel, the Phi coefficient, and Cramer's V. These statistics are described in the SAS online documentation of PROC FREQ.

The macro calls PROC FREQ, stores all the association measures in the dataset temp_chi, extracts these statistics, and stores them in the results dataset.

```
%macro ContnAna(DSin, VarX, VarY, ResDS);
/* Calculation of measures of association between
   two categorical variables (VarX, VarY)
   in a dataset (DSin) using PROC FREQ and
   arranging the results in a dataset (ResDS) */

proc freq data =&DSin noprint;
 tables &VarX * &VarY/chisq;
 output All out=temp_chi chisq;
run;

proc sql noprint;
 create table &ResDS
      (SAS_Name char(10), Description char(50), Value num);
 select _PHI_, P_MHCHI, P_LRCHI, P_PCHI, N, _MHCHI_
     , _LRCHI_, DF_MHCHI, DF_LRCHI, DF_PCHI ,_CRAMV_
     ,_CONTGY_ ,_PCHI_
   into :PHI, :P_MHCHI, :P_LRCHI, :P_PCHI, :N, :MHCHI
        , :LRCHI, :DF_MHCHI, :DF_LRCHI, :DF_PCHI, :CRAMV
        , :CONTGY, :PCHI
 from temp_chi;
insert into &ResDS
```

```
values("N", "Number of Subjects in the Stratum",&N)
values("_PCHI_","Chi-Square",&PCHI)
values("DF_PCHI","DF for Chi-Square",&DF_PCHI)
values("P_PCHI","P-value for Chi-Square",&P_PCHI)
values("_MHCHI_","Mantel-Haenszel Chi-Square",&MHCHI)
values("DF_MHCHI","DF for Mantel-Haenszel Chi-Square",
      &DF_MHCHI)
values("P_MHCHI","P-value for Mantel-Haenszel Chi-Square",
      &P_MHCHI)
values("_LRCHI_","Likelihood Ratio Chi-Square",&LRCHI)
values("DF_LRCHI","DF for Likelihood Ratio Chi-Square",
      &DF_LRCHI)
values("P_LRCHI","P-value for Likelihood Ratio Chi-Square",
      &P_LRCHI)
values("_PHI_","Phi Coefficient",&PHI)
values("_CONTGY_","Contingency Coefficient",&CONTGY)
values("_CRAMV_","Cramer's V",&CRAMV)
;
quit;
proc datasets library=work nolist;
  delete temp_chi;
quit;
%mend;
```

13.6 ANALYSIS OF ORDINAL VARIABLES

When one or both of the row or column variables, X and Y, are ordinal, the methods described in the previous sections are not appropriate. This is because the measures of association, such as X^2 and G^2, are based on the assumption that there is no ordering within the different categories. Adding an ordinal scale to the categories introduces more information in the data that should be used.

In analyzing ordinal as well as continuous variables, two types of models are usually proposed: *parametric* and *nonparametric*. Parametric models assume that the variables follow a particular probability distribution. On the other hand, nonparametric models make no such an assumption and are sometimes called *distribution-free* models.

Before we present the definition of the different measures of association between ordinal variables, we have to discuss the subject of *scores*.

When the categories of either X or Y, or both, are set on an ordinal scale, we call the values of this scale for each category the *scores*. Let us demonstrate this by an example.

Table 13.13 shows the results of cross-tabulating the average monthly rate of credit card usage versus the event of default on the card payment. To express the ordinal nature of the rate of credit card usage, we assign a scale to the different ranges. For example, we assign $1 - 2 \rightarrow 1$, $3 - 5 \rightarrow 2$, and so on. These values are the assigned

Table 13.13   Credit card usage rate versus credit default.

Average usage	Credit status Good	Credit status Default	Total	(%) Default
1–2	35,784	1,469	37,253	3.94
3–5	45,874	1,457	47,331	3.08
5–9	45,741	2,897	48,638	5.96
9–15	8,547	451	8,998	5.01
>15	6,987	359	7,346	4.89
Total	142,933	6,633	149,566	4.64

scores. Whenever scores are assigned, we have to assign *both* row and column scores. In this example of credit card default, we may assign a score of 1 to the status good and 5 to the status Default.

For most datasets, the choice of scores has little effect on the final results as long as the data is, more or less, evenly distributed over the different categories. In the preceding example, this is not really the case, because we have fewer observations for the high range of credit card use. Therefore, it is always a good practice to check the quality of the assigned scores by trying different assignment schemes.

For ordinal variables, parametric measures of association are computed using the values of the scores directly. Nonparametric measures work instead with their ranks. In most cases, the scores assigned to ordinal variables mean their ranks. Therefore, given the choice, we prefer to use nonparametric measures.

First, some notation. The row scores are denoted R_i for the score of row i, and column scores are denoted C_j for the score of column j. Furthermore, the average row score is denoted $\bar{R}$ and the average column score is denoted $\bar{C}$. Using this notation, the *Pearson correlation coefficient* is defined as

$$r = \frac{ss_{rc}}{\sqrt{ss_r ss_c}}, \tag{13.19}$$

where the terms ss_{rc}, ss_r, and ss_c are defined as

$$ss_r = \sum_{i=1}^{I} \sum_{j-1}^{J} n_{ij}(R_i - \bar{R})^2, \tag{13.20}$$

$$ss_c = \sum_{i=1}^{I} \sum_{j-1}^{J} n_{ij}(C_i - \bar{C})^2, \tag{13.21}$$

and

$$ss_{rc} = \sum_{i=1}^{I} \sum_{j-1}^{J} n_{ij}(R_i - \bar{R})(C_i - \bar{C}). \tag{13.22}$$

The value of r is between -1 and $+1$. Values close to 0, either positive or negative, indicate lack of correlation between the variables X and Y, and larger values (near -1 or $+1$) are indicators of strong correlation (or anticorrelation in the case of negative r).

The variance of the correlation coefficient r is also calculated by PROC FREQ. However, because this is a parametric measure, the confidence intervals, which can be calculated using the variance and statistical tests, are meaningful only when both the variables X and Y are normally distributed. When this condition cannot be guaranteed in real-life data, we prefer to use nonparametric measures.

PROC FREQ calculates the Pearson correlation coefficient using the option MEASURES in the TABLES and in the OUTPUT statements when we wish to store the results in a dataset. The generated dataset will contain the coefficient in the variable _PCORR_. The following macro wraps PROC FREQ and extracts r (see Table 13.14).

Table 13.14   Parameters of the macro ContPear().

Header	ContPear(DSin, XScore, YScore, M_R);
Parameter	*Description*
DSin	Input dataset
XScore	X variable name (scores)
YScore	Y variable name (scores)
M_R	Output value of r

```
%macro ContPear(DSin, XScore, YScore, M_R);

proc freq data=&DSin noprint;
 tables &XScore*&YScore / measures;
 output measures out=temp_r;
run;

data _NULL_;
 set temp_r;
 call symput("r", _PCORR_);
run;

%let &M_r = &r;

/* clean workspace */
proc datasets nodetails;
 delete temp_r;
quit;

%mend;
```

We now turn our attention to a nonparametric correlation coefficient: the *Spearman rank correlation coefficient*. Basically, it has the same definition as the Pearson coefficient, but it uses the ranks instead of the scores. It can be defined in terms of the ranks of the values of the X and Y variables directly as

$$r_s = \frac{\sum_{i=1}^{n}(R_i - \bar{R})(S_i - \bar{S})}{\sqrt{\sum_{i=1}^{n}(R_i - \bar{R})^2}\sqrt{\sum_{i=1}^{n}(S_i - \bar{S})^2}}, \qquad (13.23)$$

where R_i and S_i are the ranks of X and Y and $\bar{R}$ and $\bar{S}$ are their average ranks, respectively. Note that r_s can also be expressed in terms of the counts of the contingency matrix. The equations in this case are more complex. These expressions can be found in the SAS help on PROC FREQ. The advantage of the Spearman's coefficient is that its significance test is performed simply using the following statistic:

$$t = r_s\sqrt{\frac{n-2}{1-r_s^2}}, \qquad (13.24)$$

which follows the Student t-distribution with $n-2$ degrees of freedom (because two degrees of freedom were lost in calculating $\bar{R}$ and $\bar{S}$).

The biggest advantage of using r_s is that when its significance test shows that there is a correlation, then this result is true regardless of the underlying distribution of the variables.

To get the value of r_s, we can modify the macro ContPear() by making the DATA step read the variable _SCORR_ from the temporary dataset, as shown in the following code of the macro ContSpear() (see Table 13.15).

Table 13.15   Parameters of the macro ContSpear().

Header	ContSpear(DSin, XScore, YScore, M_RS);
Parameter	*Description*
DSin	Input dataset
XScore	X variable name (scores)
YScore	Y variable name (scores)
M_RS	Output value of r_s

```
%macro ContSpear(DSin, XScore, YScore, M_RS);
/* Calculation of Spearman correlation coefficient
   for ordinal variables using the scores given
   in XScore, YScore. The result is stored in M_RS */
```

```
proc freq data=&DSin noprint;
 tables &XScore*&YScore / measures;
output measures out=temp_rs;
run;

data _NULL_;
 set temp_rs;
 call symput("rs", _SCORR_);
run;

%let &M_rs = &rs;

proc datasets nodetails;
 *delete temp_rs;
quit;

%mend;
```

13.7 IMPLEMENTATION SCENARIOS

This chapter presented several methods of measuring the associations for nominal and ordinal variables. One may summarize possible implementation scenarios as follows.

1. Faced with a large number of variables in a candidate mining view, we could reduce the number of independent variables by considering only those that show a reasonable level of association or correlation with the dependent variable.

2. We can also test the hypothesis that two datasets, such as the training and validation partitions of the mining view, have the same distribution and interrelationships of variables. We perform this analysis by finding the level of association between each of the key variables in the analysis and a dummy variable representing the dataset label. This is particularly useful in checking that the scoring view variables have the same distribution as those used in building the models before committing to the scores produced by these models and using them at face value.

3. During the exploratory data analysis (EDA) procedures, it is always required that we investigate the relationships among the variables. The macros presented in this chapter could prove useful in automating this process.

CHAPTER 14

ANALYSIS OF CONTINUOUS VARIABLES

14.1 INTRODUCTION

This chapter presents the methods used to measure the association between two variables when one or both of them is continuous. Of course, one option to avoid dealing with continuous variables is to bin them before using them. We explore this issue in the first section of this chapter. When one of the two variables is nominal or ordinal (or a binned continuous variable), we can extend the definitions of the Gini and entropy variances to the case of continuous variables. We could also use what is known as the F-test. These methods are presented in Section 14.3. Finally, we discuss correlation analysis of continuous variables in Section 14.4.

14.2 WHEN IS BINNING NECESSARY?

Binning is used in two situations: (1) as a requirement during modeling because of either the model form or the accepted practices and (2) as a tool to facilitate data exploration.

Let us consider the first situation. Most data mining algorithms deal efficiently with continuous variables, in their raw form, if not explicitly require them, as in the case of neural networks and regression models. However, the procedures used in the implementation and presentation of the model results sometimes force the analyst to bin continuous variables into ranges or new categories.

A common example of such a case is during the construction of scorecards. In most scorecards developed using logistic regression, continuous variables are binned into ranges, and a set of new indicator variables representing these ranges is used as independent variables. This process facilitates the construction of scorecards because the scoring parameters are then given directly by the model coefficients.

Similarly, when the final score is required to be produced using a simple set of IF–THEN–ELSE rules, this type of model is naturally generated using decision trees. These models are very efficient and therefore are the most used scoring models for online transactions. Continuous variables are then binned either using the decision tree algorithm or during the original data preparation procedures.

In the second situation, binning is used only so that we can implement some of the measures used for categorical and ordinal variables. This will help the analyst to evaluate the predictive power of the variables before building the model.

When one of the two variables we study is nominal or ordinal (either originally or as a result of binning a continuous variable), we can use one of the following measures to determine the association between the variables (Breiman et al. 1998).

- F-test
- Gini variance
- Entropy variance

These methods are described in detail in the next section.

14.3 MEASURES OF ASSOCIATION

In the following, we always assume that the X variable is nominal and the Y variable is continuous.

Before we present the formulas and implementation of three association measures, we must mention that all these measures ignore the possible ordering relationships of the categories of the X variable.

14.3.1 NOTATION

Table 14.1 shows that variable X has k categories, $x_1, \ldots, x_k$. It also lists the values of the variable Y in each of these categories. For example, in the category x_i, there are n_i

Table 14.1   Notation for association measures of continuous variables.

X	Y
x_1	$y_{11} \cdots y_{1n_1}$
$\vdots$	$\vdots$
x_i	$y_{i1} \cdots y_{in_i}$
$\vdots$	$\vdots$
x_k	$y_{k1} \cdots y_{kn_k}$
Total	N records

records, with the variable Y taking the values of $y_{i1}, \ldots, y_{in_i}$. The total number of records is N, such that $N = \sum_{i=1}^{k} n_i$.

The sum of the values of Y in the category i is given as

$$y_i = \sum_{j=1}^{n_i} y_{ij}. \tag{14.1}$$

The average value of the variable Y in the category i is then calculated as

$$\bar{y}_i = \frac{y_i}{n_i}. \tag{14.2}$$

Similarly, the average of the variable Y is given by

$$\bar{y} = \frac{1}{N} \sum_{i=1}^{k} y_i. \tag{14.3}$$

The sum of the squared deviations from the average value of Y is calculated as

$$SSTO = \sum_{i=1}^{k} \sum_{j=1}^{n_i} (y_{ij} - \bar{y})^2. \tag{14.4}$$

Similarly, the weighted squared deviations of the category average from the global average is

$$SSR = \sum_{i=1}^{k} n_i (\bar{y}_i - \bar{y})^2. \tag{14.5}$$

And finally the sum of squared deviations within the categories from their means is

$$SSE = \sum_{i=1}^{k} \sum_{j=1}^{n_i} (y_{ij} - \bar{y}_i)^2. \tag{14.6}$$

Borrowing from the notation of linear regression, we can define the *mean square* (MS) values for SSR and SSE by dividing each sum by its degrees of freedom as

$$MSR = \frac{SSR}{(k-1)} \tag{14.7}$$

and

$$MSE = \frac{SSE}{(N-k)}. \tag{14.8}$$

14.3.2 THE *F*-TEST

The *F*-test is similar to the test devised for the analysis of variance in linear regression. However, in this case we are testing the association between the discrete variable X and the continuous variable Y. To perform the test, we define the value F^* as

$$F^* = \frac{MSR}{MSE}. \tag{14.9}$$

Large values of F^* suggest a high association between the two variables. F^* follows the *F*-distribution with degrees of freedom of $(k - 1, N - k)$. Therefore, we calculate the *p*-value of F^* from the inverse *F*-distribution function such that

$$p = F(F^*, k - 1, N - k). \tag{14.10}$$

Small *p*-values indicate that the variables are not associated and high *p*-values indicate that they are.

14.3.3 GINI AND ENTROPY VARIANCES

In Section 10.2.5, we defined the Gini variance when both variables are categorical. We now extend the formulation to account for the continuous variable Y. In this case, the Gini ratio is simply given as

$$G_r = 1 - \frac{SSE}{SSTO}. \tag{14.11}$$

In fact, Equation 14.11 also defines the *coefficient of determination, R^2* in the terminology of linear regression, as well as the *entropy ratio* to measure the association between the variables.

Table 14.2   Parameters of the macro `ContGrF()`.

Header	`ContGrF(DSin, Xvar, Yvar, M_Gr, M_Fstar, M_Pvalue);`
Parameter	*Description*
`DSin`	Input dataset
`Xvar`	X variable name
`Yvar`	Y variable name
`M_Gr`	Output entropy/Gini ratio (Equation 14.11)
`M_Fstar`	Output F^* used in *F*-test (Equation 14.9)
`M_Pvalue`	Output *p*-value of F^* (Equation 14.10)

The following macro calculates both the value of F^* and the ratio G_r. The macro simply calculates the values defined in Equations 14.1 through 14.11.

Step 1
Begin by using PROC FREQ to find the unique categories of the X variable XVar. Assume that it does not have missing values. The categories are stored in the dataset Temp_Cats.

```
proc freq data=&DSin noprint;
 tables &XVar /out=Temp_Cats;
run;
```

Step 2
Convert the categories X_i and their frequencies n_i into macro variables. Also find the number of categories K and the total number of records N.

```
Data _null_;
 retain N 0;
 set Temp_Cats;
  N=N+count;
  call symput ("X_" || left(_N_), compress(&XVar));
  call symput ("n_" || left(_N_), left(count));

  call symput ("K", left(_N_));
  call symput ("N", left(N));
Run;
```

Step 3
Calculate the average of the variable Y, that is, $\bar{y}$, as well as the averages for each category, $\bar{y}_i$.

```
proc sql noprint;
 /* Ybar */
  select avg(&YVar) into :Ybar from &DSin;
  /* Ybar_i */
  %do i=1 %to &K;
    select avg(&YVar) into :Ybar_&i
           from &DSin where &XVar = "&&X_&i";
  %end;
```

Step 4
Calculate the remaining terms *SSTO*, *SSE*, and *SSR*.

```
  select var(&YVar) into: SSTO from &DSin;
%let SSTO=%sysevalf(&SSTO *(&N-1));
```

```
%let SSR=0;
%let SSE=0;
  %do i=1 %to &K;
     select var(&YVar) into: ssei
            from &DSin where &Xvar="&&X_&i";
        %let SSE=%sysevalf(&SSE + &ssei * (&&n_&i - 1));
        %let SSR=%sysevalf(&SSR+ &&n_&i *
                (&&Ybar_&i - &Ybar)*(&&Ybar_&i - &Ybar));
     %end;

  quit; /* end of Proc SQL */
```

Step 5
Substitute into the equations of *MSR*, *MSE*, F^*, G_r, and *p*-value.

```
%let MSR=%sysevalf(&SSR/(&K-1));
%let MSE=%sysevalf(&SSE/(&N-&K));
%let &M_Gr=%Sysevalf(1-(&SSE/&SST0));
%let &M_Fstar=%sysevalf(&MSR/&MSE);
%let &M_PValue=
      %sysevalf(%sysfunc(probf(&Fstar,&K-1,&N-&K)));
```

Step 6
Clean the workspace and finish the macro.

```
/* clean workspace */
 proc datasets library=work nolist;
  delete temp_cats;
 run; quit;

%mend;
```

Let us demonstrate this macro with an example. The following code generates a dataset containing two variables: Loan, which varies between 0 and 2000, and Debt, which takes one of two values, Low or High.

```
data Credit;
 do CustID=1 to 10000;
  Loan=int(2000*ranuni(0));
  Err=(100-200*ranuni(0));
  /* if Loan + Err>1000 then Debt='High'; */
  /* if ranuni(0)>0.5 then Debt='High';   */
                     else Debt='Low';
  output;
 end;
 drop Err;
run;
```

The code contains two *commented* statements. You need to remove the comments from one of them for the code to work properly. The first one will generate data with strong association between the Loan value and the Debt status (high or low). The second statement will assign the status randomly independent of the value of the loan, thus creating low association between the two variables. We then invoke the macro using macro variables, as follows.

```
%let dsin=Credit;
%let XVar=Debt;
%let YVar=Loan;
%let Gr=;
%let Fstar=;
%let pvalue=;

%ContGrF(&DSin, &Xvar, &YVar, Gr, Fstar, Pvalue);

%put Gr=&Gr;
%put Fstar=&Fstar;
%put pvalue=&Pvalue;
```

If you investigate the two measures, G_r and F^*, you will discover that the p-value of the F-test saturates quickly; that is, it reaches either 1 or 0 and is less discriminant than the Gini/entropy ratio G_r.

It is worth noting that these measures are used as purity measures in *decision tree* models with continuous dependent variables (i.e., *regression trees*). Some analysts like to use decision tree software to identify the most significant variables (i.e., to *filter* them). The preceding macro is a simple alternative.

14.4 CORRELATION COEFFICIENTS

This section presents the well-known correlation concept as a way of determining the association between continuous variables. However, we have to remember that in this case, *both* variables have to be continuous or at least have to have been assigned scores on a numerical scale, as in the case of ordinal variables.

The correlation coefficient is defined in statistics as the *Pearson correlation coefficient*. It is defined as

$$r = \frac{\sum_{i=1}^{n}(x_i - \bar{x})(y_i - \bar{y})}{\left\{ \sum_{i=1}^{n}(x_i - \bar{x})^2 \sum_{i=1}^{n}(y_i - \bar{y})^2 \right\}^{1/2}}, \tag{14.12}$$

where $x_i, y_i, i = 1, \ldots, n$ are the n observations of the variables x and y, with mean values of $\bar{x}$ and $\bar{y}$, respectively.

The value of r is always between -1.0 and 1.0. Variables that have a correlation coefficient near 0 are called uncorrelated; those with r closer to 1 or -1 are said to be correlated. Figure 14.1 shows cases where r is positive, negative, and zero.

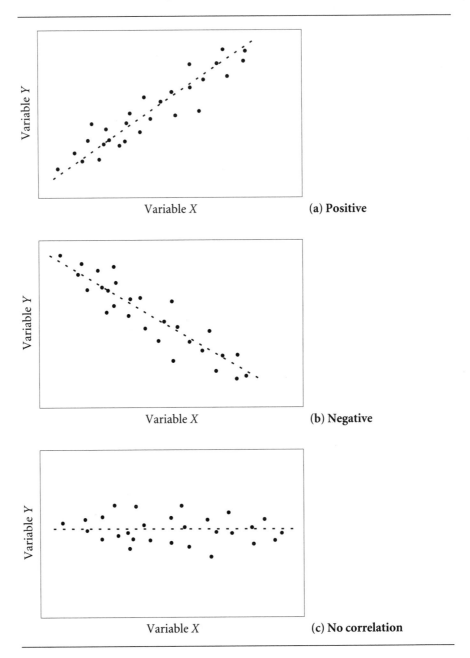

Figure 14.1   Correlation between continuous variables.

The figure shows the best linear fit in each case. It is well known that the slope of this line is the correlation coefficient defined in Equation 14.12.

Equation 14.12 does not prevent us from using a categorical variable if the two categories are represented by numbers, for example, 0 and 1.

Figure 14.2(a) shows this case. However, Figure 14.2 (b) shows that the scale of the variable x, which is not binary, *does* play a significant role in the value of r. If the variable x is normalized, between 0 and 1 in this case, we may obtain a larger value for r. Therefore, if we use any binary variables in association with the correlation coefficient, normalization is a necessary step.

Note that the normalization of two continuous variables does not change the value of r between them. It only plays a role when one of them is binary. Figure 14.3 shows the cases when r is positive, negative, and zero (after normalizing the continuous variable).

The problem with the Pearson correlation coefficient is that it is sensitive to outliers. Let us demonstrate this feature with a simple example.

EXAMPLE 14.1 The income and home value (in $1000s) of 18 individuals are shown in Table 14.3 The value of the correlation coefficient between income and home value is 0.92. Suppose now that home values of two individuals have changed, as shown in bold in Table 14.4; the new data is also shown in bold. The value of the Pearson correlation coefficient has dropped to 0.77, i.e., a difference of 16%.
◆

Table 14.3   Incomes and home values.

Income	52	64	25	37	36	100	99	31	25
Home value	285	364	136	203	269	526	613	192	205

Income	48	**40**	22	83	22	20	37	81	**100**
Home value	194	364	165	514	120	129	324	448	**419**

Table 14.4   Values of Table 14.3 with two changes.

Income	52	64	25	37	36	100	99	31	25
Home value	285	364	136	203	269	526	613	192	205

Income	48	40	22	83	22	20	37	81	100
Home value	194	**759**	165	514	120	129	324	448	**667**

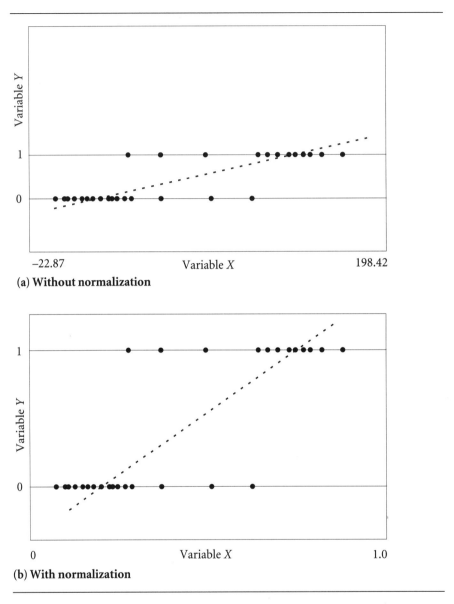

(a) **Without normalization**

(b) **With normalization**

Figure 14.2   Correlation between a continuous variable and a binary variable.

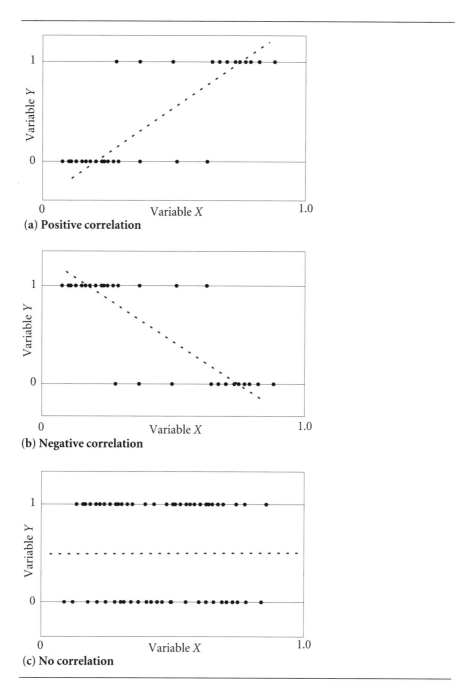

Figure 14.3 Correlation between a continuous variable and a binary variable.

To remedy this weakness of the Pearson correlation coefficient, another coefficient of correlation is suggested based on the concept of the *rank* of the observations with in the variable. This is known as the Spearman rank correlation coefficient. It is defined as

$$\theta = \frac{\sum_{i=1}^{n}(R_i - \bar{R})(S_i - \bar{S})}{\left\{ \sum_{i=1}^{n}(R_i - \bar{R})^2 \sum_{i=1}^{n}(S_i - \bar{S})^2 \right\}^{1/2}}, \tag{14.13}$$

where $R_i, S_i, i = 1, \ldots, n$ are the ranks of the variables x and y, and $\bar{R}$ and $\bar{S}$ are the mean values of these ranks, respectively.

EXAMPLE 14.2 Continuing from Example 14.1, the values of Spearman's coefficient for the two cases are 0.91 and 0.86, respectively. Therefore, the two outliers caused the Spearman's coefficient to drop 5% only. This shows that Spearman's coefficient is less sensitive to such data outliers.

◆

PROC CORR of SAS/STAT calculates these two correlation coefficients, along with other coefficients and tests of their significance. The following macro wraps the procedure and stores the resulting coefficients in a dataset with the appropriate labels (see Table 14.5).

Table 14.5   Parameters of macro VarCorr().

Header	VarCorr(DSin, VarX, VarY, CorrDS);	
Parameter	*Description*	
DSin	Input dataset	
VarX	*X* variable name	
VarY	*Y* variable name	
CorrDS	Output dataset with correlation coefficients	

```
%macro VarCorr(DSin, VarX, VarY, CorrDS);
/* Calculation of the correlation coefficients between
   VarX and VarY in the dataset DSin.
   The results are stored in the CorrDS dataset
   with the names of the coefficients */

/* Step 1: put the variable names in uppercase */
%let x=%upcase(&VarX);
%let y=%upcase(&VarY);
```

```
/* Step 2: invoke proc corr */
proc corr data=&DSin pearson spearman hoeffding kendall
 outp=temp_P outs=temp_S outh=temp_H outk=temp_K noprint;
 var &x &y;
run;
/* Step 3: Get the coefficients from the temporary datasets */
proc sql noprint;
 select &x into : xyP from temp_P where upcase(_NAME_) eq "&y";
 select &x into : xyS from temp_S where upcase(_NAME_) eq "&y";
 select &x into : xyH from temp_H where upcase(_NAME_) eq "&y";
 select &x into : xyK from temp_K where upcase(_NAME_) eq "&y";

 create table &CorrDS (Type char(10), Value num);
 insert into &CorrDS values('Pearson'  , &xyP)
                      values('Spearman' , &xyS)
                      values('Hoeffding', &xyH)
                      values('Kendall'  , &xyK);
quit;
/* Clean the workspace and finish the macro.*/
proc datasets library=work nolist;
  delete temp_P temp_s temp_H temp_K;
quit;

%mend;
```

You should have noticed by now that two more correlation measures were imple-mented in the macro VarCorr(), namely, the *Hoeffding measure of dependence D* and the *Kendall* τ_b. Like the Spearman coefficient, both of these coefficients are non-parametric measures of correlation. In fact, they are *more* nonparametric than the Spearman coefficient. Refer to the SAS/STAT help for more details on these two coefficients.

CHAPTER 15

PRINCIPAL COMPONENT ANALYSIS

15.1 INTRODUCTION

Principal component analysis (PCA) is one of the oldest and most used methods for the reduction of multidimensional data (Johnson and Wichern 2001). The basic idea of PCA is to find a set of linear transformations of the original variables such that the new set of variables could describe *most* of the variance in a relatively fewer number of variables. The new set of variables is presented, and actually derived, in a decreasing order of contribution. In addition, the first new variable, which we call the first *principal component,* contains the largest proportion of the variance of the original variable set, and the second principal component contains less, and so on.

The usual procedure, then, is to keep only the first few of the principal components, which contain, say, 95% or 99% of the variance of the original set of variables. PCA is particularly useful when

- There are too many (independent) variables

- The independent variables show a high correlation between them

As we will see later in this chapter, there are two main methods for performing PCA of a set of data. The first one involves working with the variance–covariance matrix. However, the values included in this matrix depend on the units and magnitude of each variable. Therefore, a variable representing a customer's balance will be in the range of, say, $0 to $100,000.00, and the age field will be in the range of 0 to 100. To normalize all the variables, the matrix representing the correlations, R, is sometimes used instead to calculate the principal components. There is a live and active debate in the literature about the advantages and disadvantages of these two approaches. In this chapter, we present the implementation of both methods.

The final output of PCA is the new set of variables, principal components, which represents the original dataset. The user then would normally use only the first few of these new variables because they contain most of the information of the original dataset.

In the following sections, we first present the theoretical background of PCA. However, if you are not interested in the theory, skip Section 15.2 and proceed directly to Section 15.3, which provides the macro for SAS implementation of PCA with an example. Finally, we present a modified macro that selects the most contributing variables containing the required percentage of the variance.

The final section in this chapter discusses some of the issues that frequently arise while using PCA.

15.2 Mathematical Formulations

Let us start with a set of p variables, $x_1, x_2, \cdots, x_p$, and assume that we have n observations of these variables. The mean vector μ is the vector whose p components are defined as

$$\mu_i = \frac{1}{n} \sum_{j=1}^{n} x_{ij}, \qquad i = 1, \cdots, p. \tag{15.1}$$

The unbiased $p \times p$ variance–covariance matrix (simply the covariance matrix) of this sample is defined as

$$S = \frac{1}{n-1} \sum_{j=1}^{n} (x_j - \mu)(x_j - \mu)'. \tag{15.2}$$

Finally, the $p \times p$ correlation matrix R of this sample is defined as

$$R = D^{-1/2} S D^{1/2}, \tag{15.3}$$

where the matrix $D^{1/2}$ is the *sample standard deviation matrix,* which is calculated from the covariance S as the square root of its diagonal elements or

$$D^{1/2} = \begin{bmatrix} \sqrt{s_{11}} & 0 & \cdots & 0 \\ 0 & \sqrt{s_{22}} & \cdots & 0 \\ \vdots & \vdots & \ddots & \vdots \\ 0 & 0 & \cdots & \sqrt{s_{pp}} \end{bmatrix}, \tag{15.4}$$

while the matrix $D^{-1/2}$ is the inverse of $D^{1/2}$, or

$$D^{-1/2} = \begin{bmatrix} \frac{1}{\sqrt{s_{11}}} & 0 & \cdots & 0 \\ 0 & \frac{1}{\sqrt{s_{22}}} & \cdots & 0 \\ \vdots & \vdots & \ddots & \vdots \\ 0 & 0 & \cdots & \frac{1}{\sqrt{s_{pp}}} \end{bmatrix}. \tag{15.5}$$

Let the p-pairs $(\lambda_1, v_1), (\lambda_2, v_2), \cdots, (\lambda_p, v_p)$, be the eigenvalue–eigenvectors of the covariance matrix S, with the eigenvalues arranged in descending order, $\lambda_1 \geq \lambda_2 \geq \cdots \geq \lambda_p \geq 0$.

It can be demonstrated that the ith sample principal component is given by

$$y_i = \begin{bmatrix} x_1 & x_2 & \cdots & x_p \end{bmatrix} v_i, \qquad i = 1, \cdots, p. \tag{15.6}$$

The variance of the variable y_i is equal to its corresponding eigenvalue λ_i. Therefore, the total sample variance is the sum of all the eigenvalues:

$$Tr(S) = \sum_{i=1}^{p} S_{ii} = \sum_{i=1}^{p} \lambda_i. \tag{15.7}$$

To obtain the principal components using the correlation matrix R, which is also called the *standardized observations covariance matrix*, we replace S with R in the preceding equations and denote the resulting principal components $z_i, i = 1, \cdots, p$.

In this case, the eigenvalue–eigenvector pairs of the matrix R are $(\theta_1, w_1), \cdots, (\theta_p, w_p)$, with $\theta_1 \geq \cdots \geq \theta_p \geq 0$ and the principal components of the standardized variables are given by

$$z_i = \begin{bmatrix} x_1 & x_2 & \cdots & x_p \end{bmatrix} w_i, \qquad i = 1, \cdots, p. \tag{15.8}$$

Similarly, the variance of the variable z_i is equal to its corresponding eigenvalue θ_i, and the total sample variance of the standardized variables is the sum of all the eigenvalues of R:

$$Tr(R) = \sum_{i=1}^{p} R_{ii} = \sum_{i=1}^{p} \theta_i. \tag{15.9}$$

15.3 IMPLEMENTING AND USING PCA

We may summarize the mathematical formulations in the previous section by stating that PCA works by finding the eigenvalues of the covariance matrix and using the eigenvectors as the linear transformations to obtain the principal components. The importance of each principal component is determined by the relative magnitude of its eigenvalue. Therefore, we call the principal component corresponding to the highest eigenvalue *the first principal component*; the second highest, the second principal component, and so on.

In addition to the relative ordering of the principal components, an important property of PCA is that the sum of the total variance in the original variables is equal to the sum of the eigenvalues of the covariance matrix.

Before we proceed, let us demonstrate these principles with an example.

Table 15.1 shows 20 records of credit card customers of a bank. The variables represent the average monthly balance, the average transaction value, the average monthly interest paid, and the average balance on the customer's checking account. All the variables are related to the credit card business of the bank's clients (note that

Table 15.1   Data of 20 credit card customers.

Customer ID	Average credit card balance	Average transaction value	Average interest paid	Checking account balance
1	338.55	102.66	17.9	180.00
2	149.39	30.55	8.9	210.92
3	135.47	39.33	7.4	232.76
4	26.78	7.13	1.5	200.00
5	184.91	44.21	9.9	461.13
6	333.97	106.35	19.3	263.83
7	464.49	77.14	24.0	501.01
8	26.88	6.60	1.5	439.64
9	458.13	72.39	25.6	449.92
10	395.32	108.18	22.6	188.54
11	257.60	38.24	15.0	496.47
12	98.34	15.26	5.2	463.50
13	244.86	41.45	12.8	441.58
14	388.85	55.93	20.2	429.51
15	401.28	117.87	23.3	538.55
16	426.62	65.65	24.5	250.42
17	420.27	113.09	22.1	348.48
18	247.72	38.04	13.2	469.68
19	392.29	72.17	23.2	474.02
20	210.17	49.81	11.3	381.06

the balance of the checking account is relevant because it can be assumed that the bank's clients use their checking accounts to pay credit card bills). Therefore, we may attempt to find a transformation to reduce these four variables into a smaller set while keeping all or most of the information in the data.

PROC PRINCOMP of SAS/STAT performs principal component analysis. The following listing shows its use with the data in Table 15.1.

```
PROC PRINCOMP DATA=CC COV;
  VAR AvgBalance   AvgTransValue   AvgInt  CheckBalance;;
RUN;
```

Invoking PROC PRINCOMP will result in the calculation of the covariance matrix, the eigenvalues, and the eigenvectors. The following is the listing of the SAS output of the preceding code.

The PRINCOMP Procedure

Observations	20
Variables	4

Simple Statistics

	AvgBalance	AvgTransValue	AvgInt	CheckBalance
Mean	280.0945000	60.10250000	15.47000000	371.0510000
StD	141.7152098	35.31563779	7.88309984	123.0054403

Covariance Matrix

	AvgBalance	AvgTransValue	AvgInt	CheckBalance
AvgBalance	20083.20068	4108.87486	1110.41977	2616.63039
AvgTransValue	4108.87486	1247.19427	230.09403	-462.56824
AvgInt	1110.41977	230.09403	62.14326	132.19482
CheckBalance	2616.63039	-462.56824	132.19482	15130.33835

Total Variance   36522.876561

Eigenvalues of the Covariance Matrix

	Eigenvalue	Difference	Proportion	Cumulative
1	21908.4417	7617.4826	0.5999	0.5999
2	14290.9591	13968.2050	0.3913	0.9911
3	322.7540	322.0323	0.0088	1.0000
4	0.7218		0.0000	1.0000

```
                     Eigenvectors

                Prin1       Prin2       Prin3       Prin4

AvgBalance      0.920774    -.323359    -.211416    -.054024
AvgTransValue   0.175967    -.135396    0.975021    -.006076
AvgInt          0.050739    -.018725    -.005535    0.998521
CheckBalance    0.344438    0.936353    0.067867    0.000433
```

The results show that the first two eigenvalues represent 99.11% of the variance of the original four variables. Therefore, by using the first and second principal components, it is possible to keep 99% of the information contained in the four variables.

Furthermore, the parameters of the equations defining the new variables, denoted Prin1 and Prin2, are given by components of the eigenvectors for the first and second principal components. Thus, we can define the new variables Prin1 and Prin2 as

$$\text{Prin1} = 0.920774 \, (\text{AvgBalance}) + 0.175967 \, (\text{AvgTransValue})$$
$$+ 0.050739 \, (\text{AvgInt}) + 0.344438 \, (\text{CheckBalance}), \qquad (15.10)$$
$$\text{Prin2} = -.323359 \, (\text{AvgBalance}) - .135396 \, (\text{AvgTransValue})$$
$$- .018725 \, (\text{AvgInt}) + 0.936353 \, (\text{CheckBalance}).$$

PROC SCORE of SAS/STAT allows the automatic substitution in the last two equations, provided that we store the values of the eigenvectors in a dataset and instruct PROC PRINCOMP to compute only the first two eigenvalues and eigenvectors. However, before performing a full analysis of the covariance matrix of the dataset, we would not have known that we needed only two principal components to keep more than 99% of the data variance. Therefore, in our SAS macro implementation of PCA, we adopt a two-step approach.

First, we invoke PROC PRINCOMP to analyze the full covariance matrix and obtain all the eigenvalues. Then we calculate the number of princpial components needed to preserve a certain percentage of the variance. The second step follows by using only the identified number of principal components to generate the new variables. The new variables will be denoted Prin1, Prin2, and so on. The following macro implements this strategy (see Table 15.2).

Step 1
First run PRINCOMP to calculate all the eigenvalues.

```
proc princomp data=&DSin &Method outstat=&DSEigen noprint;
var &VarList;
run;
```

Step 2
Select the top *P%* of the summation of the eigenvalues.

Table 15.2   Parameters of macro `PrinComp2()`.

Header	`PrinComp2(DSin, VarList, Method, P, DSEigen, DSout);`
Parameter	*Description*
`DSin`	Input dataset
`VarList`	List of variables
`Method`	PCA method (COV or empty)
`P`	Percentage of total variance to keep
`DSEigen`	Output dataset to store the eigenvectors
`DSout`	Output dataset with the principal components added

```
data Tempcov1;
 set &DSEigen;
 if _Type_ ne 'EIGENVAL' then delete;
 drop _NAME_;
 run;
proc transpose data=Tempcov1 out=TempCovT;
run;

data TempCov2;
 set TempCovT;
 retain SumEigen 0;
 SumEigen=SumEigen+C011;
run;

proc sql noprint;
select max(SumEigen) into :SEigen from TempCov2;
quit;

data TempCov3;
 set TempCov2;
IEigen=_N_;
PEigen = SumEigen/&SEigen;
run;


/* We now count the number of eigenvalues needed to
 reach P_Percent */

proc sql noprint;
 select count(*) into :Nh from Tempcov3 where PEigen >= &P;
 select count(*) into :NN from TempCov3;
%let N=%eval(&NN-&Nh+1);
quit;
```

Step 3

Keep only the selected set of eigenvalues and their equivalent eigenvectors. Use this reduced set for generation of new variables.

```
/* Delete from the DSEigen all the rows above
 the needed N eigenvectors */
data TempCov4;
 set &DSEigen;
run;
proc sql noprint;
%do i=%eval(&N+1) %to &NN;
 delete from TempCov4 where _NAME_ = "Prin&i";
%end;
quit;


/* And score */
proc score data=&Dsin Score=TempCov4 Out=&DSout;
Var &VarList;
run;
```

Step 4

Finally, clean the workspace and finish the macro.

```
proc datasets library=work nodetails;
delete Tempcov1 Tempcov2 Tempcov3 Tempcov4 Tempcovt;
run;
quit;

%mend;
```

15.4 Comments on Using PCA

15.4.1 Number of Principal Components

In the previous section, we presented the macro PrinComp2(), which allows the automatic selection of the top principal components by specifying the percentage of the variance that needs to be preserved. In most practical applications, it is sufficient to keep between 80% and 95% of the variance.

15.4.2 Success of PCA

Sometimes PCA may not be a suitable tool for the reduction of the given dataset or it shows that the variables cannot be reduced, at least not by using PCA. A characteristic

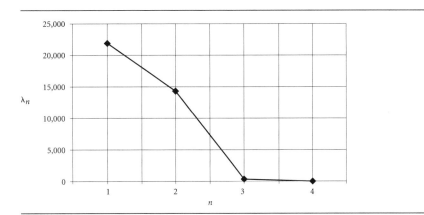

Figure 15.1   Scree plot of the credit card data.

feature of these cases is that the decline in the magnitude of the eigenvalues is very slow. This leads to taking a larger number of principal components and, therefore, achieving insignificant reduction of the number of variables.

Statisticians use a plot called *scree plot,* which displays the magnitude of the eigenvalues on a line chart, to show the rate of decay of the eigenvalues. The scree plot of the eigenvalues of the last example is given in Figure 15.1. The figure shows that the slope representing the change in the magnitude of the eigenvalues changes from very steep in the first two eigenvalues to very shallow in the third. It also shows that the fourth eigenvalue is almost zero.

Using the scree plot, it is easy to see that we need only two eigenvalues to preserve most of the variance. However, Figure 15.2 is the scree plot for a different dataset, where the magnitude of the eigenvalues is also decreasing, but very slowly. In this

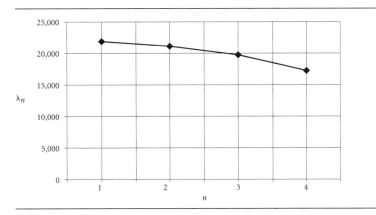

Figure 15.2   Scree plot of uncorrelated data.

case, we conclude that PCA did not find a simple reduced representation of the data and that the variables are not significantly correlated.

15.4.3 NOMINAL VARIABLES

As discussed in Section 9.4, nominal variables can be mapped into indicator (dummy) variables. These indicator variables can be used as ordinary variables in PCA. Although it is possible to perform PCA using this approach, it is not recommended because of the scant information available about the behavior of indicator variables in PCA. Only a limited number of studies have explored this approach. Therefore, we recommend using other techniques specific to the analysis of categorical variables.

15.4.4 DATASET SIZE AND PERFORMANCE

PCA is based on finding the eigenvalues of the covariance matrix. Therefore, the required computational resources depend on the number of variables more than the number of records. Therefore, performing PCA with large datasets should not pose a significant problem using SAS. The only real issue arises when the number of variables included in the analysis becomes large, say more than 50. In this case, the numerical algorithms for finding the eigenvalues and eigenvectors may themselves be pushed to the limit and provide unreliable results. Therefore, we recommend that PCA be used only with a reasonable number of variables (< 20 or so), which are believed to be correlated and could be reduced into a smaller core set. This should be based on the understanding of the data at hand.

CHAPTER 16

FACTOR ANALYSIS

16.1 INTRODUCTION

Factor analysis (FA) is similar to principal component analysis in the sense that it leads to the deduction of a new, smaller set of variables that almost describes the behavior given by the original set. However, FA is different because it does not attempt to find transformations for the given variables but aims to discover internal or hidden *factors*, which would have resulted in the current set of variables (Johnson and Wichern 2001).

Historically, factor analysis was proposed as a method to investigate intelligence as the hidden factor behind the ability of students to achieve certain levels of learning in fields such as mathematics, music, and languages. It was controversial at the time because of the interpretations' specifics, which were attached to the *discovered* factors. However, most of these arguments have been abandoned and FA is used systematically in a wide range of problems, including our subject—data reduction. Another important use of factor analysis is as a process of data exploration, which is simply called *exploratory factor analysis* (Johnson and Wichern 2001). We do not deal with the exploratory aspect of FA, but limit our presentation to its use in data reduction.

16.1.1 BASIC MODEL

The basic idea behind factor analysis is to attempt to find a set of hidden *factors* such that the currently observed variables are recovered by performing a set of *linear transformations* on these factors. Mathematically, given the set of *observed* variables x_1, $x_2, \ldots, x_p$, factor analysis attempts to find the set of factors $f_1, f_2, \ldots, f_m$, such that

$$
\begin{aligned}
x_1 - \mu_1 &= l_{11}f_1 + l_{12}f_2 + \cdots + l_{1m}f_m + \varepsilon_1 \\
x_2 - \mu_2 &= l_{21}f_1 + l_{22}f_2 + \cdots + l_{2m}f_m + \varepsilon_2 \\
&\vdots \quad \vdots \\
x_p - \mu_p &= l_{p1}f_1 + l_{p2}f_2 + \cdots + l_{pm}f_m + \varepsilon_p,
\end{aligned}
\tag{16.1}
$$

257

where $\mu_1, \mu_2, \ldots, \mu_p$ are the means of the variables $x_1, x_2, \ldots, x_p$, and the terms $\varepsilon_1, \varepsilon_2, \ldots, \varepsilon_p$ represent the unobservable part of variables $x_1, x_2, \ldots$, which are also called *specific factors*. The terms l_{ij}, $i = 1, \ldots, p, j = 1, \ldots, m$ are known as the loadings. The factors $f_1, f_2, \ldots, f_m$ are known as the *common factors*.

Equation 16.1 can be written in matrix form as

$$\mathbf{X} - \boldsymbol{\mu} = \mathbf{LF} + \boldsymbol{\varepsilon}. \tag{16.2}$$

Therefore, one could state the factor analysis problem as follows: Given the observed variables $\mathbf{X}$, along with their mean $\boldsymbol{\mu}$, we attempt to find the set of factors $\mathbf{F}$ and the associated loadings $\mathbf{L}$, such that Equation 16.2 is valid.

The different methods of estimating the loading matrix $\mathbf{L}$ and the vector of factors $\mathbf{F}$ rely on imposing some restrictions on their statistical properties. The following are the most common restrictions.

1. All the factors are independent, with zero mean and variance of unity.

2. All the error terms are also independent, with zero mean and constant variance.

3. The errors are independent of the factors.

With these three restrictions, the factor model of Equation 16.2 constitutes what is known as the *orthogonal factor model*.

Denoting the variance of the ith specific factor, ε_i, by ψ_i, it can be shown that the variance of the ith variable, x_i, is given as

$$\underbrace{\sigma_{ii}}_{\text{Var}(x_i)} = \underbrace{l_{i1}^2 + l_{i2}^2 + \cdots + l_{im}^2}_{\text{Communality}} + \underbrace{\psi_i}_{\substack{\text{Specific} \\ \text{Variance}}}. \tag{16.3}$$

Equation 16.3 shows that the variance of each observable variable is decomposed to the *communality* and the variance of the specific factor. The communality is usually given the symbol h_i^2 for the ith variable, namely,

$$h_i^2 = l_{i1}^2 + l_{i2}^2 + \cdots + l_{im}^2. \tag{16.4}$$

In evaluating the factor model, one usually performs two checks. First, the analysis of the communality shows how much of the variance of the variable is explained by the proposed set of factors. When a small proportion of the variance is explained by the factors, the factor model is suspect, to say the least. The second check is to examine the factors and try to interpret them in terms of their ability to explain the correlation between the variables.

High values of the factor loadings indicate a strong relationship between that factor and the associated variables. A cut-off value of 0.4 is commonly used to determine the significance of a factor in explaining observed variables. However, sometimes the resulting factors show no particular pattern; in such a case, *rotating* the factors is attempted. This method of *factor rotation* is explained next.

16.1.2 Factor Rotation

Any orthogonal matrix $\mathbf{T}$ such that $\mathbf{T'T} = \mathbf{TT'} = \mathbf{I}$ could be introduced into Equation 16.2 without changing the model structure. In this case, we may write the factor model as

$$\mathbf{X} - \mu = \mathbf{LF} + \varepsilon = \mathbf{LTT'F} + \varepsilon = \mathbf{L^*F^*} + \varepsilon, \qquad (16.5)$$

where $\mathbf{L^*}$ and $\mathbf{F^*}$ are the new loading matrix and vector of factors defined as

$$\mathbf{L^*} = \mathbf{LT} \quad \text{and} \quad \mathbf{F^*} = \mathbf{T'F}.$$

An orthogonal transformation matrix, such as $\mathbf{T}$, represents *rotation* of axes. Such rotation could be designed to allow the factors to have certain desired properties. These rotations could lead to easier interpretation of the model.

16.1.3 Estimation Methods

There are two methods for solving the factor model equations for the matrix $\mathbf{L}$ and the factors $\mathbf{F}$: (1) the maximum likelihood (ML) method and (2) the principal component method. The maximum likelihood method assumes that both the common and specific factors, and therefore the observed variables, are normally distributed. The validity of this assumption cannot be guaranteed for all datasets. Another limitation of the ML method is that it is computationally expensive. In fact, the SAS documentation mentions that it takes on average *100 times* the time needed to solve a problem as the principal component method takes.

The computational algorithm involves iterative procedures that may not even converge (see example in Section 16.1.5). However, the ML method allows the evaluation of the number factors' significance and is based on robust theoretical foundations. These two advantages usually make it the method of choice for statisticians. On the other hand, the principal component method is very fast, easy to interpret, and guaranteed to find a solution for all datasets.

16.1.4 Variable Standardization

Because we are not really interested in the scale of magnitude of each variable, but rather in the presence or absence of correlation between the variables, factor analysis starts by standardizing the variables. The variables are standardized such that they have a zero mean and a variance of one. In this way, the total variance of p observed variables is also equal to p. For example, starting with 7 observed variables, PROC FAC-TOR will standardize them such that when the results of the factor analysis are displayed, we speak of explaining, say 6.5, of the total variance of 7.0.

16.1.5 Illustrative Example

Recall the banking dataset of Table 15.1. The dataset contains the monthly summary of credit card average balance (AvgBalance), average value of the credit card transactions

(AvgTransValue), average value of monthly interest (AvgInt), and average balance of checking account (CheckBalance).

Note that the first three variables relate to credit card account transactions, and the last variable relates to the checking account for each customer. We invoke PROC FAC-TOR, using the principal component method. We are searching for a model that can represent all the variables. The SAS code as well as the results are as follows:

```
proc factor data=Bank method=PRIN;
 var AvgBalance AvgTransValue AvgInt CheckBalance;
run;
```

```
                    The FACTOR Procedure
           Initial Factor Method: Principal Components
                Prior Communality Estimates: ONE
```

```
   Eigenvalues of the Correlation Matrix: Total = 4  Average = 1
```

	Eigenvalue	Difference	Proportion	Cumulative
1	2.77045385	1.72791808	0.6926	0.6926
2	1.04253577	0.86144659	0.2606	0.9532
3	0.18108918	0.17516798	0.0453	0.9985
4	0.00592120		0.0015	1.0000

```
   2 factors will be retained by the MINEIGEN criterion.
```

```
                       Factor Pattern
```

	Factor1	Factor2
AvgBalance	0.98266	0.06501
AvgTransValue	0.90873	-0.23877
AvgInt	0.98395	0.05059
CheckBalance	0.10443	0.98931

```
             Variance Explained by Each Factor
```

Factor1	Factor2
2.7704539	1.0425358

```
      Final Communality Estimates: Total = 3.812990
```

AvgBalance	AvgTransValue	AvgInt	CheckBalance
0.96983992	0.88279765	0.97070795	0.98964410

Remember that PROC FACTOR had standardized the variables such that the total variance of the four analysis variables is 4.0. The output shows that we may use two principal components to calculate two factors, which could explain a variance of 3.8129. This represents 95.32% of the total variance. This result could be read directly from the cummulative sum of the eigenvalues. Using two eigenvalues of the correlation matrix, we keep 0.9532 of the total variance.

The communality of each variable is simply the summation of the square of the corresponding common loadings of the variable. For example, the communality of the variable AvgBalance is calculated as

$$(0.98266)^2 + (0.06501)^2 = 0.96984.$$

We now turn our attention to the common loadings. We observe that the loadings of the first factor for the variables AvgBalance, AvgTransValue, and AvgInt are all high (i.e., larger than 0.4). This indicates that the first factor is a summary of the *credit card* transactions, which is a distinct business entity from the second factor, which represents the balance of the checking account.

Let us now experiment with factor rotation. One method of factor rotation is the *varimax* method. In this method, a criterion is maximized (the varimax criterion) such that the absolute value of the loadings in any column is, as much as possible, either high or low. For example, examining the loadings of the second factor in the banking example, we find a high value of 0.98931 and an intermediate value of -0.23877. We attempt rotating the factors to reduce intermediate values, either by increasing the high value or, more realistically in this case, by *spreading* this intermediate value over several other factors. The SAS code in this case is as follows:

```
proc factor data=Bank method=PRIN rotate=varimax;
 var AvgBalance AvgTransValue AvgInt CheckBalance;
run;
```

The result of the code is both the original factor model and the rotated factors with the resulting new factor loadings. The second part with the rotation effects follows.

Orthogonal Transformation Matrix

	1	2
1	0.99731	0.07337
2	-0.07337	0.99731

Rotated Factor Pattern

	Factor1	Factor2
AvgBalance	0.97524	0.13693
AvgTransValue	0.92380	-0.17145
AvgInt	0.97758	0.12265
CheckBalance	0.03156	0.99431

Variance Explained by Each Factor

Factor1	Factor2
2.7611530	1.0518366

Final Communality Estimates: Total = 3.812990

AvgBalance	AvgTransValue	AvgInt	CheckBalance
0.96983992	0.88279765	0.97070795	0.98964410

The printout shows that the transformation was successful in increasing the high values and reducing the smaller ones. For example, in the loadings of the second factor, the intermediate value of −0.23877 is replaced with a smaller value of −0.17145. Note that some of the loadings have increased as a result of *spreading* the intermediate values. The factors now present an even more clear picture of the two lines of business the bank is pursuing, namely, checking accounts and credit cards.

Before we turn our attention to the automation of this process to include it as a tool for data reduction, we illustrate the occasional vulnerability of the ML method. When we attempt to solve the same factor model using the maximum likelihood, we implement the option METHOD=ML as follows:

```
proc factor data=Bank method=ML rotate=varimax;
 var AvgBalance AvgTransValue AvgInt CheckBalance;
run;
```

The code generates an error, execution stops, and the SAS engine writes the error message to the SAS Log as follows:

```
---- The SAS log ----
NOTE: 1 factor will be retained by the PROPORTION criterion.
ERROR: Communality greater than 1.0.
```

Furthermore, the preceding results in the following code in the SAS output.

```
---- The SAS Output ----
```

```
                    The FACTOR Procedure
          Initial Factor Method: Maximum Likelihood

            Prior Communality Estimates: SMC

     AvgBalance      AvgTransValue   AvgInt      CheckBalance
     0.98822342      0.73267380      0.98835067   0.18701597
```

Preliminary Eigenvalues: Total = 171.726956 Average = 42.931739

	Eigenvalue	Difference	Proportion	Cumulative
1	171.829290	171.145087	1.0006	1.0006
2	0.684203	0.971307	0.0040	1.0046
3	-0.287104	0.212328	-0.0017	1.0029
4	-0.499432		-0.0029	1.0000

1 factor will be retained by the PROPORTION criterion.

```
Iteration
Criterion   Ridge       Change          Communalities
1           0.1883987   0.0000 0.1675   0.98834 0.68228 0.99964 0.01948
2           0.1883510   0.0000 0.0008   0.98788 0.68299 1.00010 0.01865
```

ERROR: Communality greater than 1.0.

This introduction barely scratches the surface of the subject of factor analysis. You can consult many books on the subject for a deeper discussion and the various applications of factor analysis. This book focuses on the use of factor analysis in variable reduction. Therefore, we attempt to replace the original set of variables with a smaller set such that the new set would better represent the underlying structure. In this respect, factor analysis is very similar to principal component analysis (PCA). The next section discusses briefly the differences between the two techniques.

16.2 RELATIONSHIP BETWEEN PCA AND FA

As discussed, in factor analysis and specifically when using it as a data reduction technique, attention is focused on finding a *few* factors that can represent *most* of the information in the observable variables. In this regard, factor analysis is conceptually similar to principal component analysis. However, they are different in the following aspects.

1. Factor analysis assumes an underlying structure that relates the factors to the observed variables. PCA does not assume any structure.

2. PCA tries to rotate the axis of the *original* variables, using a set of linear transformations, to explain the variance. Factor analysis, on the other hand, creates a new set of variables to explain the *covariances* and correlations between the observed variables.

3. In PCA, when we use the first two principal components and then revise the model by also using the third component, the first two components do not change. This is not the case in factor analysis where, in general, a two-factor model is completely different from a three-factor model.

4. The calculations involved in PCA are straightforward and usually very fast. PCA also converges for all datasets. In factor analysis, there is a variety of methods. Furthermore, the calculations, especially in the case of the ML method, are involved and complicated. In some cases, the ML algorithm may not even converge.

The differences between factor analysis and PCA should highlight the meaning of each of the two techniques. However, in many data mining applications the meaning of the variables is not vital. Sometimes, we are interested only in creating a smaller number of variables that contain most of the information in the data, regardless of what we mean by *information*. In such cases, PCA may be more suitable because it is easier to use and interpret.

16.3 IMPLEMENTATION OF FACTOR ANALYSIS

PROC FACTOR and PROC SCORE of SAS implement the algorithms needed to perform factor analysis and score new datasets to generate the reduced set of variables (factors in this case). Our SAS implementation will be a set of macros that wrap these two procedures to facilitate their deployment.

PROC FACTOR contains many options for selecting both the estimation method and factor rotation. In our implementation, we have made the following choices.

1. The principal component method will always be used. This is motivated by its speed and the reliability of obtaining results in *all* cases.

2. We will always use factor rotation, with the varimax criterion, in an attempt to make the factors *sharply defined.*

3. No systematic attempt will be made to explain the factor model. If in a particular case we can find a good interpretation for the factors, we treat this event as a bonus, not a necessity.

16.3.1   OBTAINING THE FACTORS

The macro implementation using PROC FACTOR is straightforward. We set the option METHOD to the value PRIN to use the principal component method and store the results in the dataset DSFact. The PROption is used to control printing of the result of PROC FACTOR. Setting it to zero suppresses all output.

Table 16.1   Parameters of macro Factor().

Header	Factor(DSin, VarList, NFactors, DSFact, PROption);
Parameter	*Description*
DSin	Input dataset
VarList	List of variables
NFactors	Number of required factors
DSFactors	Dataset containing the results of the factor analysis
PROptions	Printing options (0 = no printing)

The following is the code of the macro, along with how to use it to model the data of the last example Bank (see Table 16.1).

```
%macro Factor(DSin, VarList, NFactors, DSFact, PROption);
PROC FACTOR DATA=&DSin
            Method=PRIN
            Rotate=Varimax
            nfactors=&Nfactors
outstat=&DSFact score
 %if &PROption = 0 %then noprint; ;
 var &varlist;
```

```
run;
%mend;
%let dsin=Bank;
%let varlist=AvgBalance AvgTransValue AvgInt CheckBalance;
%let nfactors=2;
%let DSFact=BankFact;
%let PROption=0;
%Factor(&DSin, &VarList, &NFactors, &DSFact, &PROption);
```

This macro requires the user to know in advance the number of factors to use. Ideally, this number would be obtained through several trials and by examining the meaning of the factors. However, when the number of observed variables is large, one can always use a smaller arbitrary number of factors without investigating the meaning of the factors. In addition, one must focus on the proportion of the explained variance to make sure that the resulting factor model *does* represent the observed variables. In most cases, this approach results in factors that have no clear interpretation, but at least they are a smaller set.

16.3.2 FACTOR SCORES

The scoring macro used to produce the factor scores is a wrapper of PROC SCORE. The only requirement is that the dataset contain the factor model. The following is the code of the macro, along with an example on its implementation (see Table 16.2).

```
%macro FactScore(DSin, VarList, DSFact, DSout);
proc score data=&dsin  score=&DSFact out=&DSout;
      var &VarList;
      run;
%mend;

%let DSin=bank;
%let DSFact=BankFact;
%let VarList=AvgBalance AvgTransValue AvgInt CheckBalance;
%let DSout=Bank_Factors;
%FactScore(&DSin, &VarList, &DSFact, &DSout);
```

Table 16.2   Parameters of macro FactScore().

Header	FactScore(DSin, VarList, DSFact, DSout);
Parameter	*Description*
DSin	Input dataset
VarList	List of variables
DSFact	Dataset containing the results of Factor() macro
DSout	Output dataset with the factors added to it

The result of this scoring macro is a dataset that contains the original analysis variables, in addition to the specified number of factors. The factors are called Factor1, Factor2, and so on. To rename these new variables, a DATA step with a RENAME option could be used.

The following macro automates this process (see Table 16.3).

```
%macro FactRen(DSin, Nfactors, Prefix, DSout);
Data &DSout;
 SET &DSin (Rename=(
  %do i=1 %to &NFactors;
   Factor&i= &Prefix&i
   %end; ));
run;
%mend;
```

For example, in order to rename the variables Factor1 and Factor2 to F1 and F2, respectively, we invoke macro FactRen() as follows:

```
%let DSin=Bank_Factors;
%let DSout=Bank_Factors;
%let Nfactors=2;
%let Prefix=F;
%FactRen(&DSin, &Nfactors,&Prefix,&DSout);
```

Table 16.3   Parameters of macro FactRen().

Header	FactRen(DSin, Nfactors, Prefix, DSout);
Parameter	*Description*
DSin	Input dataset
Nfactors	Number of factors to be renamed
Prefix	Prefix used in the new variable names
DSout	Output dataset with the factors renamed

PREDICTIVE POWER AND VARIABLE REDUCTION II

17.1 INTRODUCTION

Chapter 12 presented the main scheme of variable reduction. In that scheme there are two main reduction mechanisms: (1) the reduction of candidate independent variables with respect to a dependent variable and (2) the reduction of a set of variables into a smaller set while keeping most of the information content. To pursue the latter mechanism, there are two methods for variable reduction, namely, principal component analysis and factor analysis (discussed in Chapters 15 and 16, respectively).

This chapter pursues the first mechanism of data reduction using some of the concepts and techniques explored in Chapters 13 and 14 for the definition of measures of association between variables.

The majority of data mining predictive models focus on two tasks: classification and estimation. Most classification models have binary dependent variables. In classification models where the dependent variable (DV) has more than two categories, it is common practice to map the DV into indicator variables and use these new variables to build different models with binary DVs. In the case of estimation models, the dependent variable is always continuous. Therefore, we focus our attention now on these two types of dependent variables: binary and continuous. However, we explore *all* types of independent variables (IVs).

17.2 DATA WITH BINARY DEPENDENT VARIABLES

17.2.1 NOTATION

The following notation will be adopted for the case of binary dependent variables.

y = The binary dependent variable y (i.e., taking values 0 and 1)

N = Total number of records in the dataset

N_1, N_2 = Total number of records with y in the two categories 1 and 2

N_k^j = Number of records with $y = k$ and IV equal to the category j

n_j = Total number of records with IV equal to category j in dataset

m = Number of categories in IV

17.2.2 NOMINAL INDEPENDENT VARIABLES

We present here three common measures of predictive power based on

- The Pearson Chi-squared statistic
- The Gini diversity measure
- The entropy variance

The Pearson Chi-squared statistic was defined in Equation 13.16 (see also Agresti [2002]). The notation follows the conventions of contingency tables. Using the simplified notation just listed, we write it as

$$X^2 = \sum_{j=1}^{m} \sum_{k=1}^{q} \frac{\left(N - \left(\frac{n_j N_k}{N}\right)\right)^2}{\left(\frac{n_j N_k}{N}\right)}, \tag{17.1}$$

where q is the number of categories of the dependent variable, which is 2 in the current case of binary DV.

The statistic follows a χ^2 distribution with $(m-1)(q-1)$ degrees of freedom and is produced by PROC FREQ. The implementation of this statistic was introduced in macro PearChi() in Section 13.4.3.

The Gini ratio is defined (see Breiman et al. 1998) as

$$G_r = 1 - \frac{G_o}{G_i}, \tag{17.2}$$

where

$$G_i = 1 - \frac{\sum_{k=1}^{q} N_k^2}{N^2}, \tag{17.3}$$

and

$$G_o = \sum_{j=1}^{m} \frac{n_j G_j}{N} \left(1 - \frac{\sum_{k=1}^{q} (N_k^j)^2}{(n_j)^2}\right). \tag{17.4}$$

Finally, the Entropy ratio is defined (see Quinlan 1993) as

$$E_r = 1 - \frac{E_o}{E_i},\tag{17.5}$$

where

$$E_i = -\frac{1}{\ln q} \sum_{k=1}^{q} \frac{N_k}{N} \ln \frac{N_k}{N},\tag{17.6}$$

and

$$E_o = \sum_{j=1}^{m} \frac{n_j}{N} \left(-\frac{1}{\ln q} \sum_{k=1}^{q} \frac{N_k^j}{N} \ln \left[\frac{N_k^j}{N} \right] \right).\tag{17.7}$$

The implementation of the Gini and Entropy ratios is straightforward. It involves finding the different counts in Equations 17.2 and 17.5. The following two macros are almost identical, with the exception of the part that actually substitutes in the formulas (see Table 17.1).

Table 17.1   Parameters of macro `GiniCatBDV()`.

Header	`GiniCatBDV(DSin, XVar, DV, M_Gr);`
Parameter	Description
DSin	Input dataset
XVar	The nominal independent variable
DV	The binary dependent variable name
M_Gr	Output Gini ratio

Step 1
Count the frequencies of cross-tabulating the variable XVar versus the dependent variable DV using PROC FREQ. Also count the number of categories in the independent variable XVar by using a second TABLE statement to generate the unique categories and then count them using PROC SQL.

```
proc freq data=&DSin noprint;
 table &XVar*&DV /out=Temp_freqs;
 table &XVar /out=Temp_cats;
 run;
proc sql noprint;
  /* Count the number of categories */
  %local m;
    select count(*) into : m from temp_cats;
```

Step 2

Calculate the frequencies N_1, N_2 for DV values of 0 and 1, respectively, and substitute in the expression for G_i.

```
/* frequencies of DV=1, DV-0 , N*/
   %local N0 N1 N;
   Select sum(Count) into :N0 from temp_freqs where DV=0;
   select sum(Count) into :N1 from temp_freqs where DV=1;
quit;
%let N=%eval(&N0+&N1);

/* Gi */
%local Gp;
%let Gp=%sysevalf(1 - (&N0*&N0+&N1*&N1 ) / (&N*&N) );
```

Step 3

Extract the unique values for the independent variable XVar to use them in the queries.

```
data _null_;
 set temp_cats;
 call symput('Cat_'|| left(_N_), &XVar );
run;
```

Step 4

Loop over the categories of XVar, extract the frequencies N_k^j, n_j, and substitute in the expressions for G_o and G_r.

```
proc sql noprint;
%local ss i Ghat NN0 NN1 NN;
%let ss=0;
%do i=1 %to &m;
   /* get n_o^i (NN0) , n_1^i (NN1) */
   select max(0,sum(count)) into :NN0
     from temp_freqs where DV=0 and &XVar="&&Cat_&i";
   select max(0,sum(count)) into :NN1
     from temp_freqs where DV=1 and &XVar="&&Cat_&i";
   %let NN=%eval(&NN1+&NN0);
   %let ss=%sysevalf(&ss+ (1-((&NN0 * &NN0)+
           (&NN1 * &NN1))/(&NN * &NN)) * &NN);
%end; /* end of variable loop */
quit;
%let Ghat=%sysevalf(&ss/&N);
%let &M_Gr=%sysevalf(1-&Ghat/&Gp);
```

Step 5
Clean the workspace and finish the macro.

```
proc datasets library=work;
delete temp_freqs temp_cats;
quit;
%mend;
```

The next macro is for the calculation of the Entropy ratio E_r, defined in Equation 17.5. Since the calculation of E_r requires the same quantities needed to calculate the Gini ratio G_r, the macro is almost identical to the macro GiniCatBDV(). Except in the calculation of E_r, it follows the same steps (see Table 17.2).

Table 17.2   Parameters of macro EntCatBDV().

Header	EntCatBDV(DSin, XVar, DV, M_Er);
Parameter	*Description*
DSin	Input dataset
XVar	The nominal independent variable
DV	The binary dependent variable name
M_Er	Output Entropy ratio

Steps 1 and 2
Extract frequencies needed later in calculations and compute E_i.

```
proc freq data=&DSin noprint;
 tables &XVar*&DV /out=Temp_freqs;
 table &XVar /out=Temp_cats;
 run;
proc sql noprint;
  /* Count the number of categories */
   %local m;
   select count(*) into : m from temp_cats;

/* frequencies of DV=1, DV-0 , N*/
%local N0 N1 N;
Select sum(Count) into :N0 from temp_freqs where DV=0;
select sum(Count) into :N1 from temp_freqs where DV=1;
%let N=%eval(&N0+&N1);
/* Ei */
%local Ein;
```

```
%let Ein=%sysevalf(  -1* ( &N0 * %sysfunc(log(&N0/&N))
                          +&N1 * %sysfunc(log(&N1/&N)) )
                        /( &N * %sysfunc(log(2))        ) ) );
quit;
```

Step 3
Get the unique categories of XVar.

```
data _null_;
 set temp_cats;
  call symput('Cat_'|| left(_N_), &XVar );
run;
```

Step 4
Loop on the variables, extract the frequencies from the cross-tabulation results, and substitute in the final entropy ratio equation. The complex condition on testing zero frequencies is used to prevent numerical errors because the $\ln(\cdot)$ function does not admit a zero argument.

```
proc sql noprint;
%local ss i Eout NN0 NN1 NN;
%let ss=0;
%do i=1 %to &m;
 /* get n_o^i (NN0) , n_1^i (NN1) */
  select max(sum(count),0) into :NN0
    from temp_freqs where DV=0 and &XVar="&&Cat_&i";
  select max(sum(count),0) into :NN1
    from temp_freqs where DV=1 and &XVar="&&Cat_&i";
  %let NN=%eval(&NN1+&NN0);
  %if(&NN0>0 and &NN1>0) %then
   %let  ss=%sysevalf(&ss- &NN*
                     (&NN0 * %sysfunc(log(&NN0/&NN))
                    + &NN1 * %sysfunc(log(&NN1/&NN)) )
                      /( &NN * %sysfunc(log(2)) ) ) );
  %else %if (&NN0=0)%then
   %let  ss=%sysevalf(&ss- &NN*
                     ( &NN1 * %sysfunc(log(&NN1/&NN)) )
                      /( &NN * %sysfunc(log(2)) ) ) );
   %else
   %let  ss=%sysevalf(&ss- &NN*
                     (  &NN0 * %sysfunc(log(&NN0/&NN)) )
                      /( &NN * %sysfunc(log(2)) ) ) );
%end; /* end of variable loop */
quit;
%let Eout=%sysevalf(&ss/&N);
%let &M_Er=%sysevalf(1-&Eout/&Ein);
```

Step 5

Clean the workspace and finish the macro.

```
proc datasets library=work;
delete temp_freqs temp_cats;
quit;
%mend;
```

17.2.3 NUMERIC NOMINAL INDEPENDENT VARIABLES

The macros GiniCatBDV() and EntCatBDV() assume that the nominal independent variable XVar is a string. In the case when XVar is numeric (e.g., binary 1/0), we need to modify these two macros such that the queries, which count the frequencies n_j and N_k^j, use numeric selection criteria. This would be achieved by modifying the SELECT statements of step 4 in both macros, as follows:

```
select max(sum(count),0) into :NN0
   from temp_freqs where DV=0 and &XVar=&&Cat_&i;
 select max(sum(count),0) into :NN1
   from temp_freqs where DV=1 and &XVar=&&Cat_&i;
```

It is possible to test the type of the variable XVar before executing the queries to select the appropriate form. However, to keep things simple, we create two dedicated macros to deal with numeric nominal variables, where the preceding queries are used. These macros are GiniCatNBDV() and EntCatNBDV(). (Note the *N* in the macro name.)

17.2.4 ORDINAL INDEPENDENT VARIABLES

In the case of ordinal IVs, it is expected that the categories have been replaced by numeric scores. The Gini and entropy ratios do *not* take into account the order relationship between the categories of ordinal variables. However, the definitions given in Equations 17.2 and 17.5 could also be used to calculate G_r and E_r. Therefore, we use the macros GiniCatNBDV() and EntCatNBDV(). In addition, it is often better to keep the names of the macros applied to different variable types indicative of those types. Therefore, we make copies of these two macros under the names GiniOrdBDV() and EntOrdBDV() to stress their use with ordinal variables.

In addition to the Gini and entropy ratios, there are two correlation coefficients that could be used to evaluate the association with ordinal variables. These are the Pearson correlation coefficient and the Spearman correlation coefficient, r and r_s, defined in Equations 13.19 and 13.23, respectively.

In Section 13.6, we presented the macros ContPear() and ContSpear() for the calculation of r and r_s, respectively. They were wrappers for PROC FREQ. The following macro combines these two in one macro to calcualte both r and r_s (see Table 17.3).

Table 17.3   Parameters of macro `PearSpear()`.

Header	`PearSpear(DSin, XScore, YScore, M_R, M_RS);`
Parameter	*Description*
`DSin`	Input dataset
`XScore`	Name of the *X* variable scores
`YScore`	Name of the *Y* variable scores
`M_R`	The Pearson correlation coefficient
`M_RS`	The Spearman correlation coefficient

```
%macro PearSpear(DSin, XScore, YScore, M_R, M_RS);
/* Calculation of Pearson and Spearman correlation coefficients
    for ordinal variables using the scores given in XScore, YScore.
    The results are stored in M_R and M_RS */

proc freq data=&DSin noprint;
tables &XScore*&YScore / measures;
output measures out=temp_rs;
run;

data_NULL_;
 set temp_rs;
 call symput("rs", abs(_SCORR_));
 call symput("rr", abs(_PCORR_));
run;
%let &M_R=&rr;
%let &M_rs = &rs;
proc datasets nodetails;
 delete temp_rs;
quit;

%mend;
```

17.2.5 CONTINUOUS INDEPENDENT VARIABLES

To measure the predictive power of continuous IVs with binary dependent variables, we simply convert them to an ordinal scale using binning. We may use either equal-height or equal-width binning. Equal-width binning always allows the use of a simple linear scale to assign the ordinal scores for the resulting bins. This is not always the case with equal-height binning because the width of the bins in this case is not necessarily uniform. A simple and practical approach is to use the mid-point value of each bin as the score corresponding to that bin. However, in most cases, optimal binning (detailed in Section 10.3.3) results in better predictive power.

Once the continuous variables have been binned, they can be treated using the same macros for ordinal variables (i.e, `GiniOrdBDV()`, `EntOrdBDV()`).

Macro `VarCorr()` of Section 14.4, calculates the values of r and r_s with or without binning of the continuous IV. Therefore, we can use it directly to keep as much information in the variable distribution as possible.

We can also use the F-test, as presented in Section 14.3. In this case, we can use the macro `ContGrF()`, which computes both the Gini ratio, without the binning, and the F^*, defined in Equation 14.10, and its p-value.

17.3 DATA WITH CONTINUOUS DEPENDENT VARIABLES

17.3.1 NOMINAL INDEPENDENT VARIABLES

This case is simply the mirror image of the case of Section 17.2.5. We use the macros `GiniOrdBDV()`, and `EntOrdBDV()`, with binning of the continuous DV, and the macro `PearSpear()`. Note that these macros will work properly when the IV is binary (1/0).

In all cases, the macro `ContGrF()` provides the entropy/Gini ratio and the F^* and its p-value.

17.3.2 ORDINAL INDEPENDENT VARIABLES

In this case, the macro `VarCorr()`, of Section 14.4, provides the correlation coefficients r and r_s and the macro `ContGrF()` provides the entropy/Gini ratio and the F^* and its p-value. The only requirement is to assign the categories of the ordinal variable the appropriate scores.

17.3.3 CONTINUOUS INDEPENDENT VARIABLES

In this final case, the correlation coefficients r and r_s could be calculated using the `VarCorr()` macro. If one of the variables, preferably the IV, can be binned, then the macro `ContGrF()` can be used to calculate the entropy/Gini ratio and the F^* and its p-value. However, without binning, one can also calculate the F^* and its p-value from the original definition (Equation 14.9).

17.4 VARIABLE REDUCTION STRATEGIES

The last two sections provided several methods for the calculation of measures of the predictive power of potential independent variables. The next task is to eliminate the variables that do not show strong association with the dependent variable.

The challenge in this task arises from the fact that in almost all data mining models, all types of variables are present (i.e., nominal, ordinal, and continuous). It is not possible to compare the measures used for different variables types. For example, the Gini ratio cannot be compared to the correlation coefficient *r*. Therefore, it is possible that when comparing two variables, the use of *r* suggests using one of them, while using G_r suggests using the other.

The general strategy is to attempt to evaluate the variables using more than one criterion to make sure not to miss a possible good predictor. We propose to implement *all* possible evaluation methods for each variable. Variables that appear to be good predictors using different methods should not be removed.

To facilitate the implementation of this strategy, we present the following macro, which wraps the methods used to assess nominal variables with binary dependent variable (see Table 17.4). The macro uses a list of nominal variables to test against a binary DV and outputs all the measures of associations in different datasets.

Table 17.4   Parameters of macro PowerCatBDV().

Header	PowerCatBDV(DSin, VarList, DV, ChiDS, GiniDS, EntDS);
Parameter	*Description*
DSin	Input dataset
VarList	List of nominal independent variables to test
DV	Binary dependent variable name
ChiDS	Output dataset with the Pearson Chi-squared statistic
GiniDS	Output dataset with the Gini ratio
EntDS	Output dataset with the Entropy ratio

Step 1
Extract the variables from the input dataset and store them in macro variables.

```
%local i condition;
%let i=1;
%let condition = 0;
%do %until (&condition =1);
   %let Word=%scan(&VarList,&i);
   %if &Word =  %then %let condition =1;
          %else %do;
   %local Var&i;
    %let Var&i=&word;
   %let i = %Eval(&i+1);
      %end;
%end;
```

Step 2
Create the three output datasets to hold the results.

```
proc sql noprint;
 create table &ChiDS
         (VarName char(32), Chi2 num, PChi2 num);
 create table &GiniDS
         (VarName char(32), GiniRatio num);
 create table &EntDS
         (VarName char(32), EntropyRatio num);
quit;
```

Step 3

Loop over the variables and call the macros PearChi(), GiniCatBDV(), and EntCatBDV() to calculate the Chi-squared statistic, the Gini ratio, and the entropy ratio, respectively.

```
%local j Vx;
%do j=1 %to %EVAL(&i-1);
 %let Vx=&&Var&j;
 %let X2=;%let pvalue=;
 %PearChi(&DSin, &Vx, &DV, X2, pvalue);
 %let pvalue=%sysevalf(1-&pvalue);

%let Gr=;
%GiniCatBDV(&DSin, &Vx, &DV, Gr);

%let Er=;
%EntCatBDV(&DSin, &Vx, &DV, Er);
```

Step 4

Store the results in the output datasets.

```
 proc sql noprint;
  insert into &ChiDS values ("&&Var&j", &X2, &pvalue);
  insert into &GiniDS values("&&Var&j", &Gr);
  insert into &EntDS values("&&Var&j", &Er);
 quit;
%end;
```

Step 5

Sort the results datasets using the association measures in descending order.

```
proc sort data=&ChiDS;
by DESCENDING PchI2 Descending Chi2;
run;

proc sort data=&GiniDS;
by DESCENDING GiniRatio;
run;
proc sort data=&EntDS;
```

```
by DESCENDING EntropyRatio;
run;

%mend;
```

Examination of the three output datasets of macro PowerCatBDV() should reveal the most persistent predictive variables. To extend macro PowerCatBDV() to the cases of other independent variable types, we need to consider the following.

- Modification of step 3 to call the different macros for other IV and DV types

- Binning of continuous variables when needed

- Storing the results in different datasets to accommodate the nature of the measures being calculated

The macros PowerOrdBDV() and PowerContBDV(), listed in Section A.14, follow these steps to assess the predictive power of ordinal and continuous independent variables with binary DV. An additional macro, PowerCatNBDV(), is also provided, which is identical to PowerCatBDV(); however, it assumes that the independent categorical variables are all numeric.

CHAPTER 18

PUTTING IT ALL TOGETHER

18.1 INTRODUCTION

This final chapter provides a case study to show how all the pieces can be put together to automate the data preparation process. We start with a template, or plan, for the data flow process. The plan outlines the basic steps that will be adopted in dealing with the data in the case study. The case study simulates a complete process for the data preparation, modeling, and deployment of a model for targeted marketing. In addition to discussing the data elements and the data preparation procedures, we provide the complete implementation of the case study, including the modeling phase, to serve as a template for the user.

In the case study, we attempt to strike a balance between presenting a complex case study that resembles real-life databases and keeping the data fields simple and familiar to many readers. Therefore, a real dataset is used, after stripping many of the unnecessary details.

18.2 THE PROCESS OF DATA PREPARATION

Figure 2.1 outlined the steps of the data flow and named each resulting dataset. The chapters of this book discuss the procedures needed to move from each of those datasets and blocks to reach subsequent steps. We concentrate on the generation of two datasets: the mining view, with its training and validation partitions, and the scoring view. This section attempts to assemble all the techniques developed in the book to show where they fit into the generation of these two datasets.

Figure 18.1 shows the general plan of organizing the different data preparation procedures. The plan consists of the following steps.

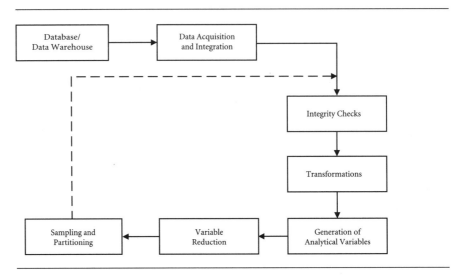

Figure 18.1   Data preparation process.

1. *Data acquisition and integration:* Invoke the macros needed to obtain the data from the data warehouse and assemble the initial form of the mining view.

2. *Integrity check, iteration (1):* Check the integrity of the data and confirm that it represents the population.

3. *Transformations:* Perform the necessary transformations to maximize the use of the available data. This step may be performed in conjunction with an initial interactive EDA. Data transformations include the treatment of missing values.

4. *Generation of analytical variables:* This can be either a separate step or part of the transformations.

5. *Variable reduction:* Reduce the number of variables to a manageable number.

6. *Sampling and partitioning:* Generate the partitions of the mining view (i.e., training, validation, and testing partitions).

7. *Iteration (2):* Use integrity checking procedures to check the validity of the partitioning and/or sampling before using the data in modeling.

8. *Iterations (3, 4, ...):* Iterate through the previous steps with EDA and modeling to discover the best set of variables for the best model.

9. *Scoring data:* Use the minimum steps of acquisition, transformations, and integrity checks to generate the scoring view. The needed variables have been already identified in previous iterations.

18.3 Case Study: The Bookstore

18.3.1 The Business Problem

The company Random Magic Books! (RMB) is a bookstore chain that offers its customers books in the following five categories.

- Children's books (Children)
- Do-it-yourself (DIY)
- Travel guides (Travel)
- Computer books (Computers)
- Fiction (Fiction)

RMB runs a customer loyalty program through which the registered customers are eligible for discounts and occasional gifts. RMB has 50,000 registered customers. To stimulate sales, RMB launched a sales campaign where 5,000 customers, selected at random, have received $10 gift vouchers. The vouchers were valid only for a specific period of 10 days.

RMB wishes to use the results of this campaign to develop a response predictive model to determine the best targets for the next sales campaign. In order to define the Response variable, the following simplifying assumptions were made.

- All purchases made by customers who received the voucher during the campaign period (20–31 December 2005) are assumed to be direct results of the campaign.

- The value of the purchases is ignored in determining the response behavior; that is, it is immaterial whether the purchases exceeded the $10 value during the campaign period.

The data available for this project is the following datasets.

- CUSTOMERS contains the details of the 50,000 registered customers.

- Books contains the details of the 10,000 volumes the bookstore carries. The table does not have the names of the books, only their serial numbers, category IDs, and prices.

- Book categories holds the descriptions of the categories IDs.

- TRANSACTIONS holds a total of 250,139 records of the sales transactions for the year 2005. Each transaction has the variables customer ID, book ID, date of purchase, method of payment, and number of units purchased.

- CAMPAIGN contains the 5000 IDs of the customers who received the $10 voucher.

18.3.2 PROJECT TASKS

The project involves the following tasks.

1. *Data acquisition and integration:* To prepare the mining view of the planned targeting model. The mining view will be based on the IDs of the customers in the dataset Campaign. However, we need to add the following fields to it:

   - Dependent variable: An indicator of whether the customer responded to the campaign by making at least one purchase during the campaign period.

   - Candidate independent variables: Include customer age (from DOB), tenure in months (from enrollment date), gender, and city.

   - Summary of transactions: Summary of customer's purchases, say in the last six months (total value of purchased books, number of purchases, most purchased category, most used payment method).

2. *Integrity checks:* The following checks are suggested:

   - Customer gender is Male, Female, or missing. Other values (wrong entries) should be converted to missing.

   - Customer age is more than 16. No customer younger than 16 is allowed to participate in the loyalty program. Therefore, values less than 16, as a result of data entry error, will be forced to be 16.

   - The date of enrollment in the loyalty program should be before the voucher mailing date (5 December 2005).

3. *Transformations:* The following transformations are proposed:

   - Mapping the city, gender, payment method, and book categories into indicator variables.

   - Binning the age variable of the customer, by finding the best five bins using the Gini ratio. Similarly, binning the calculated tenure and total value of previous purchases. After binning, new indicator variables should be generated to represent the new bins.

4. *Generation of analytical variables:*

   - New variables would be generated using the logarithmic transformation on tenure, customer age, and total purchases.

   - Generation of interaction terms between customer age, tenure, and total purchases after normalizing their values (to be between 0 and 1).

5. *Variable reduction:*

   - Calculation of the expected predictive power of all variables using the dependent variable Response.

   - The use of PCA to reduce the continuous variables.

- The use of factor analysis to reduce the continuous variables.

- Examination of different measures of predictive power and selecting the *best* variables to enter into the model.

6. *Partitioning:*

- Use random sampling to divide the mining view into training and validation partitions. Use 60% of the data for training the model and 40% for validation.

7. *Modeling:*

- This is not a main topic of this book, but in order to go through all the steps of the process, we have to build a model. We use logistic regression to develop a model that describes the response behavior in terms of all the candidate predictors. The final model includes only a subset of these variables, which should be used for scoring.

8. *Prepare the code for the scoring view:*

- Prepare a code to automatically prepare the scoring view for the continuous deployment of the model. The code is simply a stripped version of all the steps used in preparation of the mining view.

18.3.3 THE DATA PREPARATION CODE

The following printout of the file RMB_Case_Study.SAS contains the implementation code for the preceding tasks. Note that this code is only an example of how to use the macros presented in this book. It is not the only or the best way to use these macros and methods. Also note that we have not used *all* the methods presented in this book.

```
/* Preparation of the mining view for the
   Random Magic Bookstore case study */

/* Directory where the data files are */
%let DataDir=C:\BookStore;

/* Directory where the Data Preparation SAS macros are stored.
   I must end with a '\' at the end   */
%let MacroDir=C:\BookStore\Macros\;

/* Assign the Library B */
libname b "&DataDir";

/* Include ALL data preparation macros to use them at will */
%include "&MacroDir.AllMacros.SAS";
```

```
/* ========= The actual processing starts here  ========= */

/* Basic Assumption: Today = 31 December 2005 */
%let Today='31DEC2005'd;


/********** Acquisition and Integration *****************/
/* ------------------------------------------------------*/

/* Building the mining view from the dataset CAMPAIGN */
data b.MV0;
 set b.Campaign;
run;

/* Merge the Customer's data from the CUSTOMERS dataset */
proc sort data=b.MV0;
by CustID;
run;
proc sort data=b.Customers;
by CustID;
run;

Data b.MV1;
 merge b.MV0(in=Campaign) b.Customers;
 by CustID;
 if Campaign;
run;

/* Add Age and Tenure(in months) using calculations */
Data b.MV2;
 set b.MV1;
 CustAge   = intck('year', DOB , &Today);
 CustTenure= intck('month', EnrolDate , &Today);
run;

/* Now, working on the transactions: we summarize them on
   the level of the customer. Then, we extract those records
   specific to the mining view first (i.e., the customers
   included in the campaign). */

/* To find the MODE of payment method and book category,
   we use the  macro VarMode() */
/* To speed up things and divide transactions over 10 parts.
   we build an index on custID, PaymentMethod, & BookCategory */

data B.Trans1 B.Trans2 B.Trans3 B.Trans4 B.Trans5
     B.Trans6 B.Trans7 B.Trans8 B.Trans9 B.Trans10;
 set b.Transactions;
if CustID<=5000 then output B.Trans1;
```

```
if CustID> 5000 and CustID<=10000 then output B.Trans2;
if CustID>10000 and CustID<=15000 then output B.Trans3;
if CustID>15000 and CustID<=20000 then output B.Trans4;
if CustID>20000 and CustID<=25000 then output B.Trans5;
if CustID>25000 and CustID<=30000 then output B.Trans6;
if CustID>30000 and CustID<=35000 then output B.Trans7;
if CustID>35000 and CustID<=40000 then output B.Trans8;
if CustID>40000 and CustID<=45000 then output B.Trans9;
if CustID>45000                    then output B.Trans10;
run;

proc sql noprint;
create index CustID on b.Trans1;
create index PaymentMethod on b.Trans1;

create index CustID on b.Trans2;
create index PaymentMethod on b.Trans2;

create index CustID on b.Trans3;
create index PaymentMethod on b.Trans3;

create index CustID on b.Trans4;
create index PaymentMethod on b.Trans4;

create index CustID on b.Trans5;
create index PaymentMethod on b.Trans5;

create index CustID on b.Trans6;
create index PaymentMethod on b.Trans6;

create index CustID on b.Trans7;
create index PaymentMethod on b.Trans7;

create index CustID on b.Trans8;
create index PaymentMethod on b.Trans8;

create index CustID on b.Trans9;
create index PaymentMethod on b.Trans9;

create index CustID on b.Trans10;
create index PaymentMethod on b.Trans10;

quit;

%VarMode(B.Trans1, PaymentMethod, CustID, B.CustMethod1);
%VarMode(B.Trans2, PaymentMethod, CustID, B.CustMethod2);
%VarMode(B.Trans3, PaymentMethod, CustID, B.CustMethod3);
%VarMode(B.Trans4, PaymentMethod, CustID, B.CustMethod4);
%VarMode(B.Trans5, PaymentMethod, CustID, B.CustMethod5);
```

```
%VarMode(B.Trans6, PaymentMethod, CustID, B.CustMethod6);
%VarMode(B.Trans7, PaymentMethod, CustID, B.CustMethod7);
%VarMode(B.Trans8, PaymentMethod, CustID, B.CustMethod8);
%VarMode(B.Trans9, PaymentMethod, CustID, B.CustMethod9);
%VarMode(B.Trans10, PaymentMethod, CustID, B.CustMethod10);

proc sort data=b.trans1 force;
by bookid;
run;
proc sort data=b.trans2 force;
by bookid;
run;
proc sort data=b.trans3 force;
by bookid;
run;
proc sort data=b.trans4 force;
by bookid;
run;
proc sort data=b.trans5 force;
by bookid;
run;
proc sort data=b.trans6 force;
by bookid;
run;
proc sort data=b.trans7 force;
by bookid;
run;
proc sort data=b.trans8 force;
by bookid;
run;
proc sort data=b.trans9 force;
by bookid;
run;
proc sort data=b.trans10 force;
by bookid;
run;

data b.trans1;
 merge b.trans1(in=only) b.books;
 by bookid;
 if only;
run;

data b.trans2;
 merge b.trans2(in=only) b.books;
 by bookid;
 if only;
run;
```

```
data b.trans3;
 merge b.trans3(in=only) b.books;
 by bookid;
 if only;
run;

data b.trans4;
 merge b.trans4(in=only) b.books;
 by bookid;
 if only;
run;

data b.trans5;
 merge b.trans5(in=only) b.books;
 by bookid;
 if only;
run;

data b.trans6;
 merge b.trans6(in=only) b.books;
 by bookid;
 if only;
run;

data b.trans7;
 merge b.trans7(in=only) b.books;
 by bookid;
 if only;
run;

data b.trans8;
 merge b.trans8(in=only) b.books;
 by bookid;
 if only;
run;

data b.trans9;
 merge b.trans9(in=only) b.books;
 by bookid;
 if only;
run;

data b.trans10;
 merge b.trans10(in=only) b.books;
 by bookid;
 if only;
run;
```

```
%VarMode(B.Trans1, BookCat, CustID, B.CustBcat1);
%VarMode(B.Trans2, BookCat, CustID, B.CustBcat2);
%VarMode(B.Trans3, BookCat, CustID, B.CustBcat3);
%VarMode(B.Trans4, BookCat, CustID, B.CustBcat4);
%VarMode(B.Trans5, BookCat, CustID, B.CustBcat5);
%VarMode(B.Trans6, BookCat, CustID, B.CustBcat6);
%VarMode(B.Trans7, BookCat, CustID, B.CustBcat7);
%VarMode(B.Trans8, BookCat, CustID, B.CustBcat8);
%VarMode(B.Trans9, BookCat, CustID, B.CustBcat9);
%VarMode(B.Trans10, BookCat, CustID, B.CustBcat10);

data B.CustBCat;
 set B.CustBCat1 B.CustBCat2 B.CustBCat3
     B.CustBCat4 B.CustBCat5
     B.CustBCat6 B.CustBCat7 B.CustBCat8
     B.CustBCat9 B.CustBCat10;
 BookCat=mode;
 drop mode;
run;

Data B.CustMethod;
 set B.CustMethod1 B.CustMethod2 B.CustMethod3
     B.CustMethod4 B.CustMethod5
     B.CustMethod6 B.CustMethod7 B.CustMethod8
     B.CustMethod9 B.CustMethod10;
PayMethod=mode;
drop mode;
run;

data B.MV3;
 merge B.MV2(in=mv) B.CustMethod B.CustBCat;
by CustID;
if mv;
run;

/* Now, count how many transactions there are for each customer
   and the sum of their transactions in the given period */
proc sql noprint;
  create table B.sums as
    select CustID, count(*) as NoOfTrans,
           sum(Value) as TotTransValue
    from B.Transactions
where Transdate <'20DEC2005'd
     group by CustID
     order by CustID;
quit;
```

```
/* add that to the mining view */
Data B.MV4;
 merge B.MV3(in=mv) B.sums;
 by CustID;
 if mv;
 run;

 /* Generate the DV */
 proc SQL noprint;
  create table B.DV as
  select CustID, max(DV) as DV from
    (select CustID, case when TransDate >= '20DEC2005'd then 1
                   else 0
    end  as DV  from B.Transactions)
    group by CustID;
quit;

/* Only those that were mailed the voucher should
   be counted as real DV, so merge this with the MV */
data B.MV5;
 merge B.MV4(in=mv) B.DV;
 by CustID;
 if mv;
run;

/* Finally, we replace the numbers of payment method
   and book category with the actual category name
   for ease of use in modeling */

 proc sort data=B.MV5;
 by BookCat;
 run;

 data B.MV6;
  merge B.MV5 b.BookCategories;
  by BookCat;
  run;
proc sort data=B.MV6;
by PayMethod;
run;

 data B.MV7;
  merge B.MV6 b.PaymentMethods;
  by PayMethod;
  run;


/******************** Integrity Checks *****************/
/* ---------------------------------------------------*/
```

```
/* 1. Gender is either Male or Female, anything else should
      be converted to missing
    2. Age is >=16, all other ages are "clipped low"
    3. Date of enrollment in the loyalty program is before
       5 Dec 2005 (Mailing day)
    5. Number of transactions is >=0, and value is >0 (the test
       should have been performed on the raw transactions table). */
Data B.MV8;
 set B.MV7;
  if Gender not in('Male', 'Female', '') then Gender='';
  if CustAge<16 then CustAge=16;
  if EnrolDate >'05DEC2005'd then delete;
  if NoOfTrans <0 then NoOfTrans=0;
  if TotTransValue<0 then TotTransValue=0;

run;


/******************** Transformations ****************/
/*-----------------------------------------------------*/

/* Mapping the categories of Gender, Payment Method,
   Book Category and City to indicator variables.
   We use macro MappCats() */

%MappCats(B.MV8, Gender, 1, B.MV9, B.GenderCats);
%MappCats(B.MV9, City, 1, B.MV10, B.CityCats);
%MappCats(B.MV10, PayMethodName, 1, B.MV11, B.PayMethodCats);
%MappCats(B.MV11, Category, 1, B.MV12, CategoryCats);

/* Binning Age, Tenure, and value of purchases using 5 bins */
/* Age */
%GBinBDV(B.MV12, CustAge, DV, 50, 5, B.AgeGroups, B.AgeMap);
%AppBins(B.MV12, CustAge, B.AgeMap, CustAgeBins, B.MV13);
%MappCats(B.MV13, CustAgeBins, 1, B.MV14, B.AgeBinsCats);

/* Tenure */
%GBinBDV(B.MV14, CustTenure, DV, 50, 5,
        B.TenureGroups, B.TenureMap);
%AppBins(B.MV14, CustTenure, B.TenureMap,
        CustTenureBins, B.MV15);
%MappCats(B.MV15, CustTenureBins, 1, B.MV16, B.TenureBinsCats);

/* Total transaction value */
%GBinBDV(B.MV16, TotTransValue, DV, 50, 5,
        B.TransValGroups, B.TransValMap);
%AppBins(B.MV16, TotTransValue, B.TransValMap,
```

```
          TransValBins, B.MV17);
%MappCats(B.MV17, TransValBins, 1, B.MV18, B.TransValBinsCats);


/************* Generation of Analytical Variables ************/
/* ----------------------------------------------------------*/

/* Log transformation of Age, Tenure, and Total Purchases */
data b.MV19;
 set B.MV18;
  LogAge=log(CustAge);
  LogTenure=log(CustTenure);
  /* be careful about the zero!, so we add $1.00 to all
      transactions.*/
  LogTotTrans=log(TotTransValue+1);
run;


/* Interaction terms between Age, Tenure, and total purchases */

/* first, we normalize these names to X1, X2, X3, respectively */

%let OldNames=CustAge CustTenure TotTransValue;
%let NewNames=;

%NorList(&OldNames, X, NewNames, B.NameMap1);
%NorVars(B.MV19, B.NameMap1, B.MV20);

/* Then, generate interaction terms (Only cross-terms) */

%AutoInter(B.MV20, &NewNames, 1, B.MV21, B.NameMap2);


/************* Variable Reduction *************************/
/*----------------------------------------------------------*/

/* We collect all the nominal variables together and
   measure their predictive power using the macro PowerCatNBDV()
   for numeric nominal variables */

%let CatVarList = Gender_1 Gender_2 Gender_3
                  City_1 City_2 City_3 City_4 City_5
                  PayMethodName_1 PayMethodName_2
                  PayMethodName_3 PayMethodName_4 PayMethodName_5
          Category_1 Category_2 Category_3
          Category_4 Category_5
          CustAgeBins_1 CustAgeBins_2 CustAgeBins_3
          CustAgeBins_4 CustAgeBins_5
          CustTenureBins_1 CustTenureBins_2 CustTenureBins_3
          CustTenureBins_4 CustTenureBins_5
```

```
                            TransValBins_1 TransValBins_2 TransValBins_3
                            TransValBins_4 TransValBins_5;
%PowerCatNBDV(B.MV21, &CatVarList, DV,
              B.CatNChiDS, B.CatNGiniDS, B.CatNEntDS);


/* Similarly for string nominal variables (some of them were
   mapped in the above, but we leave that elimination to
   logistic regression later) */

/* first we need to replace missing values */
data b.MV22;
 set b.MV21;
  if Gender='' then Gender='Miss';
  if PayMethodName='' then PayMethodName='Miss';
  if Category ='' then Category='Miss';
run;

%let CatVarList = Gender City Category PayMethodName;
%PowerCatBDV(B.MV22, &CatVarList, DV,
              B.CatsChiDS, B.CatsGiniDS, B.CatsEntDS);


/* Ordinal variables */
%let OrdVarList=NoOfTrans;
%PowerOrdBDV(B.MV22, &OrdVarList, DV,
              B.OrdrDS, B.OrdrSDS, B.OrdGiniDS, B.OrdEntDS);


option nomprint nosymbolgen;
/* and continuous variables */
%let ContVarList=X_1 X_2 X_3 LogAge LogTenure LogTotTrans
                 M_X_1_X_2 M_X_1_X_3 M_X_2_X_3;

%PowerContBDV(B.MV22, &ContVarList, DV, 5,
              B.ContRDS, B.ContRSDS, B.ContGiniDS, B.ContEntDS);



/* merging all Results variables into one evaluation dataset */

%let DSList=B.CatNEntDS  B.CatsEntDS
            B.CatNGiniDS B.CatSGiniDS
            B.CatNChiDS B.CatSChiDS B.OrdEntDS B.OrdGiniDS
            B.OrdRDS B.OrdRSDS B.ContEntDS
            B.ContGiniDS B.ContRDS B.ContRSDS;
%let VList =VarName Varname VarName VarName Varname
            Varname Varname Varname Varname Varname
            Varname Varname Varname Varname ;
%let Mlist =EntropyRatio EntropyRatio GiniRatio GiniRatio
            Chi2 Chi2 EntropyRatio GiniRatio R RS
            EntropyRatio GiniRatio R Rs;
```

```
%BestVarsScore(&DSList, &VList, &MList, B.BestMeasures);

/* Use PCA on the continuous variables */
%let ContVarList=X_1 X_2 X_3 LogAge LogTenure LogTotTrans
              M_X_1_X_2 M_X_1_X_3 M_X_2_X_3;
%PrinComp2(B.MV22, &ContVarList, COV,0.95, B.PCAScores, B.MV23);

/* And factor analysis */
%let ContVarList=X_1 X_2 X_3 LogAge LogTenure LogTotTrans
              M_X_1_X_2 M_X_1_X_3 M_X_2_X_3;
/* we try with 3 factors */
%Factor(B.MV23, &contVarList, 3, B.FACTScores, 0);
%FactScore(B.MV23, &contVarList, B.FactScores, B.MV24);


/****************** Partitioning *************************/
/* -------------------------------------------------------*/

%let St=;
%R2samples(B.MV24,CustID,B.Training,3000,B.Validation,2000,St);

/* Merge all the variables from the mining view to the training
   and validation partitions */
proc sort data=B.Training;
by CustID;
run;
proc sort data=B.Validation;
by CustID;
run;
proc sort Data=B.MV24;
by CustID;
run;

data B.Training;
 merge B.Training (in=T) B.MV24;
 by CustID;
 if T;
run;
data B.Validation;
 merge B.Validation (in=V) B.MV24;
 by CustID;
 if V;
run;


/***************** Modeling and Validation ******************/
/* --------------------------------------------------------*/
```

```
/* Use logistic regression with some of the variables that
   were deemed useful through the reduction step */

proc logistic data=B.Training OutModel=B.ModelParam;
  Model DV(event='1')= City_1 City_2 City_3 City_4 City_5
           CustAgeBins_1 CustAgeBins_2 CustAgeBins_3
           CustAgeBins_4 CustAgeBins_5
           CustTenureBins_1 CustTenureBins_2 CustTenureBins_3
           CustTenureBins_4 CustTenureBins_5
              LogTotTrans NoOfTrans Prin1 Prin2
              Factor1 Factor2 Factor3
           / selection=stepwise;
run;

/* Score the validation partition */
/* First, rename the DV in the validation partition : trueDV */
data B.Validation;
 set B.Validation (rename=trueDV=DV);
run;

proc logistic inmodel=B.ModelParam;
  score data=B.Validation out=B.ModelEstimates;
run;

/* Confusion matrix */
proc freq data=B.ModelEstimates;
table DV * I_DV /out=B.ConfusionMatrix;
run;

/* Lift chart */
Data B.Lift;
 set B.ModelEstimates;
  keep DV P_1;
run;
proc sort data=b.Lift;
by descending P_1;
run;
Data B.Lift;
 set B.Lift nobs=N;
 Decile=int(1+(_N_-1)*10/N);
 run;
%macro LiftCurve;
/* A simple macro for the direct calculation of the
   lift in 10 deciles */
proc sql noprint;
  create table B.LiftCurve (Decile num, lift num, CumLift num);
  select sum(DV) into : S from B.Lift;
  %let CumLift=0;
  %do i=1 %to 10;
```

```
      select sum(DV) into :L from B.Lift where decile=&i;
   %let CumLift=%sysevalf(&CumLift+&L);
   insert into B.LiftCurve values( &i , %sysevalf(&L/&S) ,
         %sysevalf(&CumLift/&S) );
   %end;
quit;
%mend;
%LiftCurve;


/*********************** Scoring Code ************************/
/* ---------------------------------------------------------*/

/* We use the same code used for the scoring of the
   validation partition. We need to generate only
   the necessary fields, so we select the portions
   of the code that generate these fields.

   We only need:
   City_4
   CustAgeBins_1 ,2,3,4,5
   CustTenureBins_2,3,4,5
   Prin2
   Factor1,2,3

   This is left as a simple SAS exercise.
*/
```

APPENDIX

LISTING OF SAS MACROS

A.1 COPYRIGHT AND SOFTWARE LICENSE

All programs presented in this book (herein referred to as Code) are supplied to you by Mamdouh Refaat (herein referred to as Author) in consideration of your agreement to the following terms, and your use, installation, modification, or redistribution of this Code constitutes acceptance of these terms. If you do not agree with these terms, please do not use, install, modify, or redistribute this Code.

In consideration of your agreement to abide by the following terms, and subject to these terms, Author grants you a personal, nonexclusive license to use but not to reproduce, modify, or redistribute the Code, with or without modifications. The name of Mamdouh Refaat may NOT be used to endorse or promote products derived from the Code without specific prior written permission from Author. Except as expressly stated in this notice, no other rights or licenses, expressed or implied, are granted by Author herein, including but not limited to any patent rights that may be infringed by your derivative works or by other works in which the Code may be incorporated.

The Code is provided by Author AS IS.

AUTHOR MAKES NO WARRANTIES, EXPRESSED OR IMPLIED, INCLUDING WITHOUT LIMITATION THE IMPLIED WARRANTIES OF NONINFRINGEMENT, MERCHANTABILITY, AND FITNESS FOR A PARTICULAR PURPOSE, REGARDING THE CODE OR ITS USE AND OPERATION ALONE OR IN COMBINATION WITH YOUR PRODUCTS. IN NO EVENT SHALL AUTHOR BE LIABLE FOR ANY SPECIAL, INDIRECT, INCIDENTAL, OR CONSEQUENTIAL DAMAGES (INCLUDING BUT NOT LIMITED TO PROCUREMENT OF SUBSTITUTE GOODS OR SERVICES; LOSS OF USE, DATA, OR PROFITS; OR BUSINESS INTERRUPTION) ARISING IN ANY WAY OUT OF THE USE, REPRODUCTION, MODIFICATION, AND/OR DISTRIBUTION OF THE CODE SOFTWARE, HOWEVER CAUSED AND WHETHER UNDER THEORY OF CONTRACT, TORT (INCLUDING NEGLIGENCE), STRICT LIABILITY, OR OTHERWISE, EVEN IF AUTHOR HAS BEEN ADVISED OF THE POSSIBILITY OF SUCH DAMAGE.

A.2 Dependencies between Macros

The following is a list of the macros that call other macros. It is recommended that a master SAS file include these macros *in order* using the command %INCLUDE.

```
BoxCox()
|            —   CalcLL()


ChiSample()
|              —   ContnAna()


GBinBDV()
|              —   BinEqW2()
|              —   CalcCats()
|              —   GSplit()
|              —   FirstLast()


GRedCats()
|              —   CalcCats()
|              —   GSplit()
|              —   Decompose()


GSplit()
|            —   Decompose()


NorList()
|            —   ListToCol()


PowerCatBDV()
|              —   PearChi()
|              —   GiniCatBDV()
|              —   EntCatBDV()


PowerCatNBDV()
|              —   PearChi()
|              —   GiniCatNBDV()
|              —   EntCatNBDV()
```

```
PowerContBDV()
|                    —    BinEqW3()
|                    —    PearSpear()
|                    —    GiniOrdBDV()
|                    —    EntOrdBDV()


PowerOrdBDV()
|                    —    PearSpear()
|                    —    GiniOrdBDV()
|                    —    EntOrdBDV()


SubCat()
|            —    ModeCat()


SubCont()
|            —    VarUnivar1()
```

A.3 Data Acquisition and Integration

A.3.1 Macro TBRollup()

```
%macro TBRollup(TDS, IDVar, TimeVar,
              TypeVar, Nchars, Value, RDS);
/* This macro performs a rollup of transactions to produce
   a total balance rollup file on the level of the IDVar
   in the time variable TimeVar by accumulating the Value
   variable over the different categories of the TypeVar.
   The new names will include the values of the time
   variable TimeVar prefixed by the first Nchars of the
   categories of TypeVar.
   The input file is the transaction dataset TDS, and
   the output file is rollup file RDS */

/* First, we sort the transaction file using the ID,
   time, and type variables */
proc sort data=&TDS;
by &IDVar &TimeVar &TypeVar;
run;

/* Accumulate the values over time to a temporary _TOT
   variable  in a temporary dataset _Temp1 */
```

```
data _Temp1;
retain _TOT 0;
set &TDS;
by &IDVar &TimeVar &TypeVar;
if first.&TypeVar then _TOT=0;
_TOT = _TOT + &Value;
if last.&TypeVar  then output;
drop &Value;
   run;


proc sort data=_Temp1;
by &IDVar &TypeVar;
run;

/* Extract the categories of the TypeVar and
   store them in macro variables
   To do that, we use PROC FREQ to find all
   nonmissing categories */

proc freq data =_Temp1 noprint;
tables &TypeVar /out=_Types ;
run;

/* Ignore missing values and convert the categories
   to macro variables  Cat_1, Cat_2, ... Cat_N */
data _null_;
 set _Types nobs=Ncount;
 if &typeVar ne '' then call symput('Cat_'||left(_n_), &TypeVar);
if _n_=Ncount  then call symput('N', Ncount);
run;

/* Loop over these N categories and generate their rollup part */

%do i=1 %to &N;
proc transpose data =_Temp1 out = _R_&i
    prefix=%substr(&&Cat_&i, 1, &Nchars)_;
by &IDVar &TypeVar;
ID &TimeVar ;
var _TOT ;
where &TypeVar="&&Cat_&i";
run;

%end;

/* Finally, assemble all these files by the ID variable */
data &RDS;
 merge
 %do i=1 %to &N;
```

```
   _R_&i
  %end ; ;
   by &IDVar;
   drop &TypeVar _Name_;
  run;
  /* clear workspace */
  proc datasets library=work nodetails;
  delete _Temp1 _Types
  %do i=1 %to &N;
      _R_&i
  %end; ;
  ;
  run;
  quit;

  %mend;
```

A.3.2 MACRO ABROLLUP()

```
%macro ABRollup(TDS, IDVar, TimeVar,
                TypeVar, Nchars, Value, RDS);
/* This macro performs a rollup of transactions to produce the
   Average Balance (AB) rollup file on the level of the IDVar
   in the time variable TimeVar by accumulating the Value
   variable over the different categories of the TypeVar.

   The new names will include the values of the time
   variable TimeVar prefixed by the first Nchars of
   the categories of TypeVar.

   The input file is the transaction dataset TDS, and the
   output file is the rollup file RDS */

/* First, we sort the transaction file using the ID,
   time, and type variables */
proc sort data=&TDS;
by &IDVar &TimeVar &TypeVar;
run;

/* Accumulate the values over time to a temporary _TOT,
   and calculate the number of transactions
   for each account type and store int in _NT variable
   in a temporary dataset _Temp1. The average value is _AVG. */
data _Temp1;
retain _TOT 0;
retain _NT 0;
```

```
set &TDS;
by &IDVar &TimeVar &TypeVar;
if first.&TypeVar then _TOT=0;
_TOT = _TOT + &Value;
if &Value ne . then _NT=_NT+1;
if last.&TypeVar  then
do;
_AVG=_TOT/_NT;
output;
_NT=0;
end;
drop &Value;
   run;


proc sort data=_Temp1;
by &IDVar &TypeVar;
run;

/* Extract the categories of the TypeVar and store
   them in macro variables. To do that, we use PROC FREQ
   to find all nonmissing categories */

proc freq data =_Temp1 noprint;
tables &TypeVar /out=_Types ;
run;

/* Ignore missing values and convert the categories
   to macro variables  Cat_1, Cat_2, ... Cat_N */
data _null_;
 set _Types nobs=Ncount;
 if &typeVar ne '' then call symput('Cat_'||left(_n_), &TypeVar);
if _n_=Ncount  then call symput('N', Ncount);
run;

/* Loop over these N categories and generate
   their rollup part */

%do i=1 %to &N;
proc transpose data =_Temp1 out=_R_&i
               prefix=%substr(&&Cat_&i, 1, &Nchars)_;
by &IDVar &TypeVar;
ID &TimeVar ;
var _AVG ;
where &TypeVar="&&Cat_&i";
run;

%end;
```

```
/* Finally, assemble all these files by the ID variable */
data &RDS;
 merge
%do i=1 %to &N;
 _R_&i
%end ; ;
 by &IDVar;
 drop &TypeVar _Name_;
run;
/* Clear workspace */
proc datasets library=work nodetails;
delete _Temp1 _Types
%do i=1 %to &N;
    _R_&i
 %end; ;
 ;
 run;
 quit;

%mend;
```

A.3.3 MACRO VARMODE()

```
%macro VarMode(TransDS, XVar, IDVar, OutDS);
/* Calculation of the mode of a variable Xvar from a
   transaction dataset using the classic implementation
   in ANSI SQL */
proc sql noprint;
create table &OutDS as
SELECT &IDVar , MIN( &XVar ) AS mode
FROM (
             SELECT &IDVar,  &XVar
             FROM &TransDS p1
             GROUP BY &IDVar, &XVar
             HAVING COUNT( * ) =
                 (SELECT MAX( CNT )
                   FROM (SELECT COUNT( * ) AS CNT
                        FROM &TransDS p2
                        WHERE p2.&IDVar= p1.&IDVar
                        GROUP BY p2.&XVar
                        ) AS p3
                    )
             ) AS p
       GROUP BY p.&IDVar;
quit;
%mend;
```

A.3.4 MACRO MERGEDS()

```
%macro MergeDS(List, IDVar, ALL);
/* Match merging a list of datasets using the key IDVar */
DATA &ALL;
 MERGE &List;
 by &IDVar;
run;
%mend;
```

A.3.5 MACRO CONCATDS()

```
%macro ConcatDS(List, ALL);
/* Concatenation of a list of datasets */
DATA &ALL;
 SET &List;
run;
%mend;
```

A.4 INTEGRITY CHECKS

A.4.1 MACRO SCHCOMPARE()

```
%macro SchCompare(A,B,Result, I_St);
/* This macro compares the schemas of two datasets A and B.
It tests the hypothesis that ALL variables in B
are present in A with the same data type. The result of the
comparison is stored in the dataset Result, which contains
one row per variable of the dataset B.

The I_ST contains the status of the comparison, such that
   1=all variables in B are in A,
   0=some variables in B are not in A.

In the result dataset, we call B the "Sample", and A the "Base". */

/* Step 1: Create a table with the field names
   and types for datasets A and B. */

proc sql noprint;
create table TA as
  select name, type from dictionary.columns
  where memname = "%upcase(&A)"
  order by name;
create table TB as
```

```
        select name, type from dictionary.columns
        where memname = "%upcase(&B)"
        order by name;
  select count(*) into:N from TB;
  run;
  quit;

/* Step 2: Loop on each element in TB and attempt
      to find it in TA. We do that by converting the
      elements of TB to macro variables.  */

  data _Null_;
   set TB;
      call symput('V_'||left(_n_),name);
      call symput('T_'||left(_n_),Type);
  run;

/* Step 3: Loop on the N variables in TB and check
      whether they exist in TA and create the entries in Result */

  proc sql noprint;
   create table &Result (VarName char(32),
                           VarType char(8),
                           ExistsInBase num,
                           Comment char(80));
  %do i=1 %to &N;

     select count(*) into: Ni from TA
        where name="&&V_&i" ;
   %if &Ni eq 0 %then %do ; /* variable does not exist */
        %let Value=0;
        %let Comment=Variable does not exist
                      in Base Dataset.;
     %goto NextVar;
        %end;
     select count(*) into: Ti from TA
        where name="&&V_&i" and Type="&&T_&i";
  %if &Ti gt 0 %then %do; /* perfect match */
        %let Value=1;
        %let Comment=Variable exists in Base Dataset
                      with the same data type. ;
        %end;
  %else %do; /* same name - different type */
        %let Value=0;
        %let Comment=Variable exists in Base Dataset
                      but with the different data type.;
        %end;
  %NextVar::
  insert into &Result values ("&&V_&i",
```

```
                                    "&&T_&i",
                                     &Value,
                                    "&Comment");
     %end;
      select min(ExistsInBase) into: I from &Result;
     run;
     quit;
     %let &I_ST=&I;

     %mend;
```

A.4.2   MACRO CatCompare()

```
     %macro CatCompare(Base, Sample, Var, V_Result, I_St);
     /* Comparing the categories of the variable Var in
        the Base dataset to test if all its categories are
        present in the Sample. The results of the categories
        are stored in V_Result and the final status (1/0)
        is stored in I_St. */

     /* Step 1: obtain the categories, and count them,
        for both Base and Sample for the variable Var */

     Proc SQL noprint;
      create table CatB as select distinct &Var from &Base;
      select count(*) into:NB from CatB ;
      create table CatS as select distinct &Var from &Sample;
      select count(*) into:NS from CatS;
      create table &V_Result (Category Char(32),
                                ExistsInSample num,
                                Comment char(80));
      run;
      quit;

      /* Step 2: Convert all the categories of the Base
         into macro variables to use them in the search later */
      data _Null_;
      set CatB;
        call symput('C_'||left(_n_),&Var);
      run;

      /* Step 3: Loop over the Base categories and find whether
         all of them can be found in the sample */

      proc SQL ;
      %do i=1 %to &NB;
        select count(*) into: Nx
               from CatS where &Var = "%trim(&&C_&i)";
```

```
%if &Nx =0 %then %do;
   Insert into &V_Result
          values("%trim(&&C_&i)" ,
                                    0,
      'Category does not exist in sample.');
   %end;
%if &Nx>0 %then %do;
   Insert into &V_Result
          values("%trim(&&C_&i)" ,
                                    1,
      'Category exists in sample.');
%end;
%end;
   select min(ExistsInSample) into: Status from &V_Result;

  run;
  quit;

  %let &I_St = &Status;
/* clean workspace */
 proc datasets nodetails  library =work;
  *delete CatB CatC;
 run;
 quit;

%mend;
```

A.4.3   MACRO CHISAMPLE()

```
%macro ChiSample(DS1, DS2, VarC, p, M_Result);
/* Testing the consistency of the distribution of a
   categorical variable VarC in two datasets DS1 and
   DS2 using Chi-square analysis with p-value=p for
   accepting the similarity between the two datasets */

/* We extract only the variable in question in both datasets
   and concatenate both datasets into one new dataset */

DATA Temp_1;
 set &DS1;
 Keep &VarC DSId;
 DSId=1;
RUN;
DATA Temp_2;
 set &DS2;
 Keep &VarC DSId;
 DSId=2;
RUN;
```

```
DATA Temp_Both;
 set Temp_1 Temp_2;
RUN;
/* Then we use macro ContnAna to test the association
   between DSId and VarC */
%ContnAna(temp_Both, DSId, &VarC, Temp_Res);

/* We use the p-value of the Chi-square */
data _null_;
 set temp_res;
  if SAS_Name="P_PCHI" then call symput ("P_actual", Value);
    run;
/* compare P-Actual with P, if P_actual>P --> accept */
%if %sysevalf(&P_Actual>=&P) %then %let &M_Result=Yes;
%else %let &M_Result=No;

/* clean workspace */
proc datasets library=work nolist;
delete Temp_1 Temp_2 Temp_both Temp_res;
quit;
%mend;
```

A.4.4 Macro VarUnivar1()

```
%macro VarUnivar1(DSin,Xvar, DSUniv);
/* Calculation of the univariate statistics
   for the variable XVar and storing them
   in the dataset DSUniv */
proc univariate data=&DSin noprint;
var &Xvar;
 output out=&DSUniv
   N=Nx
   Mean=Vmean
min=VMin
max=VMax
STD=VStd
VAR=VVar
mode=Vmode
median=Vmedian
P1=VP1
P5=VP5
P10=VP10
P90=VP90
P95=VP95
P99=VP99
;
run;
%mend;
```

A.4.5   MACRO CVLIMITS()

```
%macro CVLimits(dsin, VarX, dsout, alpha);
/* Calculation of the mean and standard deviation, and their
   confidence intervals using a confidence level 1-alpha.
   The results are stored in the dataset dsout  */

proc univariate data=&dsin all noprint;
var &VarX;
output out=temp_univ
       Var=&VarX._Var
       STD=&VarX._STD
       mean=&VarX._Mean N=n;
run;
data &dsout;
set temp_Univ;
/* Alpha */
Alpha=&alpha;
MC=tinv( 1-&alpha/2,n-1) * &VarX._Std / sqrt(n);

/* Lower and upper limits on the mean */
&VarX._Mean_U= &VarX._Mean + MC;
&VarX._Mean_L=&VarX._Mean - Mc;

/* Lower and upper limits on the variance */
&VarX._Var_U= &VarX._Var * (n-1)/cinv(1-&alpha/2,n-1);
&VarX._Var_L= &VarX._Var * (n-1)/cinv(  &alpha/2,n-1);

/* Lower and upper limits on Standard Deviation */
&VarX._STD_U = sqrt (&VarX._Var_U);
&VarX._STD_L = sqrt (&VarX._Var_L);

drop MC ;
run;

%mend;
```

A.4.6   MACRO COMPARETWO()

```
%macro CompareTwo(Val1, Val2, Method, Diff);
/* Simple comparison of two values and return of the
   percentage difference (diff).
   The comparison method is set by the parameter Method:
   1- use Val1 as the base
   2- use Val2 as the base
   0- use average value as the base
*/
```

```
%if &Method=1 %then %do;
%let &diff = %sysevalf(100*(&val2-&val1)/&val1);
%end;
%else %if &Method=2 %then %do;
%let &diff = %sysevalf(100*(&val2-&val1)/&val2);
%end;
%else %if &Method=0 %then %do;
%let &diff = %sysevalf(200*(&val2-&val1)/(&val1+&val2));
%end;
%mend;
```

A.5 EXPLORATORY DATA ANALYSIS

A.5.1 MACRO EXTREMES1()

```
%macro Extremes1(DSin, VarX, NSigmas, DSout);
/* Calculation of extreme values for a continuous variable
   which are outside the range of NSigmas * STD from the
   mean. */

/* First, extract XVar to a temp dataset, and keep the
   observation number in the original dataset */
data temp;
 set &DSin;
 ObsNo=_N_;
 keep &VarX ObsNo;
run;

/* Calculate the mean and STD using proc univariate */
 proc univariate data=temp noprint;
 var &VarX;
 output out=temp_u   STD=VSTD   Mean=VMean;
run;

/* Extract upper and lower limits into macro variables */
data _null_;
 set temp_u;
 call symput('STD', VSTD);
 call symput('Mean', VMean);
run;
%let ULimit=%sysevalf(&Mean + &NSigmas * &STD);
%let LLimit=%sysevalf(&Mean - &NSigmas * &STD);

/* Extract extreme observations outside these limits */
data &DSout;
 set temp;
```

```
    if &VarX < &Llimit or &VarX > &ULimit;
run;

/* Clean workspace and finish the macro */
proc datasets library=work nodetails;
delete temp temp_u;
quit;

%mend;
```

A.5.2   MACRO EXTREMES2()

```
%macro Extremes2(DSin, VarX, NQRange, DSout);
/* Calculation of extreme values for a continuous variable
    which are outside the range of NQrange * QRange
    from the median. We use the median in place of the mean
    as a more robust estimate of the central tendency */

/* First, extract XVar to a temp dataset, and the
   observation number of the original dataset */
data temp;
 set &DSin;
 ObsNo=_N_;
 keep &VarX ObsNo;
run;

/* Calculate the median and QRange using proc univariate */
 proc univariate data=temp noprint;
 var &VarX;
 output out=temp_u   QRANGE=VQr   mode=Vmode;
run;

/* Extract the upper and lower limits into macro variables */
data _null_;
 set temp_u;
 call symput('QR', VQr);
 call symput('Mode', Vmode);
run;
%let ULimit=%sysevalf(&Mode + &NQrange * &QR);
%let LLimit=%sysevalf(&Mode - &NQRange * &QR);

/* Extract extreme observations outside these limits */
data &DSout;
 set temp;
 if &VarX < &Llimit or &VarX > &ULimit;
run;
```

```
/* Clean workspace and finish the macro */
proc datasets library=work nodetails;
delete temp temp_u;
quit;
%mend;
```

A.5.3   MACRO ROBREGOL()

```
%macro RobRegOL(DSin, DV, IVList, DSout);
 /* Extraction of "Candidate" outliers using robust regression */
 proc robustreg data=&DSin method=mm (inith=502 k0=1.8); ;
   model &DV = &IVList /leverage;
   output out=&DSout outlier=_Outlier_ Leverage=_Leverage_;
 run;
 %mend;
```

A.5.4   MACRO CLUSTOL()

```
%macro ClustOL(DSin, VarList, Pmin, DSout);
/* Inferring outliers using k-means clustering */

/* Build a cluster model with a default of 50 clusters
    to identify outliers */

proc fastclus data=&DSin MaxC=50 maxiter=100
cluster=_ClusterIndex_ out=Temp_clust noprint;
var &VarList;
run;

/* Analyze temp_clust and find the cluster indices with
    frequency percentage less than Pmin */
proc freq data=temp_clust noprint;
  tables _ClusterIndex_ / out=temp_freqs;
run;

data temp_low;
 set temp_freqs;
 if PERCENT <= &Pmin;
 _Outlier_=1;
 keep _ClusterIndex_ _Outlier_;
run;

/* We then match merge temp_low with the clustering
    output and drop the cluster index */
proc sort data=temp_clust;
by _ClusterIndex_;
run;
```

```
proc sort data=temp_low;
by _ClusterIndex_;
run;

data &DSout;
 merge temp_clust temp_Low;
 by _ClusterIndex_;
 drop _ClusterIndex_ DISTANCE;
 if _outlier_ = . then _Outlier_=0;
run;

/* Clean up and finish the macro */
proc datasets library=work;
 delete temp_clust temp_freqs temp_low;
quit;

%mend;
```

A.6   SAMPLING AND PARTITIONING

A.6.1   MACRO RANDOMSAMPLE()

```
%macro RandomSample(PopDS, SampleDS, SampleSize);
/* This macro performs simple random sampling */
proc surveyselect data=&PopDs
      method=srs n=&SampleSize noprint
      out=&SampleDS;
run;
%mend;
```

A.6.2   MACRO R2SAMPLES()

```
%macro R2samples(S,IDVar,S1,N1,S2,N2,M_St);
/*
This macro attempts to draw two random samples
S1, S2 of sizes N1, N2 from a population (Dataset S).

Before trying to do the sampling, the macro checks the
consistency conditions. If they are not satisfied, an
error message will be generated in the variable M_St.
If the data passes the checks, then Status will be set
to "OK" and the samples will be calculated and output
to the datasets S1, S2.

All sampling work is based on using the IDVar variable
in the population dataset S. It is recommended that the
dataset S contain only the ID variable for good performance.
```

```
The macro guarantees that the two samples are disjoint.
*/

/* Calculate N of the population*/
proc sql noprint;
 select count(*)into : N from &S;          /* Size of population */
 run;
 quit;

/* Check the consistency condition */

%let Nx=%eval(&N1 + &N2);
 %if &Nx > &N %then %do;
    %let &M_st = Not enough records in population
                 to generate samples. Sampling canceled. ;
 %goto Exit;
    %end;
/* Otherwise, OK */
%let &M_St=OK;

/* Draw the sample S1 with size N1 */
 proc surveyselect noprint
data =&S
    method = srs
  n= &N1
out=&S1;
 run;

/* Add a new field to S1, call it (Selected),
   and give it a value of 1. */
 data &S1;
 set &S1;
  selected =1;
  keep &IDVar Selected;
 run;

/* Merge S1 with the population S to find
   the already selected fields. */
 proc sort data=&S;
by &IDVar;
 run;

 proc sort data=&S1;
  by &IDVar;
 run;
 Data temp;
  merge &S &S1;
  by &IDvar;
```

```
   keep &IDVar Selected;
 run;

/* Draw the sample S2 with size N2 under
   the condition that Selected is NOT 1 */

 proc surveyselect noprint
    data =temp
       method = srs
    n=&N2
out=&S2;
where Selected NE 1;
 run;

/* clean S1, S2  and workspace */
 Data &S1;
  set &S1;
  keep &IDvar;
 run;

 Data &S2;
  set &S2;
  keep &IDVar;
 run;

 proc datasets library=work nodetails;
  delete temp;
 quit;

 %exit: ;  /* finish the macro */
%mend;
```

A.6.3   MACRO B2SAMPLES()

```
%macro B2samples(S,IDVar,DV,S1,N1,P1,S2,N2,P2,M_St);
/*
This macro attempts to draw two balanced samples S1, S2 of sizes
N1, N2 and proportions P1, P2 from a population (Dataset S).
The balancing is based on the values of the DV, which are
restricted to "1","0". Missing values of DV are ignored.

Before trying to do the sampling, the macro checks the
consistency conditions; if either of them is not satisfied,
an error message will be generated in the variable M_St.
If the data passes the checks, then Status will be set to
"OK" and the samples will be calculated and output to the
datasets S1, S2.
```

All sampling work is based on using the IDVar variable in the population dataset S. It is recommended that the dataset S contain only the ID and DV variables for good performance.

The macro guarantees that the two datasets are disjoint.
```
*/

/*Calculate N, P of the population*/
 proc sql noprint;
  select count(*)into : N from &S;       /* Size of population */
  select count(*) into : NP
            from &S where &DV=1; /* count of "1" */
  run;
  quit;
%let NPc=%eval(&N - &NP);       /* Count of "0" (complement)*/

/* Check the consistency conditions */

%let Nx=%eval(&N1 + &N2);
%if &Nx > &N %then %do;
%let &M_st = Not enough records in population to
            generate samples. Sampling canceled;
%goto Exit;
   %end;

/* N1 P1 + N2 P2 <= N P */

%let Nx = %sysevalf((&N1*&P1+&N2 * &P2), integer);
%if &Nx >&NP %then %do;
  %let &M_st = Count of DV=1 in requested samples exceed
                total count in population. Sampling canceled;
 %goto Exit;
   %end;

/* N1(1-P1) + N2(1-P2) <= N(1-P)*/
%let Nx = %sysevalf( (&N1*(1-&P1) + &N2*(1-&P2) ), integer);
%if &Nx > &NPc %then %do;
  %let &M_st = Count of DV=0 in requested samples
            exceed total count in population.
            Sampling canceled.;
 %goto Exit;
%end;
/* Otherwise, OK */
%let &M_St=OK;

/* Sort the population using the DV in ascending order*/
 proc sort data=&S;
by &DV;
 run;
```

```
/* Draw the sample S1 with size N1 and number
   of records N1P1, N1(1-P1) in the strata 1,0 of the DV */
%let Nx1=%Sysevalf( (&N1*&P1),integer);
%let Nx0=%eval(&N1 - &Nx1);

  proc surveyselect noprint
data =&S
    method = srs
  n=( &Nx0 &Nx1)
out=&S1;
strata &DV;
  run;

/* Add a new field to S1, call it (Selected),
   and give it a value of 1. */
 data &S1;
  set &S1;
  selected =1;
  keep &IDVar &DV Selected;
 run;

/* Merge S1 with the population S to find the
   already selected fields. */
 proc sort data=&S;
by &IDVar;
 run;

 proc sort data=&S1;
by &IDVar;
 run;
 Data temp;
  merge &S &S1;
  by &IDvar;
   keep &IDVar &DV Selected;
 run;

/* Draw the sample S2 with size N2 and number
   of records N2P2, N2(1-P2) in the strata 1,0 of the
   DV under the condition that Selected is NOT 1 */

 proc sort data=temp;
by &DV;
 run;
%let Nx1=%Sysevalf( (&N2*&P2),integer);
%let Nx0=%eval(&N2 - &Nx1);
 proc surveyselect noprint
    data =temp
     method = srs
    n=( &Nx0 &Nx1)
```

```
      out=&S2;
      strata &DV;
      where Selected NE 1;
     run;

   /* clean S1, S2  and workspace */
    Data &S1;
     set &S1;
     keep &IDvar &DV;
    run;

    Data &S2;
     set &S2;
     keep &IDVar &DV;
    run;

    proc datasets library=work nodetails;
     delete temp;
     run;
    quit;

    %exit: ;
   %mend;
```

A.7 DATA TRANSFORMATIONS

A.7.1 MACRO NORLIST()

```
   %macro NorList(ListIn, VPrefix, M_ListOut, MapDS);
   /*
   This macro normalizes the names of variables given
   in list: ListIn, and outputs the result to ListOut.
   The names of the variables are based on using the prefix
   Vprefix. We keep the mapping scheme in the dataset MapDS. */
   /*
   Decompose the input list and put the names in a
   temporary dataset Temp_Vars. We do that by calling
   the macro ListToCol. */

     %ListToCol(&ListIn, Temp_Vars, OldVarName, VIndex);

   /* Create new variable names using the prefix */
     data &MapDS;
      set Temp_Vars;
```

```
          NewVarName=compress("&VPrefix" ||'_'|| VIndex);
     run;

/* Extract the new names from the dataset MapDS to
   the ListOut */
Data _Null_;
  set &MapDS;
    call symput ("x_" || left(_N_), NewVarName);
    call symput ("N" , _N_);
  run;
%let LOut=;
%do i=1 %to &N;
  %let LOut=&lOut &&x_&i;
%end;
%let &M_ListOut=&Lout;

proc datasets library=work nolist;
 delete temp_vars;
quit;
%mend;
```

A.7.2 Macro NorVars()

```
%macro NorVars(DSin, MapDS, DSout);
/* Normalization of the names of a set of variables by applying
   the name mapping scheme obtained by macro NorList() */
/* Get list of old and new names from the map dataset */
Data _Null_;
  set &MapDS;
    call symput ("N_" || left(_N_), NewVarName);
    call symput ("O_" || left(_N_), OldVarName);
    call symput ("N" , _N_);
  run;

/* Use the dataset options to rename the variables to
   the new names */
%let RenList=;
%do i=1 %to &N;
  %let RenList=&RenList %left(&&O_&i) = %left(&&N_&i);
%end;

DATA &DSout;
  SET &DSin  ( RENAME=(&RenList)) ;
RUN;
%mend;
```

A.7.3   MACRO AUTOINTER()

```
%macro AutoInter(DSin, VListIn, Option, DSout, DSMap);
/*
This macro generates the interaction terms for a
set of variables given in the list VListIn. The input
dataset DSin is copied to the output dataset
DSout and appended with the new interaction terms.
The following naming convention is adopted:
    X1 * X2 ---> M_X1_X2. (Multiply x1 by x2)
    X1 * X1 ---> X1_2 (X1 square)

    The interaction terms can include all second-order
    terms of the variables, the product terms, or both
    depending on the value of the parameter 'Option'.
    Option=2 --> only 2nd order terms
    Option=1 --> Only interaction terms
    Option=3 --> both

    The map of the new variables is kept in a dataset DSMap */

/* First, decompose the input list and put the names of the
   variables in macro variables. */
%local i j condition Nvars iv;
%let i=1;
%let condition = 0;
%do %until (&condition =1);
   %local Var&i;
   %let Var&i=%scan(&VListIn,&i);
   %if "&&Var&i" ="" %then %let condition =1;
   %else    %let i = %Eval(&i+1);
%end;
%let Nvars=%eval(&i-1);

/* Create the empty DSMap dataset to hold the
   variables and their transformations. And for reference,
   store the base variables. */
%local iv;
%let iv=0;
 %do i=1 %to &Nvars;
  %let iv=%eval(&iv+1);
  %local V&iv E&iv;
   %let V&iv = &&Var&i;
   %let E&iv = &&Var&i; /* The first base variables
                           are simply themselves */
  %end;
```

```
/* 2nd-order terms of individual variables */
%if &Option=2 or &Option=3 %then %do;
   %do i=1 %to &Nvars;
    %let iv=%eval(&iv+1);
    %local V&iv E&iv;
%let V&iv =%sysfunc(compress(&&Var&i _2));
    %let E&iv= &&var&i * &&Var&i;
%end;
%end;

/* Interaction terms : Option=1 or 3 */
%if &Option=1 or &Option =3 %then %do;
 %do i=1 %to &Nvars;
%do j=%eval(&i+1) %to &Nvars;
    %let iv=%eval(&iv+1);
    %local V&iv E&iv;
%let V&iv =%sysfunc(compress(M_&&Var&i _ &&Var&j));
    %let E&iv =&&var&i * &&var&j ;
%end;
 %end;
%end;

/* Now, we apply these transformations on the input
  dataset by obtaining the conditions in the form of
  equations and applying them to the dataset */
data &DSmap;
 format VarName $32.;
 format Expression $200.;
%do  i=1 %to &iv;
 VarName="&&V&i";
 Expression="&&E&i";
 output;
%end;
run;

Data &DSout;
 set &DSin;
%do i=1 %to &iv;
   &&V&i = &&E&i;
 %end;
run;

%mend;
```

A.7.4   MACRO CALCCATS()

```
%macro CalcCats(DSin, Var, DSCats);
/* Get the distinct values */
```

```
proc freq data=&DSin noprint ;
tables &Var /missing out=&DSCats;
run;
%mend;
```

A.7.5   Macro MappCats()

```
%macro MappCats(DSin, var, Method, DSout, DScats);
/*
Macro for mapping categorical values into new dummy
(indicator) variables. It assumes that ALL missing values
have been replaced with something, either the word "Missing"
or any other value or character - such as ? -.
The new dummy variables will have the variable name appended
with either the category number (Method=1) or the category
value itself (Method <> 1).
The mapped values are appended to the dataset in DSout
and the categories with their frequencies are stored in DSCats.

In the case where the category itself is used to extend the
variable name, we assume that this will lead to a legal SAS
name, i.e., characters such as +, -, &, *, /, %, spaces,
or ?? are not present in the values. */


/* Get the distinct values */
proc freq data=&dsin noprint ;
tables &var /missing out=&DSCats;
run;


/* Convert them into macro variables */
data &DSCats;
 set &DSCats;
 call symput("y"||left(_n_),&var);
CatNo=_N_;
run;


/* Find how many categories there are */
proc sql noprint;
 select count(*) into :Nc from &dscats;
run;
quit;


/* Now, replace these and generate the dummy variables */
data &dsout;
```

```
  set &dsin;
   %do i=1 %to &Nc;

%if &Method=1 %then %do;
IF &var = left("&&y&i") then &var._&i=1;
ELSE     &var._&i=0;
%end;
%else %do;
  IF &Var = left("&&y&i")  then &Var._&&y&i =1;
  ELSE     &Var._&&y&i =0;
  %end;
  %end;
run;

%mend;
```

A.7.6 MACRO CALCLL()

```
%macro CalcLL(ds,N,L,X,M_LL);
/* Calculation of the likelihood function LL
   for the dataset ds and the variable X using
   the value of Lambda=L using the formula


LL = -(n/2) log{(1/n) sum(y-y_bar)^2} + (L-1) sum(log x),
where y is the transformation of x using L, and all sums
are from 1 to n, n being the number of observations
*/


/* Perform the transformation first into a variable y */
data temp;
 set &ds;
  %if %sysevalf(&L=0) %then %do;
y_temp=log(&x);
%end;
  %else %do;
y_Temp=((&x.**&L)-1)/&L;
%end;
  lx_Temp=log(&x);
run;
proc sql noprint;
select var(y_Temp)*(&N-1)/&N, sum(lx_Temp)
        into :vy , :slx from temp;
quit;
%let &M_LL = %sysevalf(-&N * %sysfunc(log(&vy))/2 +
                              (&L-1)*&slx);

%mend;
```

A.7.7 Macro BoxCox()

```
%macro BoxCox(dsin, Xvar, XVarT, dsout, W, m_Lambda, m_LL,  m_C);
/*
Calculation of the optimal Box-Cox transformation to transform
a continuous variable Xvar to an almost normally distributed
variable XVarT.

The procedure depends on trying different values of Lambda
from -3 to +3 with a step of W, calculating the Box-Cox
likelihood function and finding its maximum.

   dsin: input dataset
   Xvar: variable being transformed
   XvarT: name of transformed Xvar
   Dsout: output dataset with the transformed variable
   Lambda: optimal lambda value
   LL: value of the maximum likelihood function
   m_C: constant that has to be added to the Xvar values
      to force all of them to be positive (to allow taking the logarithm).
   W: width of the search step (accuracy of Lambda)

*/


/* Calculate C and the number of observations; note
   that we ignore missing values.  */
proc sql noprint;
 select max(&Xvar) into :C from &dsin;
 select count(&Xvar) into :N from &dsin;
quit;

/* if C is negative, then C=-C */
%if %sysevalf(&C <1e-8) %then %let C=%sysevalf(-&C + 1e-8);
%else %Let C=0;

/* Create the output dataset and add the Value of C to Xvar */
data &dsout;
 set &dsin;
   &Xvar = &Xvar + &C;
run;

/* Now start the maximization loop on the value of LL */
/* Set L_best to 3 and the maximum L to -1e50 */
%let L_best=3;
%let LL_Max=-1e50;

%do i=1 %to %sysevalf(6/&W+1);
 %let L=%sysevalf(3-(&i-1)*&W);
```

```
                  /* Calculate LL_now */
                  %let LL_Now=;
                  %CalcLL(&dsout,&N,&L,&XVar,LL_Now);

                  %if %sysevalf(&LL_Now > &LL_max) %then %do;
                       %let LL_max=&LL_now;
                   %let L_best=&L;
                     %end;
                  /* Loop */
                %end;
                /* Set the values of the optimal lambda, LL and c */
                %let &m_LL=&LL_Max;
                %let &m_Lambda=&L_best;
                %let &m_C=&C;

                /* Finally, apply the optimal transformations */

                data &dsout;
                 set &dsout;
                  %if %sysevalf(&L_Best=0) %then %do;
                &XVarT=log(&XVar);
                %end;
                  %else %do;
                &XVarT=((&XVar.**&L_best)-1)/&L_best;
                %end;
                run;
                %mend;
```

A.8 BINNING AND REDUCTION OF CARDINALITY

A.8.1 MACRO GREDCATS()

```
%macro  GRedCats(DSin, IVVar, DVVar, Mmax, DSGroups, DSVarMap);
/*
Reducing the categories of a categorical variable using
decision tree splits with the Gini-ratio criterion.
    DSin = input dataset
    IVVar = independent categorical variable considered for
            cardinality reduction
    DVVar = dependent variable used to reduce cardinality of
            IVVar
    MMax = maximum number of required categories
  DSGroups = dataset containing the new groups (splits)
    DSVarMap = dataset with categories mapping rules
    Limitations:
    - Binary DV only
```

```
            - Categorical IV only
            - Final number of categories is determined using the maximum
              number allowed
            - New variable is categorical and of length 30 characters
            - Each category is a string value and does not contain
              spaces or special characters
            - The sum of all the categories length does not exceed 500
              characters
            - No missing value
*/


/* Get the categories of the IV, and the percentage
   of the DV=1 and DV=0 in each one of them */
/* Get the categories using CalcCats macro */
%CalcCats(&DSin, &IVVar, Temp_Cats);

/* Convert the categories and their frequencies to
   macro variables using the output of macro CalcCats */
Data _null_;
  set Temp_Cats;
      call symput ("C_" || left(_N_), compress(&IVVar));
             call symput ("n_" || left(_N_), left(count));
      call symput ("M", left(_N_));
        Run;

/* Calculate the count (and percentage) of DV=1
   and DV=0 in each category using proc SQL.
   Store all these values in the dataset Temp_Freqs; */
proc sql noprint;
  create table Temp_Freqs (Category char(100), DV1 num, DV0 num,
                                                Ni num, P1 num );

%do i=1 %to &M;
select count(&IVVar) into :n1
      from &DSin where &IVVar = "&&C_&i" and &DVVar=1;
select count(&IVVar) into :n0
      from &DSin where &IVVar = "&&C_&i" and &DVVar=0;
%let p=%sysevalf(&n1 / &&n_&i);
insert into Temp_Freqs values("&&C_&i", &n1, &n0,
                                    &&n_&i, &p);
%end;
        quit;

/* Sort the categories according to the percentage of DV=1 */
 proc sort data=temp_Freqs;
  by p1;
 run;
 /* Obtain the order of the categories after sorting */
 data _Null_;
```

```
    set temp_Freqs;
      call symput("Cat_"||left(_N_), compress(Category));
  run;

/* Create the TERM dataset to keep the terminal nodes and
   their category list, and initialize the node counter
   and put ALL the categories as a starting point */

data Temp_TERM;
length node $1000;
Node='';
%do j=1 %to &M;
   Node = Node ||" &&C_&j";
 %end;
run;

%let NNodes=1;
/* Start the splitting loop: */
%DO %WHILE (&NNodes <&MMax);
/* Convert all the rows of the splits to macro
   variables; we should have exactly NNodes of them. */
   Data _Null_;
      set Temp_TERM;
       call symput ("L_" || left(_N_), Node );
   run;
/* Loop on each of these lists, generate possible splits
   of terminal nodes, and select the best split using
    the GiniRatio */
%let BestRatio =0;

%DO inode=1 %to &NNodes;
/* The current node list is &&L_&i */
/* Using this list, get the LEFT and RIGHT categories
   representing the current best split, and the
   Gini measure of these children. */
   %let List_L=; %let List_R=; %Let GiniRatio=;
%GSplit(&&L_&inode, Temp_Freqs, List_L, List_R, GiniRatio);

 /* Compare the GiniRatio; if this one is better,
    keep a record of it */
%if %sysevalf(&GiniRatio > &BestRatio) %then %do;
%let BestRatio=&GiniRatio;
%let BestLeft=&List_L;
%let BestRight=&List_R;
%let BestNode=&Inode;
    %end;

%End; /* end of the current node list */
```

```
/* Add this split to the Temp_TERM by removing the
   current node and adding two new nodes
   with their lists as their right and left parts */
Data Temp_TERM;
  Set Temp_TERM;
    if _N_ = &BestNode Then delete;
run;
proc sql noprint;
 insert into Temp_TERM values ("&BestLeft");
   insert into Temp_TERM values ("&BestRight");
quit;

 /* Increment NNodes */
%let NNodes=%Eval(&NNodes +1);

%END;   /* End of the splitting loop */

/* Now we should have a set of category groups that
   we need to map to a new set of categories for
   final output and transformation of the input dataset */

   /* We will adopt a simple naming convention by adding
      a numerical subscript to the variable name
      to denote the new categories: so that the new
      categories of variable X are X_1, X_2, ...
    The current list is in Temp_TERM */

/* Generate the DSGroups dataset */
  data &DSGroups;
    set Temp_TERM (Rename=(Node=OldCategory));
 length NewCategory $40;
NewCategory="&IVVar._"||left(_N_);
  run;

  data _NULL_;
    Set Temp_TERM;
      call symput("List_"||left(_N_), Node);
      call symput("NSplits", compress(_N_));
run;
  /* Finally, we create the new explicit mapping dataset */
  proc sql noprint;
    create table &DSVarMap (OldCategory char(30),
                            NewCategory char(30));
   quit;
   %DO ix=1 %to &NSplits;
/* Decompose each list */
%Decompose(&&List_&ix, Temp_list);
/* Convert the new list dataset to macro variables */
data _Null_;
```

```
    set Temp_list;
      call symput("CC_"||left(_N_), compress(Category));
       call symput("CM", compress(_N_));
run;
/* Insert all these values into the mapping dataset */
       proc sql noprint;
%do j=1 %to &CM;
     insert into &DSVarMap values ("&&CC_&j", "&IVVar._&ix");
 %end;
       quit;
     %END;


/* Clean up */
proc datasets library = work nolist;
 delete temp_cats Temp_freqs
         Temp_term temp_list temp_gcats;
     run;quit;
%mend;
```

A.8.2 MACRO GSPLIT()

```
%macro GSplit(Listin, DSFreqs, M_ListL, M_ListR, M_GiniRatio);
/* Given a list of categories sorted in ascending order according
   to the percentage of DV=1, this macro finds the best LEFT and
   RIGHT splits based on Gini variance.  The number of categories
   in the list is m.

   The macro loops over the list and sets the split point in
   all possible m-1 splits and finds the highest Gini ratios */


/* Extract the categories and put them in a dataset
   Temp_GCats using macro Decompose()*/
%Decompose(&Listin, Temp_GCats);
data _null_;
 set Temp_GCats;
  call symput("M", compress(_N_));
  call symput("C_"||left(_N_), compress(Category));
run;
/* Start the list loop; while we are at it, calculate the
   total number of records and the Gini for the parent node */
proc sql noprint;
    %let NL=0; %let N1=0; %let N0=0;
%do j=1 %to &M;
/* For each category, we calculate the number of
   records DV=1 and DV=0 */
     select DV1, DV0, Ni into :DV1_&j, :DV0_&j, :Ni_&j
```

```
                    from &DSFreqs where Category="&&C_&j";
        %let NL=%Eval(&NL+&&Ni_&j);
        %let N1=%eval(&N1+&&DV1_&j);
        %let N0=%eval(&N0+&&DV0_&j);
    %end;
        %let GL = %sysevalf(1 - (&N1 * &N1 + &N0 * &N0)
                                    /(&NL * &NL));

    quit;
     /* Then we loop on each split and calculate the Gini ratio
        and monitor the the maximum and its index */

        %let MaxRatio=0;
        %let BestSplit=0;
      %do Split=1 %to %eval(&M-1);
/* The left node contains nodes from 1 to Split */
%let DV1_L=0;
%let DV0_L=0;
%let N_L=0;
%do i=1 %to &Split;
   %let DV1_L = %eval(&DV1_L + &&DV1_&i);
   %let DV0_L = %eval(&DV0_L + &&DV0_&i);
   %let N_L = %eval(&N_L + &&Ni_&i);
 %end;
/* The right node contains nodes from Split+1 to M */
%let DV1_R=0;
%let DV0_R=0;
%let N_R=0;
%do i=%eval(&Split+1) %to &M;
   %let DV1_R = %eval(&DV1_R + &&DV1_&i);
   %let DV0_R = %eval(&DV0_R + &&DV0_&i);
   %let N_R = %eval(&N_R + &&Ni_&i);
%end;
       %let G_L  = %sysevalf(1 - (&DV1_L*&DV1_L+&DV0_L*&DV0_L)
                                    /(&N_L*&N_L)) ;
       %let G_R = %sysevalf(1 - (&DV1_R*&DV1_R+&DV0_R*&DV0_R)
                                    /(&N_R*&N_R)) ;
       %let G_s= %sysevalf( (&N_L * &G_L + &N_R * &G_R)/&NL);

%let GRatio = %sysevalf(1-&G_s/&GL);
        %if %sysevalf(&GRatio >&MaxRatio) %then %do;
            %let BestSplit = &Split;
     %let MaxRatio= &Gratio;
      %end;
      %end;

  /* Compose the LEFT and RIGHT list of categories and
     return the weighted Gini measure of these children */
```

```
/* The left list is: */
 %let ListL =;
%do i=1 %to &BestSplit;
  %let ListL = &ListL &&C_&i;
 %end;
 /* and the right list is: */
%let ListR=;
%do i=%eval(&BestSplit+1) %to &M;
  %let ListR = &ListR &&C_&i;
 %end;



 /* Return the output values */
   %let &M_GiniRatio=&MaxRatio;
   %let &M_ListL=&ListL;
   %let &M_ListR = &ListR;
   /* That's it */
%mend ;
```

A.8.3 MACRO APPCATRED()

```
%macro AppCatRed(DSin, Xvar, DSVarMap, XTVar, DSout);
/*
This macro applies the categories reduction using the map dataset
DSin= the input dataset
Xvar= variable to be mapped
DSVarMap= mapping rules dataset
XTVar = name of the new mapped variable in the output dataset
DSout= output dataset
*/
  /* First we extract the conditions */
  Data _NULL_;
    set &DSVarMap;
      call symput ("OldC_"||left(_N_), compress(OldCategory));
    call symput ("NewC_"||left(_N_), compress(NewCategory));
      call symput ("Nc", compress(_N_));
    run;
  /* and generate the rules, */
DATA &DSout;
  length &XTVar $40;
  set &DSin;
%do i=1 %to &Nc;
   IF &XVar = "&&OldC_&i" THEN &XTVar = "&&NewC_&i" ;
%end;
RUN;

%mend;
```

A.8.4 MACRO BINEQW()

```
%macro BinEqW(dsin, var, Nb, dsout);
/* Simple equal width binning */
/* Get max and min values */
proc sql  noprint;
 select  max(&var) into :Vmax from &dsin;
 select  min(&Var) into :Vmin from &dsin;
run;
quit;

 /* Calculate the bin size */
%let Bs = %sysevalf((&Vmax - &Vmin)/&Nb);

/* Now, loop on each of the values and create the bin boundaries
    and count the number of values in each bin */

data &dsout;
 set &dsin;
  %do i=1 %to &Nb;
  %let Bin_U=%sysevalf(&Vmin+&i*&Bs);
  %let Bin_L=%sysevalf(&Bin_U - &Bs);
  %if &i=1 %then  %do;
IF &var >= &Bin_L and &var <= &Bin_U THEN &var._Bin=&i;
  %end;
  %else %if &i>1 %then %do;
IF &var > &Bin_L and &var <= &Bin_U THEN &var._Bin=&i;
  %end;
  %end;
run;
%mend;
```

A.8.5 MACRO BINEQW2()

```
%macro BinEqW2(dsin, var, Nb, dsout, Map);
/* Modified equal-width binning where a mapping dataset
    is also produced and the boundaries of the bins are stored */
/* Get max and min values */
proc sql  noprint;
 select  max(&var) into :Vmax from &dsin;
 select  min(&Var) into :Vmin from &dsin;
run;
quit;

 /* Calculate the bin size */
%let Bs = %sysevalf((&Vmax - &Vmin)/&Nb);
```

```
/* Now, loop on each of the values and create the bin boundaries
   and count the number of values in each bin */
data &dsout;
 set &dsin;
  %do i=1 %to &Nb;
  %let Bin_U=%sysevalf(&Vmin+&i*&Bs);
  %let Bin_L=%sysevalf(&Bin_U - &Bs);
  %if &i=1 %then  %do;
IF &var >= &Bin_L and &var <= &Bin_U THEN &var._Bin=&i;
  %end;
  %else %if &i>1 %then %do;
IF &var > &Bin_L and &var <= &Bin_U THEN &var._Bin=&i;
 %end;
  %end;
run;
/* Create the map and fill it with the bin boundaries */
proc sql noprint;
 create table &Map (BinMin num, BinMax num, BinNo num);
  %do i=1 %to &Nb;
  %let Bin_U=%sysevalf(&Vmin+&i*&Bs);
  %let Bin_L=%sysevalf(&Bin_U - &Bs);
  insert into &Map values(&Bin_L, &Bin_U, &i);
  %end;
quit;
%mend;
```

A.8.6 MACRO BINEQW3()

```
%macro BinEqW3(dsin, var, Nb, dsout, KeepList);
/* Modified equal-width binning where the map is not kept.
   We also specify a list of keep variables to reduce the
   size of the output dataset. */
/* Get max and min values */
proc sql  noprint;
 select  max(&var) into :Vmax from &dsin;
 select  min(&Var) into :Vmin from &dsin;
run;
quit;

 /* Calculate the bin size */
%let Bs = %sysevalf((&Vmax - &Vmin)/&Nb);

/* Now, loop on each of the values and create the bin boundaries
   and count the number of values in each bin */
data &dsout;
 set &dsin;
  %do i=1 %to &Nb;
  %let Bin_U=%sysevalf(&Vmin+&i*&Bs);
```

```
        %let Bin_L=%sysevalf(&Bin_U - &Bs);
        %if &i=1 %then  %do;
IF &var >= &Bin_L and &var <= &Bin_U THEN &var._Bin=&i;
        %end;
        %else %if &i>1 %then %do;
IF &var > &Bin_L and &var <= &Bin_U THEN &var._Bin=&i;
      %end;
      %end;
          keep &KeepList &Var._Bin;
          run;

%mend;
```

A.8.7 MACRO BinEqH()

```
%macro BinEqH(dsin, var, Nb, dsout, Map);
/* Equal-height binning */

/* Calculate the frequencies of the values of the
   variables being binned */
proc freq data = &dsin noprint;
 tables &var / out=&var._Freqs outcum;
run;

/* Get sum of frequencies */
proc sql  noprint;
 select  max(cum_freq) into :SumFreq from &Var._Freqs;
run;
quit;

 /* Calculate the bin size */
%let Bs = %sysevalf(&SumFreq/&Nb);

/* Calculate the bin number for each unique value
   by adjusting the width of the bins to account for
   possible spillovers */

data &Var._Freqs;
 set &var._freqs;

/* starting values */
retain bin 1 used 0 past 0 spill 0 binSize &Bs;

/* If a spillover occurred in the last iteration
   then increment the bin number, adjust the bin width,
   and save the used frequencies as "past" */
if spill=1 then do;
past = used;
```

```
BinSize=(&sumFreq-used)/(&Nb-bin);
Bin=Bin+1;
Spill=0;
end;
used = used + count;

/* Check if this results in a spillover */
if used >= past +BinSize then spill =1;
else spill=0;


run;

/* Find the upper and lower limit for each bin */

proc sort data=&Var._Freqs;
 by bin;
run;

data &Var._Freqs;
 set &Var._Freqs;
  by bin;
 retain i 1;
 if first.bin then call symput ("Bin_L" || left(i), &var);
 if last.bin then do;
call symput ("Bin_U" || Left (i), &var);
i=i+1;
 end;
run;

/* Check the actual number of bins and get the frequency
   within each bin */
proc sql noprint;
 select max(bin) into :Nb from &Var._Freqs;
 %do i=1 %to &Nb;
  select sum(count) into :Bc&i from &Var._Freqs where bin=&i;
 %end;
 run;
quit;

/* Finally, add the bin number to the data */
data &dsout;
 set &dsin;
  %do i=1 %to &Nb;
IF &var >= &&Bin_L&i and &var <= &&Bin_U&i
         THEN &var._Bin=&i;
  %end;
run;
```

```
/* and the binning limits to the dataset VarBins */

data &Map;
 do BinNo=1 to &Nb;
   &var._Lower_Limit=symget("Bin_L" || left(BinNo));
   &var._Upper_Limit=symget("Bin_U" || left(BinNO));
   Frequency = 1.* symget("Bc" || left(BinNo));
   output;
 end;
run;

/* Clean workspace */
proc datasets library=work nolist;
delete &Var._Freqs;
quit;
%mend;
```

A.8.8 MACRO GBINBDV()

```
%macro  GBinBDV(DSin, IVVar, DVVar,
               NW, Mmax, DSGroups, DSVarMap);
/* Binning of a continuous variable using Gini ratio,
   with respect to a known binary dependent variable.
   DSin= input dataset
   IVVar = independent continuous variable considered
           for binning
   DVVar = dependent variable used to bin IVVar
   NW = number of initial divisions used to split the range
        between the minimum and maximum.
        The higher the value of NW, the more accurate the
        final bins, but at the cost of more computational time.
   MMax = maximum number of bins
  DSGroups = dataset with final groups of bins (splits)
   DSVarMap = dataset with mapping rules

   Limitations:
   - Binary DV only
   - Continuous IV only
   - No missing values; they should be either substituted
     with a known value or imputed
*/

/* Create an initial NW number of equal-width bins and
   generate NW categories in a new variable called CATS. To be on
   the safe side, we copy the IV and DV into a temporary
   dataset and rename the IV --> IV before working on the
   splitting. */
```

```
    Data Temp_D;
      set &DSin (rename=(&IVVar=IV &DVVAR=DV));
      keep IV DV;
    run;

  /* Use macro BinEqW2() to calculate the bins of IV in
     TEMP_D and the mapping rules for each bin.
     This creates NW bins and an output dataset TEMP_B */
%BinEqW2(Temp_D, IV, &NW, Temp_B, Temp_BMap);

/* Get the count of each bin and the percentage of
   the DV=1 and DV=0 in each one of them.
   We know that the bin numbers are from 1-NW , but some
   bins may be empty, so we use macro
   CalcCats to get only those that are present in Temp_GB */

%CalcCats(TEMP_B, IV_Bin, Temp_Cats);

/* Sort Temp_Cats by IV_Bin */
proc sort data=Temp_Cats;
   by IV_Bin;
 run;

/* Convert only the bins that are present into macro
   variables. These are our new categories */
Data _null_;
  set Temp_Cats;
      call symput ("C_" || left(_N_), compress(IV_Bin));
             call symput ("n_" || left(_N_), left(count));
      call symput ("M", left(_N_));
        Run;

/* Calculate the count (and percentage) of DV=1
   and DV=0 in each category using proc SQL.
    Store all these values in the dataset Temp_Freqs;*/
proc sql noprint;
  create table Temp_Freqs (Category char(50), DV1 num, DV0 num,
                                      Ni num, P1 num );
%do i=1 %to &M;
select count(IV) into :n1 from Temp_B
                   where IV_Bin = &&C_&i and DV=1;
select count(IV) into :n0 from Temp_B
                   where IV_Bin = &&C_&i and DV=0;
%let p=%sysevalf(&n1 / &&n_&i);
insert into Temp_Freqs values("&&C_&i", &n1, &n0,
                                    &&n_&i, &p);
%end;
       quit;
```

```
/* Create the TERM dataset to keep the terminal nodes
   and their category list, and initialize the node counter
   and put ALL the categories as a starting point */

data Temp_TERM;
length node $1000;
Node='';
%do j=1 %to &M;
   Node = Node ||" &&C_&j";
 %end;
run;

%let NNodes=1;

/* Start the splitting loop: */
%DO %WHILE (&NNodes <&MMax);
/* Convert all the rows of the splits to macro variables;
   we should have exactly NNodes of them. */
   Data _Null_;
      set Temp_TERM;
      call symput ("L_" || left(_N_), Node );
   run;
/* Loop on each of these lists, generate possible splits
    of terminal nodes, and select the best split using
    the GiniRatio */
%let BestRatio =0;

%DO inode=1 %to &NNodes;
/* The current node list is &&L_&i */
/* Using this list, get the LEFT and RIGHT categories
   representing the current best split and the
   Gini measure of these children. */
   %let List_L=; %let List_R=; %Let GiniRatio=;
%GSplit(&&L_&inode, Temp_Freqs, List_L, List_R, GiniRatio);

/* Compare the GiniRatio */
%if %sysevalf(&GiniRatio > &BestRatio) %then %do;
%let BestRatio=&GiniRatio;
%let BestLeft=&List_L;
%let BestRight=&List_R;
%let BestNode=&Inode;
    %end;

%End; /* end of the current node list */

/* Add this split to the Temp_TERM by removing the
   current node and adding two new nodes
   with their lists as their right and left parts */
Data Temp_TERM;
```

```
   Set Temp_TERM;
     if _N_ = &BestNode Then delete;
run;
proc sql noprint;
 insert into Temp_TERM values ("&BestLeft");
   insert into Temp_TERM values ("&BestRight");
quit;

 /* increment NNodes */
 %let NNodes=%Eval(&NNodes +1);

%END;   /* End of the splitting loop */

/* Now we should have a set of bin groups that we need
    to map to a new set of ranges for final output and
    transformation of the input dataset. These new ranges
    will be obtained by getting the lower and upper bounds
    on the smallest and largest bins in each node.
    The results are stored in the output dataset DSVarMap */

   /* We get all the final lists from the splits */
   data _NULL_;
     Set Temp_TERM;
       call symput("List_"||left(_N_), Node);
       call symput("NSplits",compress(_N_));
run;

   /* And we create the new explicit mapping dataset */
   proc sql noprint;
     create table &DSVarMap (BinMin num, BinMax num, BinNo num);
     quit;
     %DO ix=1 %to &NSplits;

/* Get the first and last bin number from  each list */
%let First_bin=;%let Last_bin=;
%FirstLast(&&List_&ix, First_bin, Last_bin);

/* Get the outer limits  (minimum first, maximum last)
   for these bins */
     proc sql noprint;
select BinMin into :Bmin_F from Temp_BMap
              where BinNo=&First_bin;
select BinMax into :Bmax_L from Temp_BMap
              where BinNo=&Last_bin;

/* Store these values in DSVarMap under the
   new bin number: ix */
insert into &DSVarMap values (&Bmin_F, &Bmax_L, &ix);
     quit;
```

```
      %END;
/* Generate DSGroups */
 data Temp_TERM;
       set Temp_TERM;
first=input(scan(Node,1),F10.0);
 run;
 proc sort data=Temp_TERM;
  by first;
run;

Data &DSGroups;
 set Temp_TERM (Rename=(Node=OldBin));
 NewBin=_N_;
 drop first;
run;

   /* Because the split number is not representative of
       any order, we should sort them on the basis of their
       values */
    proc sort data=&DSVarMap;
     by BinMin;
    run;
    /* and regenerate the values of BinNo accordingly. */
    data &DSVarMap;
     Set &DsVarMap;
      BinNo=_N_;
    run;

/* Clean up and finish */
 proc datasets library = work nolist;
 delete temp_b Temp_bmap Temp_cats temp_d
        temp_freqs temp_gcats temp_Term;
   run;quit;
%mend;
```

A.8.9 MACRO APPBINS()

```
%macro AppBins(DSin, XVar, DSVarMap, XTVar, DSout);
/* Applying the binning map stored in the dataset DSVarMap
    to the variable XVar in the input dataset DSin and
    saving the results in DSout.
    The new transformed variable is XTVar. */
/* The bins are sorted according to the lower limit, so we
    start the conditions by using the upper limit of the
    first bin. Similarly, for the last bin, we use only the
    lower limit. */
```

```
/* Extract the conditions */
data _Null_;
 set &DSVarMap;
  call symput ("Cmin_"||left(_N_), compress(BinMin));
  call symput ("Cmax_"||left(_N_), compress(Binmax));
  call symput ("M", compress(_N_));
run;

/* Now we generate the output dataset */
Data &DSout;
  SET &DSin;
   /* The condition loop */
   IF &Xvar <= &Cmax_1  THEN  &XTVar = 1;
   %do i=2 %to %eval(&M-1);
     IF &XVar > &&Cmin_&i AND &XVar <= &&Cmax_&i
         THEN  &XTVar = &i ;
    %end;
   IF &Xvar > &&Cmin_&M  THEN  &XTVar = &M;
 run;
%mend;
```

A.9   TREATMENT OF MISSING VALUES

A.9.1   MACRO MODECAT()

```
%macro ModeCat(DSin, Xvar, M_Mode);
/* The mode of a categorical variable in a dataset */

proc freq data=&DSin noprint order=freq;
 tables &Xvar/out=Temp_Freqs;
run;

data Temp_Freqs;
 set Temp_Freqs;
if _N_=1 then call symput('mode',trim(&xvar));
run;

%let &M_Mode=&mode;

proc datasets library=work nodetails nolist;
 delete Temp_Freqs;
quit;

%mend;
```

A.9.2 Macro SubCat()

```
%macro SubCat(DSin, Xvar, Method, Value, DSout);
/* Substitution of missing values in a categorical (string) variable
DSin: input dataset
Xvar: string variable
Method: method to be used:
1 = substitute mode
2 = substitute value
3 = delete the record
Value: used with Method
DSout: output dataset with the variable Xvar with
       all missing values treated
*/
%if &Method=1 %then %do;    /* Mode */
  /* Calculate the mode using macro ModeCat */
       %let mode=;
%ModeCat(&DSin, &Xvar, Mode);
 /* Substitute the mode whenever Xvar=missing */
 Data &DSout;
  Set &DSin;
   if &Xvar='' Then &Xvar="&mode";
  run;
    %end;

%else %if &Method=2 %then %do; /* Value */
 /* Substitute the value whenever Xvar=missing */
 Data &DSout;
  Set &DSin;
   if &Xvar='' Then &Xvar="&Value";
  run;
    %end;

%else %do; /*Delete*/
 /* Delete record whenever Xvar=missing */
 Data &DSout;
  Set &DSin;
   if &Xvar='' Then delete;
  run;
   %end;
%mend;
```

A.9.3 Macro SubCont()

```
%macro SubCont(DSin, Xvar, Method, Value, DSout);
/* Substitution of missing values for a continuous
   variable Xvar in DSin according to Method.
```

```
%VarUnivar1(&DSin,&Xvar, Temp_univ);

data _null_;
 set Temp_univ;
    Call symput('Mean'  ,Vmean);
Call symput('min'    ,VMin);
Call symput('max'    ,VMax);
Call symput('STD'    ,VStd);
Call symput('VAR'    ,VVar);
Call symput('mode'   ,Vmode);
Call symput('median',Vmedian);
Call symput('P1'     ,VP1);
Call symput('P5'     ,VP5);
Call symput('P10'    ,VP10);
Call symput('P90'    ,VP90);
Call symput('P95'    ,VP95);
Call symput('P99'    ,VP99);
run;

Data &DSout;
 set &DSin;
%if %upcase(&Method)=DELETE %then %do;
 if &Xvar=. then Delete;
         %end;
%else %do;
 if &Xvar=. then &Xvar=
   %if %upcase(&Method)=MEAN %then &mean;
   %if %upcase(&Method)=MIN %then &min ;
   %if %upcase(&Method)=MAX %then &max;
   %if %upcase(&Method)=STD %then &std;
   %if %upcase(&Method)=MODE %then &mode;
   %if %upcase(&Method)=MEDIAN %then &median;
   %if %upcase(&Method)=P1 %then &p1;
   %if %upcase(&Method)=P5 %then &P5;
   %if %upcase(&Method)=P10 %then &P10;
   %if %upcase(&Method)=P90 %then &P90;
   %if %upcase(&Method)=P95 %then &P95;
   %if %upcase(&Method)=P99 %then &P99;
   %if %upcase(&Method)=VALUE %then &Value; ;
%end;
run;

proc datasets library=work nolist nodetails;
 delete temp_univ;
run; quit;
%mend;
```

A.9.4 MACRO MISSPATT()

```
%macro MissPatt(DSin, VarList, MissPat);
/* Extraction of the missingness pattern. */

/* Convert the variable names into macro variables
   Var&i , i=1 to Nvars; we do this by looping on words of
   the input VarList */
%let i=1;
%let condition = 0;
%do %until (&condition =1);
   %let Var&i=%scan(&VarList,&i);
   %if "&&Var&i" ="" %then %let condition =1;
   %else    %let i = %Eval(&i+1);
%end;
%let Nvars=%eval(&i-1);

/* Read ONE observation and obtain the variable types
   and store them in the macro variables T1 ... TVvars */
Data _Null_;
 set &DSin (Obs=1);
 %do i=1 %to &Nvars;
  call symput("T&i", VType(&&Var&i));
 %end;
run;


/* The number of possible patterns is 2^Nvars.
   We construct a dataset to contain these patterns MissPat.
   This dataset will be the output of the macro.
   We create it first by PROC SQL, and fill it
   step by step each time we find a pattern.
*/
   proc sql noprint;
    create table &MissPat (%do i=1 %to &Nvars;
                                  &&Var&i   num ,
                           %end;
                           PatNo num);
   quit;

/* To find each pattern, we need to enumerate
   the 2^Nvar patterns such that they all
   fit into one loop. So, we generate all possible
   patterns and then search for them.
   We do that by observing that for the first variable,
   we need two rows:
     one with all 1's and one with one 0 in the first
     variable. For the second row, we need to
```

```
      copy the two rows of the first variable and
      replace the 1 for the second variable with
      0, and so on. Therefore, for variable i, we
      insert 2^(i-1) rows and replace all these
      new rows with 0 for the variable i. We use the variable
      PatNo as temporary storage for the variable index i
      for replacement */

   proc SQL noprint;
   /* First row, insert all X's and PatNo=0 */
   insert into &MissPat values (%do i=1 %to &Nvars;
                                    1 , %end;  0  );
   quit;
   /* Then start the loop on the variables */
   %do i=1 %to &Nvars;
     /* Select all the rows to a temporary table,
     and change Var&i to 0 and set PatNo to i */
 data temp;
       set &MissPat;
&&Var&i =0;
PatNo=&i;
run;

    /* Append &MissPat with the temp dataset */
    data &MissPat;
      set &MissPat temp;
     run;
   %end;
   /* We renumber the patterns from 1 to 2^Nvars,
      and create a new field called Present */
   data &MissPat;
    set &MissPat;
    PatNo= _N_ ;
    Present =0;
    run;


 /* All we need to do now is to confirm that these
    patterns really exist in the dataset DSin.
    We do that by looping on these patterns,
    extracting the equivalent condition of missing
    pattern, and then marking that pattern as present
    in the data (in the Present field).
  */


 /* Number of patterns */
 %let NPats=%sysevalf(2**&Nvars);
```

```
      %do ipat=1 %to &Npats;
      /* Extract the condition by extracting the values of
         the variables */
         proc sql noprint;
select %do i=1 %to &Nvars;  &&Var&i , %end; PatNo
   into %do i=1 %to &Nvars; :V&i, %end; :P
      from &MissPat where PatNo=&ipat;
quit;


      /* Compile the condition depending on the
         variable type 'N' or 'C' */
      %let Cond=;
      %do i=1 %to &Nvars;
   %if (&i>1) %then %let Cond=&Cond and ;
      %if &&V&i=0 %then %do;
         %if &&T&i=C %then
            %let Cond=&Cond &&Var&i = '';   /* String C */
      %if &&T&i=N %then
         %let Cond=&Cond &&Var&i=. ;      /* Numeric N */
                      %end;
      %else %do;
         %if &&T&i=C %then
            %let Cond=&Cond &&Var&i ne '' ;  /* String C */
      %if &&T&i=N %then
         %let Cond=&Cond &&Var&i ne . ;    /* Numeric N */
         %end;
      %end;


      /* Check whether the condition exists */
   %let Nc=0;
data _null_;
      set &Dsin;
      IF &Cond then do;
      call symput('Nc',1);
   stop;
   end;
     run;

      /* If the condition is valid, then flag it as present. */

      %if &Nc=1 %then %do;
      proc sql noprint;
      update &MissPat set Present=1 where PatNo=&ipat;
   quit;
     %end;

   %end;
```

```
/* Now that all the Present flags have been updated,
   we remove all patterns but those with flag =1 and
   drop PatNo and Present variables */
   data &MissPat;
    set &MissPat;
    if Present =0 then delete;
    drop Present PatNo;
    run;

/* Clean the temporary datasets */
  proc datasets library =work nodetails nolist;
   delete temp;
  run; quit;
%mend;
```

A.9.5   MACRO REMISSPAT()

```
%macro ReMissPat(VListIn, MissIn, MissOut, M_VListOut);
/* Reordering variables so that the missing pattern is
   as close as possible to monotone. */

/* Extract the variable names from the input
   variable list VlistIn */

 %let i=1;
 %let condition = 0;
%do %until (&condition =1);
   %let Var&i=%scan(&VListIn,&i);
   %if "&&Var&i" ="" %then %let condition =1;
   %else    %let i = %Eval(&i+1);
%end;
%let Nvars=%eval(&i-1);

/* Now we have Nvars (Var1, Var2, ...) in this order.
   We create the first sum of the Missing Pattern
   matrix horizontally */

 data Temp_MP;
  set &MissIn;
   _Total_V=sum(&Var1 %do i=2 %to &Nvars; , &&Var&i %end;);
run;

/* Sort using the row sum */
proc sort data=Temp_mp;
by descending _total_v;
run;
 Data Temp_MP;
  set Temp_MP;
```

```
    drop _Total_V;
  run;

  proc transpose data=Temp_mp out=Temp_mpt Prefix=P;
  run;

  data temp_mpt;
   set temp_mpt;
   _total_P=sum (P1 %do i=2 %to &Nvars; , p&i  %end; );
   _index=_N_;
  run;

  proc sort data=temp_mpt;
   by descending _total_p;
  run;
  data temp_MPT;
   set temP_MPT;
   drop _total_P;
   run;
  proc transpose data=temp_mpt out=temp_mptt prefix=v;
  run;

  /* Dataset temp_MPT contains the closest pattern to a
     monotone one with the last row containing
     the order of variables that could lead to that
     pattern; so we extract that order from the
     the variables v1 -- vNvars and compile the output list */

  proc sql noprint;
   select v1 %do i=1 %to &Nvars; , v&i %end;
          into :P1 %do i=1 %to &Nvars; , :P&i %end;
     from temp_mptt where _Name_ ='_index';
  quit;

  data &MissOut;
    set temp_Mptt;
    if _Name_='_index' then delete;
  /* Delete missing rows */
    %do i=1 %to &Nvars;
      if v&i = . then delete;
    %end;
    drop _Name_;
  run;


  /* Rename the variables to their original names */
  data &MissOut(Rename = ( %do i=1 %to &Nvars;
                             %let j=&&P&i; V&i=&&Var&j
                           %end;) ) );
```

```
   set &Missout ;
 run;

 %let ListOut=;
 %do i=1 %to &Nvars;
   %let j=&&P&i;
   %let ListOut= &ListOut &&Var&j;
 %end;
 %let &M_VListOut=&ListOut;

 /* Clean up */
 proc datasets library=work nodetails nolist;
 delete temp_mp temp_mpt temp_mptt;
 quit;
 %mend;
```

A.9.6   MACRO CHECKMONO()

```
 %macro CheckMono(MissPat, VarList, M_Result);
 /* Checking whether a given missingness pattern is monotone
    or not. This macro should be used ONLY after attempting
    to reorder the variables so that the missing
    pattern is ALMOST monotone. The Result variable
    returns 1 if the pattern is monotone and 0 if it is not. */

 /* First, convert the variable list to macro
    variables: Var1, Var2, .... VarNvars */
 %let i=1;
 %let condition = 0;
 %do %until (&condition =1);
   %let Var&i=%scan(&VarList,&i);
   %if "&&Var&i" ="" %then %let condition =1;
   %else     %let i = %Eval(&i+1);
 %end;
 %let Nvars=%eval(&i-1);

 /* Add a pattern number variable to the missing pattern
    dataset, and store their number in the macro variable Np */
 data temp_MP;
  set &MissPat;
  _PatNo=_N_;
  call symput ('Np', trim(_N_));
 run;

 /* The main pattern loop */
 %let Mono=1;    /* We assume that the pattern is monotone */
```

```
%do ipat=1 %to &Np;
/* Load pattern i to macro variable P1 to PNvars */
  proc sql noprint;
    select &Var1 %do i=2 %to &Nvars; , &&Var&i %end;
        INTO  :P1 %do i=2 %to &Nvars; , :P&i %end;
      FROM temp_MP where _PatNo=&ipat;
  quit;

/* Check the assumption of monotone missingness by finding
   the first 0 */
   %let jmin=%eval(&Nvars+1);
   %do i=1 %to &Nvars;
     %if (&&P&i = 0) %then %do;
        %if (&jmin > &i) %then %let jmin = &i;
                        %end;
   %end;
   /* This was the minimum j, which should be smaller
      than Nvars */
   %if &jmin < &Nvars %then %do;
     /* Then start the search for any value of 1 above
        this index */
     %do i=%eval(&jmin+1) %to &Nvars;
       %if (&&P&i =1) %then %let Mono=0; /* failure */
     %end;
                                %end;
%end;/* end of pattern loop */

/* Finally, store the result into Result */
%let &M_Result=%trim(&mono);

/* Clean up */
proc datasets library=work nodetails nolist;
delete temp_mp ;
quit;
%mend;
```

A.9.7 MACRO MAKEMONO()

```
%macro MakeMono(DSin, VarList, DSout);
/* Imputing continuous variables to a monotone missing pattern */
proc mi data=&DSin
   nimpute=5 seed=1000
   out=&DSout noprint;
 mcmc impute=monotone;
 var &VarList;
 run;
%mend;
```

A.9.8   MACRO IMPREG()

```
%macro ImpReg(DSin, VarList, MonoCMD, IFMono, NImp, DSout);
/* Imputing a set of variables using the regression model.
 The variables are assumed to have a monotone missing pattern.
 The variable MonoCMD contains the monotone command.
 The IFMono (Y/N) indicates whether the input dataset has been
 made monotone using the MCMC method before, and, therefore,
 contains the variable _Imputation_, which should then be
 used in the BY statement.
 Also, if the variable _Imputation_ exists, then we impute
 only 1 value, and in this case the parameter Nimp is
 ignored (but must be specified in the macro call)
*/
proc mi data=&DSin
        seed=1000   out=&DSout noprint
nimpute=%if %upcase(&IfMono)=Y %then 1; %else &Nimp; ;
&MonoCMD;
var &VarList;
%If %upcase(&IfMono)=Y %then by _Imputation_;;
run;
%mend;
```

A.9.9   MACRO AVGIMP()

```
%macro AvgImp(DSin, Nimp, IDVar, IDImp, Xvar, DSout);
/* Averaging imputed values for continuous variables */
%do i=1 %to &nimp;
Data temp_&i;
  set &dsin;
  if &IDImp=&i;
  x_&i=&Xvar;
  keep &Xvar._&i &IDvar;
run;
   proc sort data=temp_&i;
   by &IDvar;
   run;
%end;
   data temp_all;
    merge %do i=1 %to &Nimp; temp_&i %end; ;
by &IDvar;
   run;
   Data &DSout;
    set temp_all;
 &Xvar =mean( x_1 %do i=2 %to &Nimp; , x_&i %end;) ;
keep &IDvar &Xvar;
   run;
```

```
proc datasets library=work nolist nodetails;
delete temp_all %do i=1 %to &Nimp; temp_&i %end; ;
run;quit;
%mend;
```

A.9.10   MACRO NORDIMP()

```
%macro NORDImp(DSin, Nimp, Method,CVar, VarList,DSout);
/*
 Imputing nominal and ordinal variables
 DSin: input dataset
 DSout: output dataset
 Nimp: number of imputations
 Method: either Logistic or Discrim
 CVar: variable to be imputed. If CVar is ordinal,
       only logistic method could be used. If CVar
       is nominal and binary, both Logistic and Discrim
       methods could be used. If CVar is nominal and not
       binary, then only Discrim method could be used.
 VarList: list of NONMISSING variables to be used as
          predictors in the imputation models
*/
proc mi data=&DSin out=&DSout nimpute=&Nimp seed=1000 noprint;
 class &CVar;
 monotone &Method (&Cvar);
 var &VarList &Cvar;
 run;
%mend;
```

A.10   ANALYSIS OF NOMINAL AND ORDINAL VARIABLES

A.10.1   MACRO CONTINMAT()

```
%macro ContinMat(DSin, Xvar, Yvar, ContMatrix);
/* Extraction of the contingency table of a dataset
   using Xvar and Yvar */
proc freq data=&DSin noprint;
  tables &Xvar * &Yvar / out=&ContMatrix;
run;
Data &ContMatrix;
 set &ContMatrix;
 keep &Xvar &Yvar Count;
run;
%mend;
```

A.10.2 MACRO PROPDIFF()

```
%macro PropDiff(ContTable, Xvar, Yvar, Alpha,
                M_Prop, M_Upper, M_Lower);

/* Calculation of the proportion difference and
   its confidence interval */

/* Sig=Significance level (1-alpha/2) % */

/* Sort the contingency table by the categories of the Xvar */
proc sort data=&ContTable;
 by &Xvar &Yvar;
run;

/* Convert the entries n_ij of the contingency table
   into macro variables as:
      Y1  Y2
   X1 N1  N2
   X2 N3  N4 */
data _NULL_;
 set &ContTable;
 call symput ("n_"||left(_N_), COUNT);
run;

/* calculate N1* , N2*, P1, P2 */
%let N1star=%eval(&N_1+&N_2);
%let N2star=%eval(&N_3+&N_4);
%let P1=%sysevalf(&N_1/&N1star);
%let P2=%sysevalf(&N_3/&N2star);
/* Calculate |P1-P2| (absolute value of the difference) */
%let P1P2=%sysfunc(abs(&p1-&P2));

/* Substitute in the formula for Sigma(P1-P2) */
%let sigma=%sysfunc(sqrt(((&P1*(1-&P1))/&N1star)+
                   ((&P2*(1-&P2))/&N2star)));

/* Store proportion difference, upper and lower limits
   in their return variables. */
%let &M_Prop = &P1P2;
%let &M_Upper=%sysevalf(&p1p2 + &sigma *
                               %sysfunc(probit(1-&alpha/2)));
%let &M_Lower=%sysevalf(&p1p2 - &sigma *
                               %sysfunc(probit(1-&alpha/2)));
%mend;
```

A.10.3   MACRO ODDSRATIO()

```
%macro OddsRatio(ContTable, Xvar, Yvar, Alpha,
                 M_Theta, M_Upper, M_Lower);
/* Calculation of the odds ratio and its confidence interval */
/* Sig=Significance level (1-alpha/2) % */

/* Sort the contingency table by the categories of the Xvar */
proc sort data=&ContTable;
 by &Xvar &Yvar;
run;

/* Convert the entries n_ij of the contingency table
   into macro variables as:
       Y1  Y2
    X1 N1  N2
    X2 N3  N4 */
data _NULL_;
 set &ContTable;
 call symput ("n_"||left(_N_), COUNT);
run;

/* Calculate OddsRatio (Theta) using the modified formula */
%let Theta=%sysevalf((&N_1+0.5)*(&N_4+0.5)/
                       ((&N_2+0.5)*(&N_3+0.5)));

/* ASE(log theta) using the modified formula */
%let ASE_log=%sysfunc(sqrt(1/(&N_1+0.5) +
                        1/(&N_2+0.5) +1/(&N_3+0.5) +
                        1/(&N_4+0.5) ) );

/* Calculate log (theta) and  confidence
   interval of Log(theta) */
%let LogT=%sysfunc(log(&Theta));
%let LogU= %sysevalf(&LogT + &ASE_Log *
                          %sysfunc(probit(1-&alpha/2)));
%let LogL= %sysevalf(&LogT - &ASE_log *
                          %sysfunc(probit(1-&alpha/2)));

/* Store Odds ratio, upper and lower limits in
   their return variables */
%let &M_Theta = &Theta;
%let &M_Upper = %sysfunc(exp(&LogU));
%let &M_Lower = %sysfunc(exp(&LogL));
%mend;
```

A.10.4   Macro PearChi()

```
%macro PearChi(DSin, XVar, Yvar, M_X2, M_pvalue);
/* Calculation of the Pearson Chi-squared statistic and its
   p-value for two categorical variables (Xvar, Yvar)
  of dataset (DSin) */

proc freq data =&DSin noprint ;
 tables &Xvar * &Yvar/chisq;
 output All out=temp_chi chisq;
run;

/* Now extract X2 and its p-value */
Data _Null_;
set Temp_chi;
call symput("Mpvalue", P_PCHI);
call symput("MX2", _PCHI_);
run;
%let &M_Pvalue=&Mpvalue;
%let &M_X2 =&MX2;
proc datasets library=work nolist;
  delete temp_chi;
quit;
%mend;
```

A.10.5   Macro LikeRatio()

```
%macro LikeRatio(DSin, XVar, Yxar, M_G2, M_pvalue);
/* Calculation of the likelihood ratio and its p-value
   for two categorical variables (Xvar, Yvar)
   in a dataset (DSin) */

proc freq data =&DSin noprint ;
 tables &Xvar * &Yvar/chisq;
 output All out=temp_chi chisq;
run;

/* Now extract the likelihood ratio and its p-value */
Data _Null_;
set Temp_chi;
call symput("Mpvalue", P_LRCHI);
call symput("MG2", _LRCHI_);
run;
%let &M_Pvalue=&Mpvalue;
%let &M_G2 =&MG2;
proc datasets library=work nolist;
  *delete temp_chi;
```

```
quit;
%mend;
```

A.10.6 MACRO CONTPEAR()

```
%macro ContPear(DSin, XScore, YScore, M_R);
/* Calculation of Pearson correlation coefficient for
    ordinal variables using the scores given in XScore,
    YScore. The result is stored in M_R */

proc freq data=&DSin noprint;
tables &XScore*&YScore / measures;
output measures out=temp_r;
run;

data _NULL_;
 set temp_r;
 call symput("r", _PCORR_);
run;
%let &M_r = &r;
proc datasets nodetails;
 *delete temp_r;
quit;
%mend;
```

A.10.7 MACRO CONTSPEAR()

```
%macro ContSpear(DSin, XScore, YScore, M_RS);
/* Calculation of Spearman correlation coefficient for ordinal
    variables using the scores given in XScore, YScore.
    The result is stored in M_RS. */

proc freq data=&DSin noprint;
tables &XScore*&YScore / measures;
output measures out=temp_rs;
run;

data _NULL_;
 set temp_rs;
 call symput("rs", _SCORR_);
run;
%let &M_rs = &rs;
proc datasets nodetails;
 *delete temp_rs;
quit;
%mend;
```

A.10.8   MACRO CONTNANA()

```
%macro ContnAna(DSin, VarX, VarY, ResDS);
/* Calculation of measures of association between
   two categorical variables (VarX, VarY)
   in a dataset (DSin) using PROC FREQ and
   arranging the results in a dataset (ResDS). */

proc freq data =&DSin noprint;
 tables &VarX * &VarY/chisq;
 output All out=temp_chi chisq;
run;

proc sql noprint;
 create table &ResDS
       (SAS_Name char(10), Description char(50), Value num);
 select _PHI_, P_MHCHI, P_LRCHI, P_PCHI, N, _MHCHI_
      , _LRCHI_, DF_MHCHI, DF_LRCHI, DF_PCHI ,_CRAMV_
      ,_CONTGY_ ,_PCHI_
    into :PHI, :P_MHCHI, :P_LRCHI, :P_PCHI, :N, :MHCHI
       , :LRCHI, :DF_MHCHI, :DF_LRCHI, :DF_PCHI, :CRAMV
       , :CONTGY, :PCHI
  from temp_chi;
insert into &ResDS
values("N", "Number of Subjects in the Stratum",&N)
values("_PCHI_","Chi-Square",&PCHI)
values("DF_PCHI","DF for Chi-Square",&DF_PCHI)
values("P_PCHI","P-value for Chi-Square",&P_PCHI)
values("_MHCHI_","Mantel-Haenszel Chi-Square",&MHCHI)
values("DF_MHCHI","DF for Mantel-Haenszel Chi-Square",
       &DF_MHCHI)
values("P_MHCHI","P-value for Mantel-Haenszel Chi-Square",
       &P_MHCHI)
values("_LRCHI_","Likelihood Ratio Chi-Square",&LRCHI)
values("DF_LRCHI","DF for Likelihood Ratio Chi-Square",
       &DF_LRCHI)
values("P_LRCHI","P-value for Likelihood Ratio Chi-Square",
       &P_LRCHI)
values("_PHI_","Phi Coefficient",&PHI)
values("_CONTGY_","Contingency Coefficient",&CONTGY)
values("_CRAMV_","Cramer's V",&CRAMV)
;
quit;
proc datasets library=work nolist;
  delete temp_chi;
quit;
%mend;
```

A.11 ANALYSIS OF CONTINUOUS VARIABLES

A.11.1 MACRO CONTGRF()

```
%macro  ContGrF(DSin, Xvar, YVar, M_Gr, M_Fstar, M_Pvalue);
/* Calculation of the Gr and F* values for a continuous
    variable Y and a nominal variable X
DSin = input dataset
XVar = X variable
YVar = Y Variable
M_GR = returned Gr ratio
M_Fstar = returned F*
M_Pvalue = returned p-value of F*
*/
/* Get the categories of the XVar */
proc freq data=&DSin noprint;
tables &XVar /missing out=Temp_Cats;
run;

/* Convert the categories (X_i) and their frequencies
    n_i to macro variables */
Data _null_;
retain N 0;
  set Temp_Cats;
  N=N+count;
      call symput ("X_" || left(_N_), compress(&XVar));
              call symput ("n_" || left(_N_), left(count));
      call symput ("K", left(_N_));
    call symput ("N", left(N));
        Run;

/* Calculate the quantities needed to substitute in
    SSTO, SSR, SSE, MSR, MSE, F*, Gr */

    proc sql noprint;
    /* Ybar */
     select avg(&YVar) into :Ybar from &DSin;

      %do i=1 %to &K;
/* Ybar_i */
select avg(&YVar) into :Ybar_&i
        from &DSin where &XVar = "&&X_&i";

    %end;

/* SSTO, SSR, SSE */
    select var(&YVar) into: SSTO from &DSin;
```

```
%let SSTO=%sysevalf(&SSTO *(&N-1));
%let SSR=0;
%let SSE=0;

    %do i=1 %to &K;
  select var(&YVar) into: ssei
          from &DSin where &Xvar="&&X_&i";
      %let SSE=%sysevalf(&SSE + &ssei * (&&n_&i - 1));

  %let SSR=%sysevalf(&SSR+ &&n_&i * (&&Ybar_&i - &Ybar)*
                                    (&&Ybar_&i - &Ybar));
    %end;

  quit; /* end of Proc SQL */

/* MSR, MSE , F*, Gr, Pvalue */
%let MSR=%sysevalf(&SSR/(&K-1));
%let MSE=%sysevalf(&SSE/(&N-&K));
%let &M_Gr=%Sysevalf(1-(&SSE/&SSTO));
%let &M_Fstar=%sysevalf(&MSR/&MSE);
%let &M_PValue=%sysevalf(%sysfunc(probf(&Fstar,&K-1,&N-&K)));

/* clean workspace */
proc datasets library=work nolist;
 delete temp_cats;
run; quit;
%mend;
```

A.11.2 Macro VarCorr()

```
%macro VarCorr(DSin, VarX, VarY, CorrDS);
/* Calculation of the correlation coefficients between
   VarX and VarY in the dataset DSin.
   The results are stored in the CorrDS dataset with
   the names of the coefficients. */

/* Put the variable names in uppercase */
%let x=%upcase(&VarX);
%let y=%upcase(&VarY);

/* Invoke proc corr */
proc corr data=&DSin pearson spearman hoeffding kendall
    outp=temp_P outs=temp_S outh=temp_H outk=temp_K noprint;
var &x &y;
run;
/* Get the coefficients from the temporary datasets */
proc sql noprint;
select &x into : xyP from temp_P where upcase(_NAME_) eq "&y";
```

```
select &x into : xyS from temp_S where upcase(_NAME_) eq "&y";
select &x into : xyH from temp_H where upcase(_NAME_) eq "&y";
select &x into : xyK from temp_K where upcase(_NAME_) eq "&y";

create table &CorrDS (Type char(10), Value num);
insert into &CorrDS values('Pearson'  , &xyP)
                      values('Spearman' , &xyS)
                      values('Hoeffding', &xyH)
                      values('Kendall'  , &xyK);
quit;
/* Finally, clean the workspace */
proc datasets library=work nolist;
  delete temp_P temp_s temp_H temp_K;
quit;

%mend;
```

A.12 PRINCIPAL COMPONENT ANALYSIS

A.12.1 MACRO PRINCOMP1()

```
%macro PrinComp1(DSin,  VarList, Method, DSEigen );
 /* A wrapper for proc princomp */
   proc princomp data=&DSin &Method outstat=&DSEigen noprint;
   var &VarList;
   run;
%mend;
```

A.12.2 MACRO PRINCOMP2()

```
%macro PrinComp2(DSin, VarList, Method, p, ScoreDS, DSout);
/* Reducing a set of variables (VarList) using PCA,
   by keeping fraction p (p<=1) of the variance.
   The output is stored in DSout and the model is stored
   in ScoreDS. */

/* First run PRINCOMP to get All the eigenvalues */

   proc princomp data=&DSin
                 &Method
                 outstat=Temp_eigen
                 noprint;
   var &VarList;
   run;
```

```
/* Then select only the top fraction p of the variance */
data Tempcov1;
 set temp_Eigen;
 if _Type_ ne 'EIGENVAL' then delete;
 drop _NAME_;
 run;
proc transpose data=Tempcov1 out=TempCovT ;
run;

data TempCov2;
 set TempCovT;
 retain SumEigen 0;
 SumEigen=SumEigen+COl1;
run;

proc sql noprint;
select max(SumEigen) into :SEigen from TempCov2;
quit;

data TempCov3;
 set TempCov2;
IEigen=_N_;
PEigen = SumEigen/&SEigen;
run;

/* Count the number of eigenvalues needed to
   reach p */

proc sql noprint;
 select count(*) into :Nh from Tempcov3
                       where PEigen >= &P;
 select count(*) into :NN from TempCov3;
%let N=%eval(&NN-&Nh+1);
quit;

/* Delete from the DSEigen all the rows above
   the needed N eigenvectors */
data &ScoreDS;
 set Temp_Eigen;
run;
proc sql noprint;
%do i=%eval(&N+1) %to &NN;
 delete from &ScoreDS where _NAME_ = "Prin&i";
%end;
quit;


/* And score */
proc score data=&Dsin Score=&ScoreDS Out=&DSout;
```

```
Var &VarList;
run;

/* Finally, clean workspace */
proc datasets library=work nodetails;
delete Tempcov1 Tempcov2 Tempcov3 Temp_eigen Tempcovt;
run;
quit;
%mend;
```

A.13 FACTOR ANALYSIS

A.13.1 MACRO FACTOR()

```
%macro Factor(DSin, VarList, NFactors, DSFact, PROption);
/* Implementation of factor analysis. The macro results
   in the output dataset which could be used with the
   scoring macro FactScore() to create factor scores
   in a scoring dataset. The number of factors MUST be
   specified.
   DSin: input training dataset
   VarList: variable for factor analysis model
   NFactors: number of needed factors
   DSout: output dataset containing the factor model
   PROption: option to suppress the output of proc Factor
   values: 0--> no printing
   Anything else --> printing
*/

PROC FACTOR    DATA=&DSin
               Method=PRIN
               Rotate=Varimax
               nfactors=&Nfactors
          outstat=&DSFact score
 %if &PROption = 0 %then noprint; ;
 var &varlist;
run;
%mend;
```

A.13.2 MACRO FACTSCORE()

```
%macro FactScore(DSin, VarList, DSFact, DSout);
/* Scoring a dataset using the factor model stored in DSFact.
   The result is a dataset with additional new variables
   with the names Factor1, Factor2, ..., etc. */
```

```
proc score data=&dsin  score=&DSFact out=&DSout;
      var &VarList;
      run;
%mend;
```

A.13.3   MACRO FACTREN()

```
%macro FactRen(DSin, Nfactors, Prefix, DSout);
/* Renaming the names of the variables Factor1, Factor2, ...
   to the new names starting with the prefix PreFix to become
   Prefix1, Prefix2, etc. All the other variables are
   copied from DSin to DSout (which could be the same dataset).
*/
Data &DSout;
 SET &DSin (Rename=(
  %do i=1 %to &NFactors;
   Factor&i= &Prefix&i
   %end; ));
run;
%mend;
```

A.14 PREDICTIVE POWER AND VARIABLE REDUCTION II

A.14.1   MACRO GINICATBDV()

```
%macro GiniCatBDV(DSin, XVar, DV, M_Gr);
/* Calculation of the Gini ratio for a categorical (string)
   independent variable using a binary dependent variable DV.
   The output is stored in M_Gr. The categories of the DV
   must be 1/0. No missing values are allowed. */

/* Count the frequencies of the categories of variable XVar
   versus the categories of the DV using proc freq */

proc freq data=&DSin noprint;
 table &XVar*&DV /out=Temp_freqs;
 table &XVar /out=Temp_cats;
 run;
proc sql noprint;
  /* Count the number of categories */
   %local m;
   select count(*) into : m from temp_cats;

/* Frequencies of DV=1, DV-0 , N*/
   %local N0 N1 N;
```

```
      Select sum(Count) into :N0 from temp_freqs where DV=0;
      select sum(Count) into :N1 from temp_freqs where DV=1;
   quit;
   %let N=%eval(&N0+&N1);

   /* Gp */
   %local Gp;
   %let Gp=%sysevalf(1 - (&N0*&N0+&N1*&N1 ) / (&N*&N) );

   /* Get unique categories of XVar and store them in macro
      variables */

   data _null_;
    set temp_cats;
     call symput('Cat_'|| left(_N_), &XVar );
   run;

   /* Start the variable loop */
   proc sql noprint;
   %local ss i Ghat NN0 NN1 NN;
   %let ss=0;
   %do i=1 %to &m;
     /* Get n_o^i (NN0) , n_1^i (NN1) */
     select max(0,sum(count)) into :NN0
            from temp_freqs where DV=0 and &XVar="&&Cat_&i";
     select max(0,sum(count)) into :NN1
            from temp_freqs where DV=1 and &XVar="&&Cat_&i";
     %let NN=%eval(&NN1+&NN0);
     %let ss=%sysevalf(&ss+ (1-((&NN0 * &NN0)+(&NN1 * &NN1))/
                                       (&NN * &NN)) * &NN);
   %end; /* end of variable loop */

   quit;

   %let Ghat=%sysevalf(&ss/&N);
   %let &M_Gr=%sysevalf(1-&Ghat/&Gp);

   proc datasets library=work;
   delete temp_freqs temp_cats;
   quit;
   %mend;
```

A.14.2 MACRO ENTCATBDV()

```
%macro EntCatBDV(DSin, XVar, DV, M_Er);
/* Calculation of the entropy ratio for a categorical
   (string) independent variable using a binary dependent
   variable DV. The output is stored in M_Gr.
```

The categories of the DV must be 1/0. No missing values
are allowed. */

```
/* Count the frequencies of the categories of variable XVar
   versus the categories of the DV using proc freq */

proc freq data=&DSin noprint;
 tables &XVar*&DV /out=Temp_freqs;
 table &XVar /out=Temp_cats;
 run;
proc sql noprint;
  /* Count the number of categories */
   %local m;
   select count(*) into : m from temp_cats;

/* frequencies of DV=1, DV-0 , N*/
%local N0 N1 N;
Select sum(Count) into :N0 from temp_freqs where DV=0;
select sum(Count) into :N1 from temp_freqs where DV=1;
%let N=%eval(&N0+&N1);

/* Ein */
%local Ein;
%let Ein=%sysevalf(  -1* ( &N0 * %sysfunc(log(&N0/&N))
                          +&N1 * %sysfunc(log(&N1/&N)) )
                    /( &N * %sysfunc(log(2))          ) );

quit;
/* Get the unique categories of XVar and store them
    in macro variables. */

data _null_;
 set temp_cats;
  call symput('Cat_'|| left(_N_), &XVar );
run;

/* Start the variable loop */
proc sql noprint;
%local ss i Eout NN0 NN1 NN;
%let ss=0;
%do i=1 %to &m;

 /* get n_o^i (NN0) , n_1^i (NN1) */
  select max(sum(count),0) into :NN0
        from temp_freqs where DV=0 and &XVar="&&Cat_&i";
  select max(sum(count),0) into :NN1
        from temp_freqs where DV=1 and &XVar="&&Cat_&i";
  %let NN=%eval(&NN1+&NN0);
  %if(&NN0>0 and &NN1>0) %then
```

```
%let  ss=%sysevalf(&ss- &NN*( &NN0 *%sysfunc(log(&NN0/&NN))
                           + &NN1 * %sysfunc(log(&NN1/&NN)) )
                          /( &NN * %sysfunc(log(2))      ) );
  %else %if (&NN0=0)%then
  %let  ss=%sysevalf(&ss- &NN*( &NN1 * %sysfunc(log(&NN1/&NN)))
                          /( &NN * %sysfunc(log(2)) ) );
    %else
    %let  ss=%sysevalf(&ss- &NN*(&NN0 * %sysfunc(log(&NN0/&NN)))
                          /( &NN * %sysfunc(log(2)) ) );

%end; /* end of variable loop */
quit;
%let Eout=%sysevalf(&ss/&N);
%let &M_Er=%sysevalf(1-&Eout/&Ein);

proc datasets library=work;
delete temp_freqs temp_cats;
quit;
%mend;
```

A.14.3 MACRO PEARSPEAR()

```
%macro PearSpear(DSin, XScore, YScore, M_R, M_RS);
/* Calculation of Pearson and Spearman correlation coefficients
   for ordinal variables using the scores given in XScore, YScore.
   The result is stored in M_R and M_RS */

proc freq data=&DSin noprint;
tables &XScore*&YScore / measures;
output measures out=temp_rs;
run;

data _NULL_;
 set temp_rs;
 call symput("rs", abs(_SCORR_));
 call symput("rr", abs(_PCORR_));
run;
%let &M_R=&rr;
%let &M_rs = &rs;
proc datasets nodetails;
delete temp_rs;
quit;

%mend;
```

A.14.4 MACRO POWERCATBDV()

```
%macro PowerCatBDV(DSin, VarList, DV, ChiDS, GiniDS, EntDS);
/* Calculation of all the predictive power measures of
   a set of categorical variables against a binary
   dependent variable. The used measures are
   Chi-square, Gini measure, and Entropy variance.
   The output is three datasets  ChiDS, GiniDS, EntDS,
   giving the predictive powers of the three measures.

Dependencies: PearChi(), GiniCatBDV(), EntCatBDV()
*/

/* First extract the variables from the list and put
   them in a list of macro variables */

%local i condition ;
%let i=1;
%let condition = 0;
%do %until (&condition =1);
   %let Word=%scan(&VarList,&i);
   %if &Word =  %then %let condition =1;
           %else %do;
   %local Var&i;
    %let Var&i=&word;
   %let i = %Eval(&i+1);
      %end;
%end;

/* We loop on these variables and find their
   chi2, pchi2 using the macro PearChi, and each
   time we store the variable name and
   the values of Chi2, PChi2 in the dataset.
   Similarly, for the Gini and the Entropy variance measures.
*/

proc sql noprint;
 create table &ChiDS  (VarName char(32), Chi2 num, PChi2 num);
 create table &GiniDS (VarName char(32), GiniRatio num);
 create table &EntDS  (VarName char(32), EntropyRatio num);
quit;

%local j Vx;
%do j=1 %to %EVAL(&i-1);
 %let Vx=&&Var&j;
 %let X2=;%let pvalue=;
 %PearChi(&DSin, &Vx, &DV, X2, pvalue);
 %let pvalue=%sysevalf(1-&pvalue);
```

```
%let Gr=;
%GiniCatBDV(&DSin, &Vx, &DV, Gr);

%let Er=;
%EntCatBDV(&DSin, &Vx, &DV, Er);

 proc sql noprint;
  insert into &ChiDS values ("&&Var&j", &X2, &pvalue);
  insert into &GiniDS values("&&Var&j", &Gr);
  insert into &EntDS values("&&Var&j", &Er);
 quit;
%end;

/* Finally, we sort the list using the p-values in ascending
   order (to give most correlated variables higher priority) */
proc sort data=&ChiDS;
by DESCENDING PchI2 Descending Chi2;
run;

proc sort data=&GiniDS;
by DESCENDING GiniRatio;
run;
proc sort data=&EntDS;
by DESCENDING EntropyRatio;
run;

%mend;
```

A.14.5 MACRO POWERORDBDV()

```
%macro PowerOrdBDV(DSin, VarList,DV,RDS, RSDS, GiniDS, EntDS);
/* Calculation of all the predictive power measures of
   a set of ordinal variables against a binary
   dependent variable. The measures used are
   r, rs, Gini measure, and Entropy variance.
   The output is four datasets  rDS, rsDS, GiniDS, EntDS,
   giving the predictive powers of the three measures.

Dependecies: PearSpear(), GiniOrdBDV(), EntOrdBDV() */

/* First extract the variables from the list and put them
   in a list of macro variables */

%local i condition ;
%let i=1;
%let condition = 0;
%do %until (&condition =1);
```

```
    %let Word=%scan(&VarList,&i);
     %if &Word = %then %let condition =1;
             %else %do;
     %local Var&i;
      %let Var&i=&word;
     %let i = %Eval(&i+1);
        %end;
  %end;


  /* We then loop on these variables and find their r and rs
     using the macro PearSpear, and each time we store the
     variable name and the values of r, rs in a dataset.
     Similarly, for the Gini and the Entropy variance measures.
  */

  proc sql noprint;
   create table &RDS   (VarName char(32), R num);
   create table &RSDS   (VarName char(32), Rs num);
   create table &GiniDS (VarName char(32), GiniRatio num);
   create table &EntDS (VarName char(32), EntropyRatio num);
  quit;

  %local j Vx;
  %do j=1 %to %EVAL(&i-1);
   %let Vx=&&Var&j;
   %let R=;
   %let RS=;

  %PearSpear(&DSin, &Vx, &DV, R, RS);

  %let Gr=;
  %GiniOrdBDV(&DSin, &Vx, &DV, Gr);

  %let Er=;
  %EntOrdBDV(&DSin, &Vx, &DV, Er);

   proc sql noprint;
    insert into &RDS values ("&&Var&j", &R);
    insert into &RSDS values ("&&Var&j", &Rs);
    insert into &GiniDS values("&&Var&j", &Gr);
    insert into &EntDS values("&&Var&j", &Er);
   quit;
  %end;

  /* Finally, we sort the list using the measures in
     ascending order (to give the most correlated first) */
  proc sort data=&RDS;
  by DESCENDING R;
```

```
run;
proc sort data=&RSDS;
by DESCENDING Rs;
run;

proc sort data=&GiniDS;
by DESCENDING GiniRatio;
run;
proc sort data=&EntDS;
by DESCENDING EntropyRatio;
run;

%mend;
```

A.14.6 MACRO POWERCATNBDV()

```
%macro PowerCatNBDV(DSin, VarList, DV, ChiDS, GiniDS, EntDS);
/* Calculation of all the predictive power measures of
   a set of categorical variables against a binary
   dependent variable. The measures used are
   Chi-square, Gini measure, and Entropy variance.
   The output is three datasets  ChiDS, GiniDS, EntDS,
   giving the predictive powers of the three measures.
   The categorical variables are numerical in this case.

Dependecies: PearChi(), GiniCatBDV(), EntCatBDV() */

/* First extract the variables from the list and put them
   in a list of macro variables */

%local i condition ;
%let i=1;
%let condition = 0;
%do %until (&condition =1);
   %let Word=%scan(&VarList,&i);
   %if &Word =  %then %let condition =1;
            %else %do;
   %local Var&i;
    %let Var&i=&word;
   %let i = %Eval(&i+1);
      %end;
%end;


/* We then loop on these variables and find their chi2,
   pchi2 using the macro PearChi, and each time we store
```

```
       the variable name and the values of Chi2, PChi2 in
       the dataset. Similarly, for the Gini and the Entropy
       variance measures. */

proc sql noprint;
 create table &ChiDS  (VarName char(32), Chi2 num, PChi2 num);
 create table &GiniDS (VarName char(32), GiniRatio num);
 create table &EntDS  (VarName char(32), EntropyRatio num);
quit;

%local j Vx;
%do j=1 %to %EVAL(&i-1);
 %let Vx=&&Var&j;
 %let X2=;%let pvalue=;
 %PearChi(&DSin, &Vx, &DV, X2, pvalue);
 %let pvalue=%sysevalf(1-&pvalue);

%let Gr=;
%GiniCatNBDV(&DSin, &Vx, &DV, Gr);

%let Er=;
%EntCatNBDV(&DSin, &Vx, &DV, Er);

 proc sql noprint;
  insert into &ChiDS values ("&&Var&j", &X2, &pvalue);
  insert into &GiniDS values("&&Var&j", &Gr);
  insert into &EntDS values("&&Var&j", &Er);
 quit;
%end;

/* Finally, we sort the list using the p-values in
   ascending order (to give the most correlated first). */
proc sort data=&ChiDS;
by DESCENDING PchI2 Descending Chi2;
run;

proc sort data=&GiniDS;
by DESCENDING GiniRatio;
run;
proc sort data=&EntDS;
by DESCENDING EntropyRatio;
run;


%mend;
```

A.15 OTHER MACROS

A.15.1 LISTTOCOL()

```
%macro ListToCol(List,DSOut,ColX, VIndex);
/* Decomposing a list of words and storing them in a
   dataset dsOut in the column ColX */
/* Create the empty dataset */
proc sql noprint;
 create table &DSOut (&ColX char(32), &VIndex int);


%let i=1;
%let condition = 0;
%do %until (&condition =1);
   %let Word=%scan(&List,&i);
   %if "&Word" ="""  %then %let condition =1;
           %else %do;
   insert into &DSOut Values("&word", &i);
   %let i = %Eval(&i+1);
      %end;

%end;
run; quit;
%mend;
```

BIBLIOGRAPHY

Adamo, J. M. (2001) *Data Mining for Association Rules and Sequential Patterns: Sequential and Parallel Algorithms*, Springer-Verlag, New York.

Agresti, A. (2002) *Categorical Data Analysis, Second Edition*, John Wiley & Sons, New York.

Berry, M., and Linoff, G. (2004) *Data Mining Techniques: For Marketing, Sales, and Customer Relationship Management, 2nd Edition*, John Wiley & Sons, New York.

Bishop, C. (1996) *Neural Networks for Pattern Recognition*, Oxford University Press, New York.

Box, G., Jenkins, G., and Reinsel, G. (1994) *Time Series Analysis: Forecasting & Control*, Prentice-Hall, Englewood Cliffs, New Jersey.

Breiman, L., Friedman, F., Olshen, R., and Stone, C. (1998) *Classification and Regression Trees*, Chapman & Hall/CRC, Washington, D.C.

Cristianini, N., and Shawe-Taylor, J. (2000) *An Introduction to Support Vector Machines and Other Kernel-Based Learning Methods*, Cambridge University Press, New York.

Hatsie, T. (2001) *The Elements of Statistical Learning: Data Mining, Inference, and Prediction*, Springer-Verlag. New York.

Hosmer, D., and Lemeshow, S. (1989) *Applied Logistic Regression*, John Wiley & Sons, New York.

Johnson, R. A. and Wichern, D. W. (2001) *Applied Multivariate Statistical Analysis*, Prentice-Hall, Upper Saddle River, New Jersey.

Levy, P. S., and Lemeshow, S. (1999) *Sampling of Populations: Methods and Applications, Third Edition*, John Wiley & Sons, New York.

Mitchell, T. M. (1997) *Machine Learning*. McGraw-Hill, New York.

Pyle, D. (1999) *Data Preparation for Data Mining*, Morgan Kaufmann, San Francisco.

Reyment, R., and Jöreskog, K. (1993) *Applied Factor Analysis in the Natural Sciences*, Cambridge University Press, New York.

Quinlan, R. (1993) *C4.5: Programs for Machine Learning*, Morgan Kaufmann Series in Machine Learning, San Francisco.

Rubin, D. B. (1987) *Multiple Imputation for Nonresponse in Surveys*, John Wiley & Sons, New York.

SAS Institute (2004) *SAS 9.1 Macro Language: Reference*, SAS Publishing, Cary, North Carolina.

SAS Institute (2005) *SAS 9.1 SAS/STAT: User Manual*, SAS Publishing, Cary, North Carolina.

Schafer, J. L. (1997) *Analysis of Incomplete Multivariate Data*, Chapman & Hall, New York.

Tukey, J. W. (1977) *Exploratory Data Analysis*, Addison-Wesley, Reading, Massachusetts.

Wickens, T. (1995) *The Geometry of Multivariate Statistics*, Lawrence Erlbaum Associates, Hillsdale, New Jersey.

INDEX

ABOUT THE AUTHOR

Mamdouh Refaat has been active in consulting, research, and training in various areas of information technology and software development for the last 20 years. He has worked on numerous projects with major organizations in North America and Europe in the areas of data mining, business analytics, and engineering analysis.

He has held several consulting positions for solution providers including Predict AG in Basel, Switzerland, and at ANGOSS Software Corporation, he was the Director of Professional Services.

Mamdouh received his PhD in engineering from the University of Toronto and his MBA from the University of Leeds, UK.

LIMITED WARRANTY AND DISCLAIMER OF LIABILITY

ELSEVIER, INC. AND ANYONE ELSE WHO HAS BEEN INVOLVED IN THE CREATION OR PRODUCTION OF THE ACCOMPANYING CODE ("THE PRODUCT") CANNOT AND DO NOT WARRANT THE PERFORMANCE OR RESULTS THAT MAY BE OBTAINED BY USING THE PRODUCT. THE PRODUCT IS SOLD "AS IS" WITHOUT WARRANTY OF MERCHANTABILITY OR FITNESS FOR ANY PARTICULAR PURPOSE. ELSEVIER WARRANTS ONLY THAT THE MAGNETIC DISC(S) ON WHICH THE CODE IS RECORDED IS FREE FROM DEFECTS IN MATERIAL AND FAULTY WORKMANSHIP UNDER THE NORMAL USE AND SERVICE FOR A PERIOD OF NINETY (90) DAYS FROM THE DATE THE PRODUCT IS DELIVERED. THE PURCHASER'S SOLE AND EXCLUSIVE REMEDY IN THE EVENT OF A DEFECT IS EXPRESSLY LIMITED TO EITHER REPLACEMENT OF THE DISC(S) OR REFUND OF THE PURCHASE PRICE, AT ELSEVIER'S SOLE DISCRETION.

IN NO EVENT, WHETHER AS A RESULT OF BREACH OF CONTRACT, WARRANTY, OR TORT (INCLUDING NEGLIGENCE), WILL ELSEVIER OR ANYONE WHO HAS BEEN INVOLVED IN THE CREATION OR PRODUCTION OF THE PRODUCT BE LIABLE TO PURCHASER FOR ANY DAMAGES, INCLUDING ANY LOST PROFITS, LOST SAVINGS, OR OTHER INCIDENTAL OR CONSEQUENTIAL DAMAGES ARISING OUT OF THE USE OR INABILITY TO USE THE PRODUCT OR ANY MODIFICATIONS THEREOF, OR DUE TO THE CONTENTS OF THE CODE, EVEN IF ELSEVIER HAS BEEN ADVISED ON THE POSSIBILITY OF SUCH DAMAGES, OR FOR ANY CLAIM BY ANY OTHER PARTY.

ANY REQUEST FOR REPLACEMENT OF A DEFECTIVE DISC MUST BE POSTAGE PREPAID AND MUST BE ACCOMPANIED BY THE ORIGINAL DEFECTIVE DISC, YOUR MAILING ADDRESS AND TELEPHONE NUMBER, AND PROOF OF DATE OF PURCHASE AND PURCHASE PRICE. SEND SUCH REQUESTS, STATING THE NATURE OF THE PROBLEM, TO ACADEMIC PRESS CUSTOMER SERVICE, 6277 SEA HARBOR DRIVE, ORLANDO, FL 32887, 1-800-321-5068. ELSEVIER SHALL HAVE NO OBLIGATION TO REFUND THE PURCHASE PRICE OR TO REPLACE A DISC BASED ON CLAIMS OF DEFECTS IN THE NATURE OR OPERATION OF THE PRODUCT.

SOME STATES DO NOT ALLOW LIMITATION ON HOW LONG AN IMPLIED WARRANTY LASTS, NOR EXCLUSIONS OR LIMITATIONS OF INCIDENTAL OR CONSEQUENTIAL DAMAGE, SO THE ABOVE LIMITATIONS AND EXCLUSIONS MAY NOT APPLY TO YOU. THIS WARRANTY GIVES YOU SPECIFIC LEGAL RIGHTS, AND YOU MAY ALSO HAVE OTHER RIGHTS WHICH VARY FROM JURISDICTION TO JURISDICTION.

THE RE-EXPORT OF UNITED STATES ORIGINAL SOFTWARE IS SUBJECT TO THE UNITED STATES LAWS UNDER THE EXPORT ADMINISTRATION ACT OF 1969 AS AMENDED. ANY FURTHER SALE OF THE PRODUCT SHALL BE IN COMPLIANCE WITH THE UNITED STATES DEPARTMENT OF COMMERCE ADMINISTRATION REGULATIONS. COMPLIANCE WITH SUCH REGULATIONS IS YOUR RESPONSIBILITY AND NOT THE RESPONSIBILITY OF ELSEVIER.